Siam's New Detectives

Southeast Asia

POLITICS, MEANING, AND MEMORY

David Chandler and Rita Smith Kipp

SERIES EDITORS

Siam's New Detectives

Visualizing Crime and Conspiracy in Modern Thailand

SAMSON LIM

UNIVERSITY OF HAWAI'I PRESS *Honolulu*

Printed in the United States of America

21 20 19 18 17 16 6 5 4 3 2 1

Library of Congress Cataloging-in-Publication Data

Names: Lim, Samson W., author.
Title: Siam's new detectives : visualizing crime and conspiracy in modern Thailand / Samson Lim.
Description: Honolulu : University of Hawaiʻi Press, 2016. | Includes bibliographical references and index.
Identifiers: LCCN 2015038301 | ISBN 9780824855253 cloth : alk. paper
Subjects: LCSH: Police—Thailand—History. | Criminal investigation—Thailand—History.
Classification: LCC HV8252.55.A2 L56 2016 | DDC 363.2509593—dc23
LC record available at http://lccn.loc.gov/2015038301

University of Hawaiʻi Press books are printed on acid-free paper and meet the guidelines for permanence and durability of the Council on Library Resources.

Series design by Rich Hendel

CONTENTS

ACKNOWLEDGMENTS

There are many people that I need to thank for their help in writing this book. I would like to begin by thanking Tamara Loos, who provided me unwavering support during the research and writing process. Annelise Riles introduced me to many of the ideas that give this project its form. Eric Tagliacozzo offered encouragement and a good example of how to be a gracious scholar. Thak Chaloemtiarana steered me toward the wonders of Thai literature. Ngampit Jagacinski enabled me to read that literature. My gratitude goes out to each of them.

In addition to this group of mentors, many others have helped me. When I first considered conducting research on Thailand, Michael Montesano provided advice and guidance. When I began the project, I was aided by a number of generous "seniors," including Jane Ferguson, Tyrell Haberkorn, Nina Hien, Doreen Lee, Richard Ruth, and Erick White. I was also surrounded by a group of wonderful peers: Claudine Ang, Trais Pearson, John Phan, and Ivan Small. I am particularly grateful to Christopher Ahn, Akiko Ishii, Hajimu Matsuda, and Honghong Tinn for having read and commented on the formative drafts of this book. I also have to thank Craig Reynolds for supporting my project despite my not being his student. At MIT, where I spent two semesters as a visiting scholar, I would like to thank Jeffrey Ravel and the History Section for making me feel welcome.

While conducting research in Bangkok, I had the great luck to work with several Thai scholars. These include Thosaeng Chaochuti, Thanaphol Limaphichat, Viengrat Netipho, Nipaporn Ratchatapattanakul, Suvimol Roongcharoen, Chalong Soontravanich, Jutharat Ua-amnoey, and especially the late Somboon Siriprachai. I was also aided by a number of Thai graduate students, many of whom are now professors in Thailand: Meng, Pong, Prakan, Preeya, Puey, Tai, Tai, and Thikan. I thank them for their patience with all my questions and the invaluable help they extended me while I was in Thailand. I also thank Thongchai Likhitphonsawan for opening his private library to me.

There are also the people who have been much more than colleagues: Lawrence Chua, my office mate and a role model; Scot Hislop, who has been like a brother to me for over twenty years; and Arjun Subramanyam, who needs to return my cable box. I would not have finished this work without these three individuals. Finally, I especially need to thank my parents and sister for being so patient. Their support was the most crucial of all.

Financial assistance for the research for this project was provided by the Fulbright-Hays Program, the American Council of Learned Societies, the Singapore University of Technology and Design, and the Graduate School, the Southeast Asia Program, and the History Department at Cornell University. Institutional support was provided by the National Research Council of Thailand, the National Archives of Thailand, the National Library of Thailand, the Library and Museum of the Attorney General's Office of Thailand, the History Department at Chulalongkorn University, and the History Section at MIT.

NOTE ON TRANSCRIPTION

In general, I follow the Royal Thai General System of Transcription (RTGS). However, I have replaced "ch" with "j" for the character จ, as this helps those familiar with the Thai language distinguish between จ and ช and ฉ, both of which sound like "ch" in English. I have kept the "ch" transliteration of จ in proper names and other words commonly spelled with "ch" (for example, Chao Phraya River).

Introduction

Sherry Ann Duncan, a sixteen-year-old Thai American girl, did not return home from school on July 22, 1986. Three days later, a man out clearing weeds found her body in a forest just east of Bangkok. Working from a tip given by a trishaw peddler named Pramoen Photphalat, the police moved quickly to arrest five men. The day after the arrests, the police released one of the suspects and took the other four to Suan Phlu Lane in central Bangkok to reenact Pramoen's story, which described four men dragging a girl with "golden hair" out the back of a building there at 11:30 p.m. on the night Sherry Ann disappeared. The police took photos of the reenactment and included them in their case files. Eventually, they sent the four men to trial, and, in the absence of any smoking gun, Pramoen became a key witness and his testimony, acted out and recorded, became critical evidence linking the suspects to the scene of the crime. In July 1990, a provincial court in Samut Prakan province, just east of Bangkok, found all four defendants guilty and sentenced them to death.[1]

The attorneys for the four defendants immediately appealed the provincial court's guilty verdict, arguing that the prosecution's evidence did not prove the men's involvement. In 1993, the case reached the Supreme Court of Thailand (*san dika*), which declared the four suspects innocent for lack of sufficient, direct evidence connecting them to the murder. It then ordered their release. In the time between the initial verdict and the Supreme Court's decision, one defendant died, another contracted a disease that would eventually kill him, and a third became crippled—all while in prison.

In 1996, a second trial for the same crime took place in which the presiding judges found three new suspects guilty of premeditated murder and sentenced each to life in prison. The key evidence? A reenactment, again by Pramoen. This time the police took Pramoen to a shabby love motel in eastern Bangkok, the location where he had apparently met with police officers involved in the investigation into Sherry Ann's murder in 1986. That year, police officers sat with Pramoen at the hotel and instructed him on what he had "seen" the night of Sherry Ann's death. Ten years later, Pramoen was at the hotel again, pointing out the "scene of the crime" and letting a different set of police officers know that the testimony he gave in the first trial had been fabricated. The proof that had helped the provincial court in Samut Prakan order four men to death, ostensibly a representation of the night of July 22, 1986, referred to nothing that ever actually happened.

One might dismiss the Sherry Ann case as just another example of the police misconduct that is common in developing countries, a cautionary tale about the justice system in the Third World. The case, however, is an extreme one, even for Thailand, where stories of wrongdoings perpetrated by police officers often fill the news. What is not unusual, however, is the method the police used to solve the crime and to produce evidence for the court; the reenactment (popularly referred to in Thai as *phaen prathut-sakam*) and its recording are common practice in Thailand. In part, this is a story about that particular practice, whose product is an object of evidence that the police materialize, the press makes public, and the courts accept as proof of a voluntary confession in the adjudication of criminal cases in Thailand. More broadly, however, this is a history of the visual evidence and the techniques for their production that an array of agents including police officers, reporters, photographers, and fiction writers generate and use in Thailand to picture the past and shape legal outcomes. In short, it is a study of the visual culture of policing, an epistemological history of how people, as actors in separate but overlapping social, political, and legal institutions, make visible a specific category of action called crime.[2] There is real-world relevance, then, to this academic story: Innocence or guilt, justice and outrage, are in part effects of simulations of the past created by the police and the press through overlapping practices of knowledge production. The objects of visual evidence that police officers, newspaper reporters, and fiction writers produce on a daily basis become, in turn, the forms through which what is known about criminal violence takes shape in the public imagination.

As in many modern societies, visual evidence occupies a privileged position in the Thai criminal justice system. The perception that objects like pictures, maps, and fingerprints provide neutral representations of things, people, and events allows them to tether police investigations and criminal trials to an external reality. In various archival sources from the early twentieth century, for example, high-ranking Thai police officers and government officials often noted the ability of photographs and maps to depict reality more accurately than other methods of representation. More recently, the anthropologist Rosalind Morris has noted a strong "willingness to embrace photographic evidence" in Thailand.[3] The view that visual images, particularly mechanically produced ones, are more objective than other forms of evidence is also present in legal systems outside of Thailand. Jennifer Mnookin writes that although a group of legal professionals disputed the reliability of photographs when they first entered the trial process in America, there were many who thought photos were "not just a piece of evidence or a link in a causal chain. [They were] the determining evidence, evidence so strong that it renders any trial merely an unfolding of the inevitable."[4] Lorraine Daston and Peter Galison, meanwhile, write that in Europe a "strong association between the visual and the factual" developed over the nineteenth century, and this connection has given mechanical techniques of reproduction such as photography their status as unbiased modes of representation. They add that by the middle of the nineteenth century, mechanically produced images had become the "standard bearer of objectivity" in scientific representation and in the law.[5] Yet the Sherry Ann example, exceptional as it is, shows that photographs and other visualizations, even those intended as true representations of reality, are not always factual and are hardly objective.

Why, then, is there the stubborn impression that visual representations make for better evidence? From what do visualizations derive their privileged epistemological status? In response to this question, I offer two related arguments. First, various objects of evidence used in the criminal justice system, such as fingerprints, maps, and photographs, derive their facticity from aesthetic rules—proper lighting in a crime scene photo, black ink fingerprints on white paper, and standard markings on maps and diagrams. By aesthetic rules I mean a set of criteria for judging the merits of a product of human craft (with the product being one meant to convey a meaning symbolically), especially if the judgment is of the relative sensory or intellectual "pleasing-ness" of the product. These rules, or conventions, emerged over time through the interaction of a range of actors employed both inside and outside what might conventionally be seen as the legal system. I refer primarily to individuals working in the field of mass media, including popular fiction and film. So, aside from police officers and lawyers—the people most often associated with the law—agents including fiction writers, news reporters, and photographers are also involved in determining what facts used in the criminal justice system look like. In short, aesthetic conventions ensure the facticity of visual evidence as much as the brute existence of the things that they are supposed to represent. Moreover, these conventions developed as part of ongoing interactions between diverse groups of seemingly unrelated actors and artifacts.

Second, some objects of visual evidence, once created (and even during their creation), do more than represent existing things. They act as diagrams—standardized depictions of natural phenomena used to perform logical operations that generate new information. Visual evidence, in other words, includes images that function as tools to facilitate the discovery of truths not stated or known in the creation of the images themselves. One might think of crime scene maps, for example, as representing a geographical space in the world, but they are also instruments for knowledge production that allow the police to generate facts about crime, such as the location of a gunman or the escape route of a suspect, that would otherwise not have been accessible. In a similar way, photos of reenactments and other visualizations used by the police do more than capture and present preexisting facts; they are diagrams of detection that the police work with to produce the criminal past. Frederik Stjernfelt, a Danish scholar who works in the field of semiotics, defines this type of visual tool as a "special sort of icon which represents the internal structure of [its referent] in terms of interrelated parts, facilitating reasoning possibilities."[6] Stjernfelt derives this definition from Charles Peirce, the nineteenth-century philosopher, who writes, "A great distinguishing property of the icon is that by the direct observation of it other truths concerning its object can be discovered than those which suffice to determine its construction."[7] In other words, through the contemplation of a diagram, new information about the world can be learned. Maps, as explained above, are a good example as they are "rule bound depictions of aspects of the shape of phenomena" used to determine information such as distance, routes, and locations.[8]

It is this generative power, as much as any mimetic function, that makes images useful as investigative tools. This means that scholars cannot analyze images produced by the police solely in terms of representational fidelity or just interpret them for deeper meaning. Examining how legal officers interact with their visual tools to generate information about the past is more important than simply critiquing the accuracy (or inaccuracy, as the case may be) of their representations. As such, the analysis of the primary sources—old police training manuals, court records, news reports, crime fiction, and archival documents—that serve as this study's foundation requires a different tack. Instead of treating these sources only as straightforward, even if incomplete, reflections of society and mining them for data with which to retell the past, I analyze their formal attributes, tracing how the look of a specific type of document or category of evidence has emerged and evolved. This tactic allows me to demonstrate how various objects typically considered fixed and inert (i.e., facts) are also artifacts, products of human activity. Just as scholars in science and technology studies have shown how scientific facts about the natural world emerge through trial and error in a laboratory, so, too, do facts used in the law. Specific actors engage in set routines, using specialized techniques developed over time to produce fingerprints, crime scene maps, and other types of visual evidence. Facts about crime used in criminal investigation are not things that exist out there in the world just waiting to be found. Again, take the crime scene map. In the early decades of the twentieth century, the idea of the crime scene did not exist in Siam, as people called Thailand until 1939, or in many European countries, for that matter. What one was and how it looked were not clear, not so much because the Thai police were incompetent, but because the notion of a crime scene had not yet fully developed and become naturalized as a category through which the world could be ordered. In other words, the crime scene map could not represent a crime scene, even if that is what police officers see it doing now, because the latter had not yet come into being. Instead, the map is the material object that helped make the modern geography of crime "real."

The appearance of the modern map and the type of space it presents were in turn shaped by a host of factors, including such non-law, non-"real" things as fictional stories, especially the popular detective novels serialized in the vernacular press beginning in the late nineteenth century. The detective stories that were transplanted from England, the United States, and France included descriptions and examples of what a crime scene was and how one might investigate it. One of the first crime scene maps in Siam can be found in a detective story written by King Vajiravudh (then crown prince) in 1904.[9] This helped the police and public visualize what a space of crime might look like and how to produce and use it to solve cases. The drawing of crime scene maps eventually became standard procedure for the Thai police force, which introduced the practice into their training program during the early decades of the twentieth century. It is therefore no surprise that objects of evidence, from photographs of criminals to maps of crime scene reconstructions, show up today both in trials as proof and in the press and on television as news and entertainment. They have been shared objects from the very beginnings of their existence. The standing of various forms of visual evidence commonly used in the criminal justice system as objective, factual representations of the world developed through a deliberate program of training as well as through experimentation and chance. This does not mean that there is no independent reality or that legal facts are created from thin air. Instead, what one knows about the past is a combination of representational techniques and the physical world. Understanding how modern legal systems operate, then, ultimately requires a critical examination of the visual culture of the law, specifically the aesthetic rules that govern the production and use of material evidence.

What is gained from the historical study of aesthetics or, more accurately, a historical analysis of form? For one, the approach provides a way for scholars to conceptualize and trace the interaction between the law and the media. As suggested above, specific images on paper, such as photographs of reenactments, are both units of information and physical objects that travel from one social, professional, or epistemological field to another. In the process of moving, these objects can help create new phenomena or facilitate change in existing ones. As the example of the map indicates, specific items of fiction traveled across the epistemological divide into the factual forms being developed at the same time by criminal investigators, generating a new type of space known as the crime scene. By focusing on the way these images look and how they change over time, scholars can begin to plot out the trajectory of their evolution, identify the players shaping change, and study how actors in different fields of society use them. A historical analysis of form may therefore shed light on the processes of social, cultural, and professional change.

The historical study of form also opens up avenues for potentially fruitful comparative work, both temporally and geographically. Examining the similarities that exist between different systems of representation allows scholars to think of images less in terms of distinctions such as "primitive" or "traditional" and "modern" than as different—sometimes competing, sometimes complementary—schemes of diagrammatic logic that people have developed under varying circumstances to perform cognitive operations. The anthropologist Alfred Gell has compared objects from vastly different time periods and societies, such as the works of Duchamp and Dali and those of the Maori and the Marquesas, by highlighting their analogous formal attributes. In both Western high art and non-Western craft objects, one finds complex entities that their producers, whether as "artists" or "natives," attempt similarly to imbue with symbolic intention.[10] In both instances, the artifacts are clearly part of a larger network of meaning, even if the more exotic items are sometimes seen only as practical instruments for everyday life. By bringing together these seemingly distinct types of things, Western art and non-Western artifact, Gell is able to subject them to the same critical analysis and thus bridge the gulf, in some ways an artificial one, that the concept of modernity has created between the West and the rest of the world. A similar move can be made with visual evidence in the study of policing and the law. Police officers produce photographs and maps as material artifacts with the intention of signifying something within the criminal justice system, itself a complex system of representations. The design and use of these images are influenced by theories and conventions that cross social, institutional, geographic, and conceptual borders, making them ideal objects through which to study how modern societies establish, maintain, and exploit epistemological borders visually.

An approach that emphasizes form is also useful in thinking about visual images as primary sources more broadly. In Thailand, the use of images as both symbols and tools has a long history and remains quite commonplace. The *duang chata* is one example (Figure I.1). It is a circle divided counterclockwise into twelve sections, one for each *rasi* or sign of the zodiac. J. C. Eade writes,

> This circle can be visualized as representing the sun's annual circular paths as seen from its pole, though it also does duty for the circular paths of all the other planets, brought for this purpose to the same plane. At the same time it represents the daily rotation of the heavens through 360 degrees, in that the ascendant [the *lagna* or *lakhana*] is also plotted in the circle. Here the clockwise angular distance from the *lagna* to the sun marks the time interval from dawn.[11]

Fortune-tellers and astrologers regularly use *duang chata* to predict possible future outcomes as well as explain past events by performing specific operations with the diagram. What is the difference between a "traditional" visualization like this and a "modern" one like a crime scene map? The question might sound absurd or even foolish, but both examples share a basic property in that they are symbols that are also operable: they allow users to work on reality. In this sense, diagrams are more than things to be read for meaning. Material images tell their observers about something in the world but they also, as in the example of modern criminal detection, help their creators operate in that world.

What this book contributes to the discipline of history and to the study of Thailand, therefore, is both historiographical and methodological. While not an institutional history of the Thai police in any strict sense, it does offer

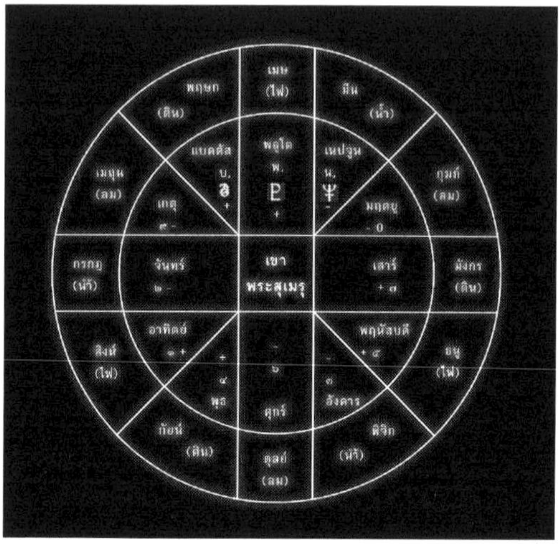

FIGURE I.1. *Duang chata*. A diagrammatic representation of the cosmos used in astrology. Image by Wasin Rangsikansong for the author.

the first extended overview of the development of the force in English. The study begins in the late nineteenth century, when local elites and foreign consultants first introduced modern policing to Siam and concludes with the end of the Cold War, by which time many of the practices used today for visualizing violent crime had already become entrenched. It is also during this period that the police grew to take on an active, independent role in shaping political, social, and cultural conditions in the kingdom. By detailing the evolution of detective practices over this period, I provide a window into the Thai police's role in a larger cultural system of knowledge production about crime, violence, and history.

Methodologically, I show how a historical analysis of form can supplement the way many scholars have traditionally approached visual sources, as symbols that require a close reading. For example, a historian may interpret an image as signifying some abstract idea that proves an existing theory (about modernity, the unconscious, or a dominant discourse), but this most often tells us only what we already know—that capitalist relations of production are exploitative, that the bureaucratic state is repressive, that discourse and power produce each other. By acknowledging the productive nature of images, in addition to their symbolic functions, one can see that policing is fundamentally an interactive, creative endeavor as much as a disciplinary one. In other words, the police state, or more precisely the detective state, that developed in Thailand in the 1950s persists today in part through the use of terror and physical force but also because the public has unwittingly engaged the police and the media in a spectacular game of detection, a social murder mystery unfolding in real time through which the deployment of state violence is seen as justified, desirable, and necessary.

1

Kingdom of Crime

On July 23, 1986, at about 1:00 a.m., Phrimphrao Wongjinda, or "Daeng," whose house was located near Khlong Chonprathan (a canal) in Samut Prakan province heard the hum of a car's engine during an otherwise quiet night. It is unclear whether she made anything of the noise. At 6:20 a.m. that same day, Buakhao Kingkaew found a pink schoolbag in the same canal, off Sukhumvit Road at kilometer 30, not too far from Phrimphrao's house. In the bag were eight books, six notebooks, one pair of glasses, one small purse, one pencil box, and a book belt without a buckle. Buakhao kept the bag, thinking that she would later look for its owner.[1] In a field, a forest, or a crowded city, people hear countless sounds every day, every minute, including sometimes that of a car engine idling during the middle of the night. They are also likely to find miscellaneous objects associated with human activity—a soda can, a cigarette butt, a schoolbag—lying on the ground almost anywhere they look. Most of the time, people ignore or forget the sounds they hear, the white noise of life, and pass over the things they see on the street, the debris of everyday existence. In a place like Bangkok during the mid-1980s, noise and trash were certainly common, and mostly meaningless. Bangkok was, after all, a big, sprawling, messy city. Sometimes, though, the things left behind and the sounds in the air signify something. They just need to be connected.

On July 26, *Thai rat,* the kingdom's top-selling daily newspaper, ran a short story appearing toward the bottom of its front page—buried under the other, more important noise of the day—with a small headline: "Schoolgirl Disappears: Mysterious Taxi Takes Her Away after School."[2] The last paragraph of the story reported that the missing girl's caretaker, Winai Chaiphanit, was offering a 20,000 baht reward for the return of the girl or for information leading to her return. The story also provided his phone number. At 8:00 a.m. the next day, Prasit Kingkaew, Buakhao's husband, called Winai to tell him that one of the notebooks in the schoolbag his wife found had "Sherry Ann" written in it. Whether motivated by the reward or not, Prasit had recognized the name from reading the newspaper and made the call.[3] Connected to a story about a missing girl, a schoolbag and the sound of a car engine became clues, information that gave form to and could perhaps help solve a mystery unfolding in "real time" in Bangkok in 1986.

Thais had, by the time Sherry Ann Duncan was murdered, a relatively clear conceptual framework with which they could recognize, order, and act on signs of violence. A missing child and a dead body act as triggers, setting off specific, routine actions performed by people employed by the state as police and those working on behalf of the press as reporters. The police went to inspect the dead body, look for clues, and question potential witnesses. The press made the investigation public, updating readers of new developments on a daily basis and bringing otherwise unconnected individuals together. The predictability of the process, if not its specific outcome, indicates the high level of familiarity Thai society has for the investigation ritual, for the detection process.

One hundred years earlier, the institution of the police was in its infancy, having a presence only in Bangkok. The provinces, not yet having been created as such, boasted no police from the capital.[4] The press, too, was only just getting off the ground, with a few newspapers published by missionaries and a handful of journals read by the educated elite. In this chapter, I begin telling the story of how the modern investigation process became commonplace in Thailand. I start by describing in broad strokes the chaotic situation that confronted the Siamese government between the 1890s and the 1930s, and then I detail its strategy for dealing with that chaos. In many ways, the establishment of a standing police force was part of a larger reaction to perceived social turmoil, a way to control an unruly kingdom. It was also the beginning of a new investigative culture, on display for all the wrong reasons in the Sherry Ann murder case, that would see the police evolve into something much more than just a second army over the course of the twentieth century.

A MESSY PLACE

From descriptions given by foreign visitors, one gets the impression that Siam's capital during the late nineteenth century was rather disorganized. Public spaces like streets were

> nearly all very narrow and crooked, and only adapted to the Siamese, who until lately never pretended to use carriages. . . . They [streets] are also very uneven, with here and there great holes, crossed by rough stepping stones, and during the highest tides are overflowed with water, sometimes knee-deep, for several hours each day. . . . The back lanes and bypaths . . . are in a chronic state of filth, wet or dry.[5]

Semipublic spaces, including commercial ones built for entertainment and pleasure, were similarly disorganized. Gambling houses, for example, were simply "large bamboo sheds, with an attap roof, devoid of furniture, and many of them without even a floor, only the bare earth, over which are laid mats for the players to sit on." These makeshift casinos were, in turn, frequented by "men, women, and little children," who, when tired of gambling, could "adjourn to the neighboring theatre," where they could "spend an hour or two watching the . . . performances [of *lakhon,* a type of Siamese stage drama]."[6] The sacred spaces of the city often did not look very different from these profane ones: "Next to gambling-hells, theatres, and perhaps dram-shops, the structures which are most numerous . . . [were] the temples."[7] These, in turn, held fairs, hawker stalls, beggars, and all manner of activity. A report from 1911 showed an illegal gambling ring had made its base at a *wat* (a Buddhist temple complex) in Phetchabun province.[8] As late as 1932, one American in Bangkok concluded, "The temple is not sacred. It is a town hall."[9] So even though the *wat* is typically thought of today as a religious center, it was in the past a multipurpose community center.

That people did not maintain the structures of their city added to the experience of being in a ramshackle, transient place: "It is a curious fact that the Siamese, though ever building, seem seldom, if ever, to take steps to keep their edifices, sacred or secular, in repair. And more often than not what they do build they leave uncompleted. It is quite an exception to see any building which has been completed 'out of hand,' and still more exceptional to find repairs going on."[10] One visitor in the early 1880s summed up his impression of the city with these words:

> As the reality of the interior of the city, in its filth, its foetid odours, and the poverty of its buildings, is very different from the idea which the view from the river conveys to the mind, so a close acquaintance with the temples which look the most magnificent from a distance shows them in a very different light from that in which they reflected the brilliant rays of the midday or the setting sun.[11]

Another similar account of Bangkok from the mid-nineteenth century goes like this: "The town looked as a supper-room does the morning after a ball; there was nothing left of the feast save the odds and ends; jellies had melted to nauseous looking water, and gaily-ornamented cakes crumbled into indescribable pieces of nastiness. So it was with Bangkok."[12]

The impression of messiness extended to the private spaces of the family home, which, like the gambling parlor and the public thoroughfare, was often seen as unkempt or makeshift:

> The middle class dwell in houses built of wood, usually unpainted teak, and roofed with earthen tiles. They are small and illy ventilated, and here the people huddle together, from the parents to the children of the third and fourth generation. . . . They have very little furniture. . . . The lower class dwellings are built on posts . . . which elevate them five or six feet from the ground, and are reached by ladders, which at night are drawn up to prevent dogs or thieves coming into the house. But the very poor have . . . huts made of palm leaves tied to a bamboo frame, and with . . . the bare earth for a floor.[13]

The slapdash, sometimes shoddy character of these homes was complicated by their seemingly unhindered mobility: "Owners can also move at will, letting their dwellings float up- or downstream with the incoming or outgoing tide, where they can tie them up at a new mooring place."[14] Nothing was stable. Expectations of an intimate space in the family home, perhaps guided by a Victorian sensibility, were thus disappointed.[15] Instead, the Siamese house was the location of conflicting, jumbled activities, not all typically associated with home life. Cruising along the muddy waters of the Chao Phraya River, one could "look inside open houses and observe the inhabitants going about their daily business . . . [and] see them cooking, eating, sleeping, sitting together around a teapot with their friends, listening to a priest sermonizing, or playing with their children. A craftsman can be seen industriously pursuing his profession, an idler smoking, and a woman, whose legs are bound because she has run away or committed some other misdemeanor, meekly washing and knocking about some kitchen utensils. Then one can find buyers and sellers involved in lengthy negotiations, can hear the shrieking voices of bickering women, or find oneself stuck in a jam of boats, which one can only escape unscathed from if one's pilot is giving his undivided attention to the matter."[16] All manner of activity, it seemed, could take place in the home, just as anything could happen at the temple or on the street.

To this muddle a series of rapid physical changes were added. These involved a range of development projects initiated by the royal government, private companies, or individuals through the market, including technological adaptations in communications and information technology such as the introduction of paved streets, trains, automobiles, typewriters (for Thai characters), printing presses, filing systems, and a postal service. In Bangkok

> during the first decade of this century [the twentieth] modern construction proceeded with a certain rapidity, and by the end of his [King Chulalongkorn's] reign a discernible change had been wrought in the appearance of the capital. . . . Great sections of the massive crenellated wall [that surrounded the old city] had been demolished to provide road metal for some of the hundred and twenty miles of carriage ways that crossed the network of canals on substantial bridges of iron and marble, including the 200-foot-wide, two mile long, tree-lined boulevard [Ratchadamnoen] connecting the recently built Grand Palace with the complex of ornamental gardens, princely villas and the summer palace [Dusit] which had been laid out immediately north of Khlong Padung Krung Kasem, and the Samsen Road—New Road's complement to the northeast.[17]

In 1890, Prince Naritsaranuwatiwang proposed building eighteen roads in the Sampheng area to facilitate commerce and increase land values in the area. In 1899, as part of the Suan Dusit palace construction, several more roads were built. Before this building spree, there were few paved roads, and those that did exist did so mostly because of canal digging; they were made from dirt dredged from various waterways.[18]

With the roads came tramways, electricity, the telegraph, and a sewer system. In 1888, a group of Danes introduced the horse tramway. This was electrified and extended in 1893. In 1903, the tram system carried about ten million passengers annually. The major routes at the time were along Charoenkrung, Bangkholaem, Samsen, Atsadang, and Ratchawong Roads. The system totaled 17.3 km of lines, with "receipts on the routes from Charoenkrung to Bangkoalam [*sic*] and Samsen between 1899 and 1907 show[ing] increasing demand for trams."[19] The trams, which first served commercial areas, were eventually extended into the suburbs and helped trigger a move away from canals and rivers. More roadways also meant more cars, which grew in number from 401 in 1910 to 3,361 in 1929.[20] In addition, many modern services were established:

> Banking facilities, hotels, a hospital and a nursing home, a university and several secondary schools, a library and a museum, one of the finest race-courses in the East and a number of social-cultural-athletic clubs were provided among the other of the amenities necessary for modern living. Water was piped into the city and available from a number of artesian bores, and electricity lit street lamps and moved the trams that shared the clogged roadways with a never-ending stream of jinrikishas [rickshaws], horse-drawn carriages, bullock carts, bicycles, small omnibuses and an increasing number of motor cars.[21]

In monetary terms, by the beginning of 1926, 202 million baht had been spent on "works of development: Railway construction, 172,435,797, Irrigation Construction, 22,709,703, Bangkok Waterworks, 4,922,129, Samsen Power Station, 2,044,339."[22]

The provision of paved roads also spurred other changes, such as the gradual introduction of row housing developments and new palaces for nobles. From 1880s onward, "settlements gradually moved from the banks of waterways to along major roads, at that time mainly Charoenkrung and Bumrungmuang [Bamrungmueang]."[23] By the 1910s, the city had taken on a whole new look: "A revision of the 1910 census undertaken in 1913 shows that by the early 1910s, settlements had already moved away from the river and canals. Bangkok's population (excluding Thonburi) clustered around the districts of Chakkrawat, Prarajawang, Samphuntawong [Samphanthawong], Pomprab, Bangrak, and Pahurad [Phahurat], where roads were concentrated."[24] At that point, not more than 7 to 8 percent of the city's population lived in floating houses. By 1910, "the map of Bangkok had changed remarkably from its appearance of the 1880s. Many industrial, residential, and commercial areas developed along the arterial roads: Sampeng [Sampheng], Dusit, Sarapratum, Bangrak, Bangkoalam [Bangkholaem], Banglumpoo Lang, the part of Bangsue west of Klong Prem Prachakorn, and the district within the city wall."[25] Southern Bangkok was an especially active area for development: "Roads had significant effects on the growth of this [Bangrak] district. Consulates, the residences of foreigners, the port, rice mills, and saw mills were located in this area. Charoenkrung Road became the hub of commercial Bangkok and remained so until the 1950s, the headquarters of many of the principle trading houses, banks, and other enterprises, and containing most of the leading hotels."[26] The landscape in and around Bangkok was changing rapidly and without much oversight.

It did not help that the people who inhabited these cluttered, mixed-up spaces represented many ethnicities, and many did not speak central Thai. There were, in addition to the Siamese, tens of thousands of Chinese of many different dialect groups. G. William Skinner, in his encyclopedic book on the Chinese in Thailand, notes that about 185,000 Chinese, overwhelmingly male, lived in Bangkok in 1904.[27] The relatively small total number of people in the capital, which was an estimated 120,000 in 1883 and was no more than about 360,000 by World War I, meant these Chinese men comprised about half (or more) of the city's population at the turn of the century.[28] More than their sheer numbers, it was the speed of the increase that contributed to the feeling among government officials that Chinese immigrants were inundating the city. Skinner shows that the total number of net arrivals of Chinese to Siam between 1882 and 1892 was 78,000. This jumped to 193,200 between 1893 and 1905 and remained high at 180,200 between 1906 and 1917.[29] The Chinese, in addition to having a "Chinatown" in Sampheng, were located in large numbers throughout the city. Constance Wilson, from a detailed analysis of Siam's first postal census, writes, "Chinese were well distributed throughout the city where they could be found in every neighborhood."[30] They could also be found in almost all sectors of the economy, controlling trade activities and tax collection duties and providing a source of labor for the expanding city and provincial hubs from Nakhon Sawan to Phuket. Significant numbers of Laotians, Malays, Annamites, Mons, Khmers, and South Asians and a handful of vocal, influential Europeans in the capital made the situation more complex. Though mostly spread throughout Bangkok, some groups did have their own streets or districts—Vietnamese in Samsen, Lao in Tanao, *farangs* (Caucasians) in Bangrak, and Indians in Phahurat. The capital and select townships, including Phuket, Chiang Mai, and places along what are now the kingdom's borders, were as diverse ethnically as they were physically messy, at least in terms of present-day city-planning notions of distinct, organizable zones of land uses. Rather than benignly cosmopolitan or simply pluralistic, however, many viewed this diversity, for different reasons, as problematic.

THE CRIME PROBLEM

For the administrations of Kings Chulalongkorn (r. 1868–1910), Vajiravudh (r. 1910–1925), and Prajadhipok (r. 1925–1935), one of the chief problems posed by the kingdom's messiness was crime, which, according to government statistics and anecdotal evidence from newspaper reports, increased dramatically throughout Siam in the first two decades of the twentieth century. Today, people still sometimes refer to Siam at the turn of the nineteenth century as a "kingdom of crime" (*anajak haeng jon*).[31] As with most crime waves in the era of mass media, it is difficult to say whether the rise in crime associated with this period was real or something that can be attributed to the increased reporting of violence around the kingdom. The statistics that exist for the period do indicate a large number of violent crimes and increases in these crimes in certain areas at different times. But these increases could also be attributed to improvements (however uneven) in data gathering. In any case, someone scanning the daily papers published in Bangkok in the late nineteenth century would have come away with the impression that incidents of banditry, very often accompanied by physical assault and murder, were commonplace across the kingdom. On May 19, 1902, for example, someone picking up a copy of the *Bangkok Times* would have come across an article entitled, "Gang Robbery at Paklat." The report describes a group of forty men raiding a gambling house in southern Bangkok. Eleven were killed and many injured during that incident.[32] Another report tells of an official in charge of an area just north of the city requesting permission to organize a posse of men to control the rampant crime there.[33] Things were so out of hand at the turn of the century that even monks were kidnapped.[34] One British police officer serving in the Metropolitan Constabulary in Bangkok in 1906 recounts a story that A. J. A. Jardine, another British national and head of the Metropolitan Constabulary from 1897 to 1902, was fond of relating: "One evening, not long after his [Jardine's] arrival in Siam, he had occasion to call at a large [police] station on the way from the club to dinner. He found the shutters down and the place closed. On seeking the reason from an old inspector who resided above the station, he was informed that they usually barred the station for the night to prevent theft of rifles and other Government property."[35] The officer went on to describe Bangkok by saying, "Rarely a night passed in which we [the police] had not to turn out to keep order. The floor of the Bangkok [Police] Station was often covered with blood. People carried knives and swords as a matter of course until the 'Arms Act' was put into force, when things became more peaceable."[36]

Almost two decades later, however, things had hardly become any "more peaceable." An article from the newspaper *Jinosayam warasap* dated June 4, 1921, said that incidents of banditry in Samut Prakan and Phraprapadaeng provinces, adjacent to Bangkok, were common, causing citizens to feel extremely frightened. A few days before that report, on May 24, a group of bandits robbed a house in Phra Khanong district in what is now eastern Bangkok, taking property and kidnapping a woman. Later that night, the same bandits robbed a local notable in Bangna district not far from Phra Khanong. The police eventually found the woman but they never arrested the bandits. The report goes on to say that these incidents point clearly to the fact that citizens in the provinces adjacent to Bangkok did not live in peace (*sangop sabai suk*), and it called on local officials and the Ministry of Local Government (*krasuang nakhonban*) to deal with the situation swiftly.[37] It also suggested a special police unit be put together to subdue the bandits hunkered down in Phrapradaeng, just southwest of Bangkok.[38] A report dated April 24, 1923, describes a funeral-turned-gambling-den in Samut Prakan, east of the capital, at which a dead man with several assault wounds was found. Another report, from March 13 of the same year, says that on March 11, police officers and a local resident went to arrest a man named Waek, a suspected criminal, at his residence, also in Samut Prakan. A shootout ensued in which Waek was shot in the chest and captured. His associates fled the scene.[39]

It is common today to link the city in general and rapid urbanization in particular with increased rates of crime. The violence in Siam, however, was not limited to urban Bangkok and its suburbs. The situation throughout the central plains was quite dire. In 1882, King Chulalongkorn reportedly told Jao Phraya Surasakmontri (given name Joem Saengchuto), the commander of the "front army" (*thahan na*), "At this time, incidents of serious crime including murder and armed robbery occur every evening [in Suphanburi in the central plains]. Many people have lost their lives and have been physically assaulted as a result of these robberies."[40] Surasakmontri claimed that at least two to three cases of murder or robbery occurred there each day.[41] A *Bangkok Times* correspondent wrote in 1892 that in the *monthon* (administrative district) of Ayutthaya, "not a week passes without some fresh act of violence and bloodshed."[42] In Nakhon Nayok, a province just north of Bangkok, reports indicated that talk of various criminals (*phu rai*) was commonly heard in villages there.[43] As if on cue, a story from February 22, 1917, tells of four or five men entering a house and beating up its owner before robbing him of his possessions. A few weeks before that, reports from the same province came in about a man shooting a soldier to death just across from the home of the provincial governor.[44]

Banditry and assaults were also common in other parts of the central plains, including Sawankhalok in Phitsanulok *monthon,* now a six-hour drive from Bangkok. A news report dated February 24, 1917, stated that it was difficult to determine the cause for all the crime occurring there, but the situation was simply frightful (*na wat siao mak*). For example, a report from May 26, 1917, tells of a shooting at the house of a man named Won that occurred during the evening. Fortunately, no one was injured.[45] A few weeks earlier, a man named Yok was shot near Wat Bong in *tambon* (subdistrict) Wang Phanit while taking his pigs to sell at market. The paper called the situation in the area extremely grave. A report from March 24 says that someone robbed the house of a woman named Su in Amphoe Mueang, Sawankhalok. Shots were fired but no one was hit. The bandit then set fire to the victim's house after locking the owners and their child inside. The woman and her husband could not escape the blaze and died. Their child fell from the house in a flaming heap. It was not clear whether he survived. Even the governor was not spared from violence, as someone fired shots into his compound (*juan*) on the night of February 16, 1917, when he was hosting a party.

Prince Damrong, King Chulalongkorn's brother and minster of interior at the time, visited Sawankhalok in January 1917 despite being warned of the violence. The night he arrived, the sound of five gunshots was heard. A paper reporting the incident cheekily suggested that this may have been a five-gun salute to the prince. The next morning, the chatter of merchants at the local market claimed that one of the bullets had hit a woman named Liam while she was in her house. Another hit a woman who had come out to see what was going on. The third bullet hit a woman in *tambon* Yan Khao Thong. They did not know if the fourth and fifth bullets hit anyone. The year before, Police Inspector (*jare*) J. Jarmer, one of several Danish nationals serving in the provincial police in the 1910s and 1920s, reported that that the area was awash in guns and that gunfire could be heard nightly.[46] There were 2,103 registered guns in the province, he wrote, adding that many more were not registered. He claimed that the crime problem there was exacerbated by unspecified problems between a *Daily Mail* reporter, the provincial governor, and the local judge.[47]

Reports from areas outside the central plains show similar patterns of banditry. Along the eastern seaboard, incidents of crime were on the rise, and, as with the monks in the Bangkok area, no one was safe. In Chonburi several *palat amphoe* (deputy district chiefs) were shot to death in the 1910s.[48] The situation did not appear qualitatively better in the northeast. In Nakhon Ratchasima, a report from February 1924 claimed that people there were living in a state of unease because criminals had gathered en masse and that at least two to three incidents of crime took place each night. Bandits there had no fear, and they particularly targeted homes headed by old people and women. The police, it was reported, were not doing anything to stop the crime wave. According to the paper, they just sat around collecting their salaries.[49] Even the north, seen today as an idyllic getaway from chaotic Bangkok, did not escape the violence. A report from 1916 by Police Colonel Jao Ratchabut, police inspector for Lampang, to Mom Jao Khamrop, the director-general of police, stated that incidents of banditry, some that included murder, were increasing in his region. The cause, he wrote, was the lack of police officers, which was due in turn to the police department's small budget and poor pay.[50]

Of course, actual levels of violent crime varied from location to location and over time. It was higher in certain places for some periods and lower in others. One newspaper reported in October 1916 that crime was down for the whole of Ayutthaya *monthon,* mostly because it had been a particularly cold few weeks and this discouraged would-be bandits. The decline may have stemmed from more than just cold weather, though, as news from the Thanaburi area in Ayutthaya *monthon* showed that crime there was down, due in large part to the hard work of the police. Bangkok papers praised the police for their quick work on January 22, 1918, reporting that they had captured two murderers in one hour in the city of Ayutthaya.[51] Lopburi, to the north of Ayutthaya, was reportedly also doing well in late 1916, despite reports of the murder of two government officials. One news story noted that the situation had improved because of the good work of the new governor. The province experienced only "crime as usual," but nothing of epic proportions.[52]

There is also data that shows that the number of crimes reported fell significantly during the first few years of the 1920s in the north and northeast. One foreign visitor noted,

> It is generally accepted that Siam was visited by a wave of crime which followed in the wake of [World War I], and this probably does account for a good proportion of the cases reported in the Southern and Central portions of the country, but it seems this wave did not reach as far as the North (or, at most, only its back-eddies), for the figures show nothing but a normal amount of crime among a people who are still no less subject to the frailties of the human race than any other agricultural population.[53]

He added, "nothing is so remarkable or augurs so well for the future as the absence of serious crime, when compared with some of the central and southern Provinces of Siam."[54] For a twelve-month period in 1923–1924, he reports that the number of criminal cases reported for the whole kingdom was 42,800. The population at that point was approximately 9,200,000, giving a crime rate of 1 for every 215 persons. This is relatively high, but when looking at the distribution, it becomes clear that much of the crime was concentrated in the central region during the early 1920s. The rate of crime per person in the *monthon* of Bangkok was highest, at 1 in 60. Phitsanulok's was 1 in 121, Ayutthaya's was 1 in 164, and Ratchaburi's was 1 in 143. The rates in the north and northeast, however, were much lower. In Phayap, the average fell to 1 in 357, and in Maharat it was only 1 in 480. Evidently, the rates in northeastern *monthon* like Ubon Ratchathani, Udonthani, and Roi Et were the lowest of all.[55]

Despite the temporal and geographical variation, it is clear that the press and the government began noticing periodic spikes in the level of crime in the 1890s, and this intensification was common to both city and country. An article entitled "Ayutthia" in the *Bangkok Times* indicates that as early as 1892, when the article was published, people (or at least the English reporters of the *Bangkok Times* and its foreign and elite Siamese readership) were becoming alarmed that the number of incidents of crime were increasing.[56] As the preceding sampling of news reports indicates, the press presented this violent crime as a strong, destabilizing force in the lives of people throughout the kingdom at one point or another between 1890 and 1930. The constant flow of news stories suggests that people were living in fear, and the media made regular calls for the central government to act quickly and decisively or to send people with "ability" (*khwam samat*) to administer townships outside Bangkok. The press was in essence amplifying the effects of crime and bringing it to "national" attention in Bangkok. It is also clear that the government, which archived the newspaper clippings from which much of this information was obtained, was quite aware of the problem and was looking for ways to deal with the disorder.[57]

The paradox of this situation is that during the reform years, or between the 1890s and the 1920s, ample information about criminals did exist. People often knew who was doing what, or thought they did, especially outside the cities. A report from the *Bangkok Times* about crime from 1907, for example, states, "No one would be surprised . . . when as often happened, bandits killed during raids were found to be people living in the immediate neighborhood."[58] Another newspaper report from February 1917 indicated that on the seventh day of the month a pregnant woman named Saeng was shot to death near the local market during the evening. The next day the governor went to investigate the incident along with the deputy governor and local police officers, only to discover that the shooter lived nearby and was quite well known. However, the provincial prosecutor, or magistrate (*ayakan jangwat*), investigated the case and found that the person named by the police was not the shooter. Instead, the policeman himself was the culprit. Witnesses later confirmed that the shooter was the police officer, who subsequently confessed and stated that the cause was his failed marriage.[59] In another news story, from 1913, a reporter bemoaned the cheapness of life in Siam, saying that while murder was a crime according to law, a simple payment from the perpetrator, say 300–400 baht, to a victim's relatives was enough to keep things quiet.[60] English residents in Siam at the time reported a similar situation. A Mr. Fitzmaurice wrote,

> There have been recent cases of murders and other serious crimes in which the perpetrators have not been brought to justice; amongst others a case in which two traders were murdered in Palao, on the road between Phe [Phrae] and Pong. After shooting and robbing the men, the assailants fled, but left behind a hat bearing one of their names and a poll tax paper belonging to another of their number. It appears that it was generally known who these assailants were, but that, although the men and the fact of their return to [Phrae] are said to have been known to the Mung [Mueang] Song authorities (fifteen miles from Palao) no steps were then taken to arrest either of the men whose names were betrayed by what they had left behind them in their flight.[61]

In other words, locals often knew the identities of criminals in cases of violent crime.

In fact, this information was part and parcel of local social networks. One report claimed that anyone who went to the Nongkhai city market could hear every day that people in the area knew that resident toughs made a living from questionable means but that village leaders weren't able to do anything and could never find evidence against the troublemakers.[62] A report from April 17, 1917, supported this, stating that several bandits had made their base in Sawankhalok and regularly committed crimes against the locals and merchants. Local officials knew who they were but took no action to arrest the criminals. The article then urged the government, as usual, to assign people with ability to suppress the criminals.[63] In several cases in the subdistrict of Wat Bung, victims of shootings said they could identify perpetrators and often told the local authorities. But when cases went to court, defendants would be freed because the suspects were able to produce dozens of witnesses on their own behalf. After a shooting, it was alleged that perpetrators would go to people's houses and convince them to be defense witnesses by offering them material rewards (*sombat*). Meanwhile, plaintiffs could rarely produce enough evidence because many witnesses were afraid of the suspects. This was reported to be the case in several other provinces as well.[64] Prince Damrong, in a famous tract in which he interviewed a captured bandit named Jan, active in Pathumthani, Ayutthaya, and Suphanburi around 1903, asked, "How does the *sai* [informer, here for the bandit, not the state] know who the *nakleng* [local tough] is?"[65] Jan replied that in the circle of *nakleng,* identities are not kept secret.[66] Local residents had information about the identities of perpetrators of crimes, violent or otherwise, and in many cases village officials knew as well. In fact, local residents, officials, and bandits were often in cahoots. For example, in 1885 in Mueang Phichit, residents in five subdistricts provided food for a group of bandits, and in 1890 it was said that people were similarly supporting bandits with food in Nakhon Nayok.[67] All this was part of a social order in which crime and knowledge were intricately tied to localized systems of patronage.

Despite the wealth of existing information about criminals, central government officials found themselves stymied in their efforts against crime. Many crimes were never solved, no one was ever arrested, and police and reporters appeared to have no idea who the perpetrators were. As such, crimes reported in the press read as unexplained acts of violence lacking clues, suspects, and motivations—real-life mysteries for a kingdom in transition. In part because locals already knew who the bad guys were, the solution to crime that newspapers put forth was that the government should simply assign people with ability or send out military expeditions to suppress criminals, which the government did do regularly. Jao Phraya Surasakmontri, for instance, made his name in part from successfully quashing bandits in the central region. In one expedition to Suphanburi in 1882, he claimed to have captured three hundred criminals.[68] The problem with military solutions was that their victories were short lived. One newspaper article notes that there was a decrease in crime in Chonburi after a military expedition in 1916, but that by early 1917 it was once again on the rise.[69] Military raids also did not address the basic problem for the government that crime exposed: officials working during Chulalongkorn's reign were faced with an increasing number of crimes for which vital information (such as the identity of the culprit) existed but that they could not access.

The government's ability to act against crime was also complicated by extraterritoriality rights enjoyed by foreign subjects in Siam. Siam agreed to a treaty of "friendship and commerce" with the British in 1855. The agreement, known today as the Bowring Treaty, contained a number of provisions, three of which are most often cited as being critical. First, export duties were capped at 3 percent on all products except opium and bullion, which were to be traded without any duty. Second, British merchants were granted the right to trade with individual Siamese merchants without the interference of any third party. This meant the effective end of monopoly trade. Third, and most important with respect to criminal investigation, British subjects were placed under consular jurisdiction, meaning that charges against them would be processed by judges in the British consulate rather than in a Siamese court.[70] Several similar treaties with countries including France and the United States followed the Bowring Treaty. So in cases where a foreign subject was arrested on suspicion of a crime, that suspect would have to be handed over to foreign officials to be tried. This meant that the large number of Chinese, Indian, Malay, and Lao people who were living in Siam but were subjects of European, U.S., or Japanese governments could effectively escape Siamese law. Many claimed upon arrest that they were not Siamese subjects, something that took time to verify. Extraterritoriality therefore posed an additional hurdle for the reforming government in tackling high crime rates.[71]

The issue for the government, therefore, was not simply that crime was being committed, but that the crimes were seemingly inexplicable, an impression the papers in Bangkok reinforced with their style of reporting—short, simple blurbs devoid of context, teasing readers with violence without any closure. The practices of modern police investigation like those involved in the Sherry Ann case had yet to take hold, but the beginnings of a socio-legal mystery were being put in place by the press and agents of the state.

THE STATE'S DETECTIVES

To address the crime problem, the government adopted an administrative innovation—the police—that was simultaneously taking hold in Europe, its colonies, and the United States. In the early years of the twentieth century, there were two separate police units in Siam, the Metropolitan Constabulary (then known in Thai as the *kong trawen*), which operated primarily in Bangkok, and the Provincial Gendarmerie (*tamruat phuthon*), which functioned outside the capital. The Metropolitan Constabulary dates back to 1860, when King Mongkut established the Police Constabulary Division. Before this, "Bangkok's nearest approach to police officers consisted of a body of men clad in civilian clothing who carried bundles of canes and whose functions in assisting magistrates were somewhat akin to those of the Bow Street Runners."[72] Their headquarters flanked a frying pan factory (now the Siam Commercial Bank head office) and fronted a fortress and the residence of a district officer in what is currently the Samphanthawong area of Bangkok. The unit was headed by an Englishman named Samuel Bird Ames. Ames is described alternatively as a merchant, a trader, and a wanderer. In 1860 he was running a construction company in Bangkok. His main achievement in Siam prior to being appointed as chief of police was the construction of a bridge near the government's Custom House. The police in Ames' force were mostly Indians (Sikhs) and Malays. Cecil H. Forty, an English officer serving in Siam during the early decades of the twentieth century, wrote in 1906 that the early constabulary "consisted of Malays whom he [Ames] had himself recruited from the ranks of men who had served in the army of police in Singapore. These were augmented, and in time replaced, by Siamese and Indians, though a few individuals remained on in the capacity of detectives [a title more than a function] long after the original circumstances of their enlistment had been forgotten by the public."[73] According to Forty, the new policeman "must indeed have been a droll figure. It soon became a familiar sight for the neighborhood to behold burly turbaned Indians walking their beats. Practical jokes were frequently played upon them; but, due to the strict enforcement of discipline, the men were able to keep their composure under all circumstances."[74] One of their first tasks was dealing with "rampaging Chinese secret societies,"[75] indicating that the police were, in part, a tool introduced to pacify the diverse, messy population. Accordingly, their first patrol was of Sampheng, the Chinese sector of Bangkok.[76] These police constables walked a beat and responded to disturbances or calls for help. They were also tasked with keeping an eye on public sanitation conditions, beggars, and loiterers. In other words, their work comprised keeping order, making arrests, and helping put down disturbances in ethnic enclaves. The investigative work now associated with modern policing around the world was not part of normal police practice.

This began to change in 1890, when the royal government under Chulalongkorn began its ambitious reform programs, including wholesale changes to the police force. Their model, as with so many of their other development projects, was a colonial one, specifically British in the case of the metropolitan police.[77] Prince Naretworarit, fresh from a stint in England and duly impressed by the London Police, proposed that the Metropolitan Constabulary be reorganized with the English model as a guide.[78] King Chulalongkorn had been impressed with the British colonial police in Singapore. He visited the colony in 1890, and that same year he approved the reorganization proposal.[79] He also went personally to observe the Dutch colonial police in Batavia. A few years later, in the 1890s, the government sent officials to study the operations of the colonial police force in British Burma. Reports from that mission were published in the late nineteenth-century journal of the Royal Wachirayan Library called *Wachirayan*.[80] A cynical, but accurate, view of the calls for aid from Bangkok to fight crime is to see them as an excuse, a pretense, for the central government to extend its control out into the provinces and to consolidate its authority over the capital. As the study missions indicate, the central government's reaction to escalating crime was in fact a self-conscious, systematic reformation of the law, the courts, and the metropolitan police, as well as the establishment of the new Provincial Gendarmerie. The police force was an administrative innovation that could be adopted and used internally. It was also, quite conveniently, a sign of modernity that European colonists recognized.[81]

Initially, the reformed Metropolitan Constabulary had two main units, the *kong tai suan thot luang* (roughly, the criminal investigation department) and the *kong raksa* (operations department). The criminal investigation department combined the old *kong trawen sai* and *kong trawen khwa* (or the "left" and "right" constabulary), which were under the control of the *nai amphoe* (district head) and the *kamnan* (subdistrict head).[82] A *kong sot naem* (detective division) was part of this investigative department. Officers in the investigation department technically had the power to inspect dead bodies, question witnesses, investigate individual criminals, and send cases for minor offenses to court. The operations department was in charge of keeping the peace in assigned districts in the capital and carrying out orders of the court such as arresting suspects for trial. Part of this unit was tasked with policing areas outside the capital proper (that is, in the "suburbs" outside *phranakhon*, the Thai term for "capital city").[83] The 1890 reform was accompanied by the establishment of magistrates' courts, or *politsapha,* which tried minor offenses.[84] Chulalongkorn had also issued a new set of regulations called the "Fifty-Three Rules for the Police in the Capital and outside the Capital" in 1875 to guide the work of the city's new police.[85] In theory and on paper, the police had a clear mandate and set of procedures, a point I will return to later.

For now it is enough to note that by 1908, the Metropolitan Constabulary had become well established in Bangkok's landscape, appearing regularly in newspaper reports and even in the kingdom's early fiction. King Vajiravudh's well-known detective stories from 1904–1905 featured a private detective named Thong-in and often included references to the constabulary and occasionally to its *farang* chief inspector, who was portrayed as condescending and incompetent. The real-life *farang* chief of the Metropolitan Constabulary between 1902 and 1915, Eric St. John Lawson, gives us a more concrete picture of how much the new police had become part of the capital's landscape. He wrote that the *monthon* of Bangkok was "policed by a force consisting of 3,398 men, of whom 2,679 are employed in the town of Bangkok and the remainder in the outlying districts."[86] He described the unit as follows: "The force is divided into seven divisions, five of which were in the town proper and two outside the town. One of these is the Chinese branch, whose duties are connected with all matters appertaining to the large Chinese community, and in addition there is the Special Branch."[87] The largest station had 120 men and the smallest had 24. Outposts were set up where the population was thin. The total number of stations and outposts was eighty-eight. The force at that point consisted of several nationalities, mostly Siamese, but also many Lao. These men were recruited by examination after they had gone through a period of training. Gradually, it was these men who would take over the investigation of crime in the capital.

The Provincial Gendarmerie was not established until almost forty years after its metropolitan counterpart. Uncontrolled crime in the "border" areas was a convenient excuse that the French could use to expand their presence into "Siamese territory," and, because the central government in Bangkok could not deploy its army within twenty-five kilometers of the Mekong River according to a treaty signed after the Gunboat Crisis of 1893, the number of incidents of banditry in that area increased.[88] The creation of the Provincial Gendarmerie, technically not part of the army, in 1897 was a way to circumvent this prohibition.[89] The model for the new unit was the French gendarmerie, a uniformed and armed police force similar to a military cavalry unit. Once established, the Provincial Gendarmerie was put under the command of Gustav Schau, a Danish national, and housed within Prince Damrong's Ministry of Interior. Schau and other Danish officers were enlisted to run the Provincial Gendarmerie in part because it was thought that their presence in sensitive territories would be less likely to provoke the French than would that of British officers.[90] The first unit was set up in Prachinburi, not far from the Siamese "border" with French Indochina. By 1908, the Provincial

Gendarmerie had officers in every *monthon,* the last being Phuket. In 1918, the provincial police force numbered 9,651 men.[91] While there are no accurate statistics for the period, some estimates show that the kingdom had a population of approximately nine million, or one officer for every one hundred subjects.[92]

As with its French prototype, the Provincial Gendarmerie operated like a military unit more than a police force, despite being tasked with such police responsibilities as suppressing banditry and gathering information from local district and subdistrict heads on incidents of crime, illegal weapons, suspicious people, and sources of corruption. To do this they were assigned patrols of the countryside, which were to last no more than fifteen days, and to report their findings. The gendarmerie, however, was undermanned and ill trained. Records show that they did not often go on their reconnaissance missions. Sometimes they did not leave their base camp more than once every four or five months.[93] Neither did they get much cooperation from local authorities, who viewed them with distrust. Even if the constabulary had gone out regularly, it is unclear that they would have made much difference in crime solving. Lawson wrote that gendarmes "undergo the usual military discipline, following the rules and regulations of the Siamese Army, and are armed with the Mannlicher magazine carbine, each man being allowed eighty cartridges a year for practice. The force is recruited by conscription from the army recruiting list, and the men, after serving for two years in the gendarmerie, are transferred to the army reserve."[94] In other words, they were not trained in criminal investigation.

Furthermore, the Provincial Gendarmerie did not have the same legal powers as its metropolitan counterpart. According to successive laws on local administration, one in 1897 and another in 1914, local civilian officials, not the police, were in charge of keeping peace and order as well as gathering evidence for trials in the provinces. The Provincial Gendarmerie generally only aided civilian administrative authorities, accompanying *amphoe* officials when dealing with an incident, even though its role officially included helping with the initial inspection of a crime scene, looking for clues, and rounding up witnesses to compile case reports. These reports were then supposed to be given over to the *amphoe,* who would review the file and question witnesses to decide whether to take case to trial. This arrangement between civilian authorities and the police lasted well into the Sixth Reign. In many cases, however, the *krommakan amphoe* (district officials) were too busy or were uninterested in going out to conduct investigations. Instead, some would use the opportunity to enrich themselves by taking bribes. In other instances, they left it up to the police or hired an underling to do their work.[95] The problem with this delegation of duties was that police officers and flunkies were not trained to solve crime. This is not a knock on the police, since, in actuality, no one was. So, police officers and civilian officials used force to extract confessions, a practice (known colloquially as *jarit nakhonban*, roughly translated as "administrative tradition") that, though outlawed by the end of the nineteenth century (1895), was still employed with regularity well into the 1920s and 1930s (and some would say is still today). The Provincial Gendarmerie was in many cases simply the local officials' "muscle" (*kamlang*), sent out to make arrests.[96] If there was ever a situation that could not be handled locally, a special force from Bangkok could be sent to deal with it.

In 1915, the Metropolitan Constabulary and the Provincial Gendarmerie were placed under the Ministry of Local Government, then headed by Jao Phraya Yommarat (given name Pan Sukhum), before both were shifted to the Ministry of Interior, to which Yommarat also moved, in 1922.[97] After the consolidation, officers outside the capital still did not have the power to investigate cases or bring a case to court. In fact, the combined police force was envisioned along functional as well as geographical lines. In a Ministry of Interior document dated April 28, 1926, the unified force was described in terms of legal power. The police officials who could arrest suspects, question them, and compile a report for trial in the *politsapha* were called the *tamruat nakhonban* (the police in Bangkok). The *tamruat phuthon* (the police outside of Bangkok), on the other hand, could arrest suspects but had to send them to the district head for questioning. And it was the district head, not the police, who compiled case reports for the public prosecutor to use in trials in provincial courts.[98] The power to gather evidence and question witnesses (*sop suan*) was only gradually shifted to police officers in the provinces. On October 1, 1935, the new Criminal Procedure Code was promulgated by royal decree. It held that, in the provinces outside Bangkok and Thonburi, local civilian administrators (*phanakngan fai pokkhrong*) or high-ranking police officers, deputy district heads, and police with the rank of police sublieutenant or above had the power to gather and compile evidence within their jurisdictions. In 1938, the Ministry of Interior under Rear Admiral Thawan Thamrongnawasat finally transferred the power to compile evidence and question witnesses from district-level administration officials to the police.[99] The slow, problematic shift from a crime suppression unit to a full investigative police like the one involved in the Sherry Ann case can therefore be explained as the result of several factors including a lack of experienced trainers, resistance from local authorities who traditionally dealt with crime, infighting among ministries, and the fear of placing too much power in a police force quickly earning itself a bad reputation.

At the same time that the government was tinkering with the structure and function of the two police forces, it began to experiment with a special unit of plainclothes detectives, first for the capital and later for the countryside. The first attempt at establishing an undercover unit, excluding previous spy units such as the *kong mon* (Mon division), took place in 1890, when a formal police detective department for the capital and its suburbs called the *kong sot naem* (detective division) was established.[100] This unit was proposed by Jardine, the British inspector general of police on loan to Siam from British Burma between 1890 and 1902, as part of the general restructuring of the Metropolitan Constabulary at the time. The purpose of establishing a *kong sot naem* was to create a more reliable source of information than district-level officials, who were, as alluded to earlier, often in allegiance with local bandits. In addition, the government regularly used criminals to catch criminals, a policy called "bandit catch bandit" (*jon jap jon*). This practice, however, caused confusion and was eventually stopped. If initially the uniformed police's duties had more to do with keeping the peace—making arrests, breaking up fights, picking up litter—than with investigation, then these new detective units were their opposite.

Unlike their uniformed counterparts in the Metropolitan Constabulary, the primary job of officers in the *kong sot naem* was detection—to find out the identities and whereabouts of wanted criminals, solve mysterious crimes, and access and deliver to the central government information contained in local social networks of knowledge. The initial proposal was for one or two officers from the *kong sot naem* to be located in each district of the capital to act as informants. For this unit, officers who showed a good understanding of the rules and regulations of the police and who were believed to be trustworthy and reliable were chosen from the Metropolitan Constabulary. In the field, the police detective would report to either the *nai amphoe* (district head) or the *phon trawen* (district constable). The unit started off small, as Jardine's plan was implemented only on a trial basis and in a few *tambon* (subdistricts) in Bangkok. Over time, the program was expanded to other *tambon,* and the group eventually became its own or *kong* (department).[101] Because it was difficult to tell who was an authorized agent of the government and who was a criminal, officers carrying out undercover duties were issued a document with an official seal and the signature of the chief officer of the Metropolitan Constabulary to prove their status as agents of the state.[102] In 1899, Jardine asked for permission to expand the *kong sot naem* and have it placed under his direct control. His request was not approved because it was felt that the unit was not showing any positive results.[103] The main problem was the difficulty in finding trustworthy and capable men to fill the unit's ranks. As the years passed, the unit did less and less investigative work; its duties shifted to include the registration of Chinese secret society members, prostitutes, and pawnshops.[104]

In 1902, the *kong sot naem* was dissolved when Lawson took over as the head of the Metropolitan Constabulary. Lawson held the post for twelve years, during which time it was said that "many improvements, extensions, and changes were made. Among the more important of them was founding of the Special Branch (*kong phiset*), an institution very much of the nature of the London Criminal Investigation Department."[105] Along with the Special Branch, Lawson credits himself with the introduction of the system of identification by fingerprints, the opening of schools for the training of officers, and the publication of a police manual in Siamese and English. Lawson's proposal for a new Special Branch was approved on May 10, 1902. By 1903, Lawson reported that the Special Branch consisted of one assistant superintendent of police, one chief inspector, six inspectors, four head constables, eighteen sergeants, and ninety-one constables. The unit's responsibilities included investigation, especially in complex or mysterious cases beyond the ability of local civil officials (e.g., the *nai amphoe*) or normal police officers to solve. The unit could also investigate and compile reports for sending a case to trial and, like its predecessor, the *kong sot naem,* it supervised the operations of the pawnshops, the enforcement of the pawnbrokers law, the registration of prostitutes, and the arrest of professional criminals.[106]

Other detective units were created afterward. These included the short-lived *tamruat phuban* (detective police), which was supposed to operate as a plainclothes detective unit for the provinces. The unit, initiated by Prince Damrong in 1913, actually grew out of calls for an undercover police force for areas outside Bangkok as early as 1904. In that year, at a meeting of superintendent commissioners (*khaluang thesaphiban*) under the Ministry of Interior, a proposal to create a secret police force throughout the provinces was suggested that "would strengthen the commune and village elders' efforts to maintain law and order in the countryside."[107] This suggestion was rejected on the grounds that men recruited to be secret police would themselves likely become criminals. Two years later, Prince Damrong, then minister of interior, authorized plainclothes policemen that he called *yokrabat tamruat phuthon* to secretly collect information on "thugs, bandits, and receivers of stolen goods" in Nakhon Chaisi *monthon.*[108] This group evidently proved something of a success, prompting Prince Damrong to set up the aforementioned *tamruat phuban* as a sort of criminal investigative unit he called the *krom nak suep,* literally "the detective unit," in September 1913.[109] The *tamruat phuban* operated for just two years before being disbanded. Damrong noted that the failure was due in part to a lack of qualified teachers. The unit's demise may also have had to do with the placement of both the Metropolitan Police and the Provincial Gendarmerie under the Ministry of Local Government in 1915. After the restructuring, Jao Phraya Yommarat became minister while Prince Damrong resigned from his post in the government.

Despite the failure of this initial effort, talk of setting up a permanent undercover police unit for the entire kingdom continued. In 1918, for example, the idea of creating a secret police force within the Provincial Gendarmerie and procedures for reforming the police investigation unit was mooted in the department and within the ministry. In a letter to the Minister of Local Government dated February 13, 1919, Lawson, then the adviser to the Ministry of Interior, described the workings of the British secret police as a possible model.[110] Nothing happened immediately, and the old *kong phiset* continued to operate. Then, in the late 1920s, talk of setting up a new secret police unit gained steam. On May 16, 1928, a letter from Prince Paribatra, the minister of interior after Jao Phraya Yommarat, to King Prajadhipok (Rama VII) asked for approval to set up a *kong tamruat phuthon klang* (central investigation division) to help catch bandits in locations throughout the country.[111] The reason put forth was that crime during the period was extremely high and was not limited by district boundaries. A report, dated May 15, 1928, by Luang Phraya Phetinthara (given name P. L. E. Warming), a Danish officer in the Provincial Police, showed that the number of murders and armed robberies in the five years before 1928 was 6,734, or about 1,347 per year. The total population at that time, he noted, was about ten million, making the murder and robbery rate 134 per one million persons. According to the same report, Burma in 1924 had a population of thirteen million and only 817 cases of murder and armed robbery, or about 56 cases per one million persons. The prince thus asked for a special unit, a sort of Siamese FBI, to be established to tackle these high crime rates.[112] At the end of 1932, this FBI-style unit, the *santiban,* was finally created. Its jurisdiction was not limited by local boundaries. The investigative police had at last become an administrative technology with true "national" reach that could be used to consolidate and control Siam through the production and control of knowledge about crime.

Over the early decades of the twentieth century, the foundations of the modern Thai police force emerged. The force expanded slowly and not without serious problems. Its mission grew from law enforcement and crime suppression to include investigation. Meanwhile, its leadership shifted from foreign advisers to the local elite, just as its rank and file moved from including Indians and Malays to become predominantly Siamese. While relatively small and arguably inefficient and ineffective in many ways, the force quickly became part of Siam's social fabric. Today, as evident in the Sherry Ann Duncan murder case, when a murder or other offense takes place, the police and the public engage in a particular set of routines to help them make sense of the noise of daily life, to come to grips with the violence and crime that plague Thai society. These routines have their origins in institutional changes initiated during the late nineteenth and early twentieth centuries.

2

Facts about Crime

Pridi Phanomyong, one of the leaders of the 1932 revolution against the absolute monarchy, noted in a lecture at the teachers society of Thailand (*samakhom samakhayajan*) on August 10, 1928, that crime was a "problem of knowledge" (*sat,* or *sastra*), because the reasons for people's actions, legal or otherwise, could be discovered through various scientific disciplines such as economics, medicine, or psychology.[1] Although Pridi did not accept wholeheartedly the idea that criminals were simply born or that biologically determined criminal types existed, he did not reject the notion that crime could be understood, and thus dealt with, by the methods of generating, organizing, and presenting information being used with increasing frequency during the late nineteenth century in England, France, Italy, and the United States.[2] In Siam in the 1920s and 1930s, high-ranking police officers and government officials shared Pridi's sentiment that scientific, modern methods of investigation were key to solving the crime problem, which became a permanent part of Thai life through the press. For example, Luang Bannasanprasit (given name Sithi Rojanawiphat), a former *nai amphoe* (district head) in Chonburi province, wrote a criminal investigation manual published in 1929 in which he stated that the causes of crime included gambling, alcohol, opium, poverty, and education level, but not genetics, and he argued that methods to deal with crime should address these social issues.[3] Thus, the police force set out on an ambitious program of reform that revolved around rationalizing their detective practices, one that would usher in a new way of seeing crime that, unlike in Europe and America, did not result so much in the creation of a new criminal type as in the introduction of novel techniques with which to visualize information about society's criminal past. These methods included compiling statistics, keeping criminal records, making fingerprints, taking photographs of convicted criminals and crime scenes, and drawing maps, charts, and diagrams.

These practices led, in turn, to the creation of a new corpus of objects that have shaped the way generations of police officers and the general public have come to imagine crime. In this chapter, I describe how these ostensibly scientific objects were adopted and why they are in some ways akin to art as much as they are neutral and objective representations of the physical world.

PROBLEMS OF PROOF

The kingdom's new police force faced a number of problems that hindered its effectiveness in dealing with the onslaught of crime that seemed to overwhelm the country in the late nineteenth and early twentieth centuries. Some of these problems, including extraterritoriality, networks of patronage, and the lack of trained officers, have already been mentioned. High-ranking police officers and government officials also saw the problem as one stemming from the legal system's inability to convict suspects in criminal trials. A lengthy report written in 1917 by Police Major General Eric St. John Lawson shows that between 1910 and 1916 the number of criminal cases in Siam recorded by the police increased sharply. Of these, the number of murders increased twice as fast as other criminal cases. For all the *monthon* (administrative districts), there were 496 murders recorded in 1910, and this more than doubled to 1,124 in 1916. The total for the six-year period was 6,280. More disturbing for the government was the general failure of the police and local officials to bring perpetrators to justice. The arrest rate over the six-year period was just 47 for every 100 murder cases. The conviction rate in these arrests was an abysmal 13 out of 100 cases. Of the total 6,280 murders, only 736 people were sentenced. Excluding Bangkok, there were 51,314 criminal cases in all the kingdom's *monthon* for 1916. A total of 40,415 arrests were made in these cases, but only 21,972 convictions were obtained. For cases of murder in the same year, the conviction rate was just 15 out of 100. For robberies, only 12 out of 100 cases resulted in a conviction. Perhaps even more embarrassing for the Siamese government, the number of murders in British Burma during the same period was not even half that of Siam, and the conviction rate was an astounding 81 out of 100 for murder cases. For robberies, Burma managed a conviction for 74 out of every 100 cases. In cases of destruction of property, Burmese officials gained a conviction in 66 out of every 100 cases. For physical assaults, the conviction rate was 71 out of 100 cases.[4]

To get to the root of the problem, Lawson interviewed a number of police officers, and, from their replies, he generated a long list of factors contributing to the Thai police's seeming ineptitude. As noted earlier, some of the factors had to do with local politics or basic logistical issues. Officers, for example, claimed that local officials, including village leaders (*phu yai ban*) and subdistrict heads (*kamnan*), were not cooperating with them. They often reported crimes late, thus allowing time for suspects to flee and witnesses to leave a crime scene. In some situations, local officials did not just delay reporting crimes; they went as far as to obstruct criminal investigations. This usually occurred when local officials wanted to protect members of their entourage or the local toughs in their employ. Another reason respondents gave was that people did not like being witnesses in criminal cases because they feared retribution from local hooligans. Lawson wrote, "Very often the villagers know perfectly well who has killed another. But if they speak and he is acquitted they know that probably they will be the next victim."[5] Many also felt the entire legal process was a waste of time, having sometimes to travel great distances to get to court. The police inspector of Nakhon Sawan *monthon* wrote that cases from the district of Mae Sot had to be tried in the district of Tak, forty miles away, and witnesses were loath to make the long trip.[6]

There were also issues of legal authority and expertise. Provincial police officers lacked the legal power to conduct investigations and question witnesses (activities referred to in the early twentieth century as *tai suan,* later *sop suan*) in a criminal case and were not able to send cases to court. These powers belonged to district-level administrators (*krommakan amphoe*) including the district head (*nai amphoe*) and the deputy district head (*palat amphoe*). Jao Phraya Yommarat noted the problem, saying that in some cases the Provincial Police would investigate a crime but could not send a suspect to court, since it was only the district head who was legally allowed to do so.[7] Also, many police privates were conscripts who worried that after their two-year term the people they arrested would seek revenge on them and their families. Lawson wrote that most just wanted to "get away" after their stint was over. Compounding the issue, many conscripts were not adequately trained for investigative work. Police Inspector J. Jarmer, a Danish officer in the Provincial Gendarmerie, stated in a meeting on the future of the police training school in 1923 that because conscripts were forced to be police officers, they had no incentive to actually learn the orders and laws related to police work.[8] Moreover, local district officials had too many responsibilities outside of peacekeeping to act as police detectives. Thus, they often could not and did not investigate cases. Lawson explained, "The investigation of crime by *amphurs* [*sic*] is a failure" because they did not have the time, knowledge, or number of subordinates needed to do the work properly.[9] Finally, provincial prosecutors were not directly responsible for crime suppression and thus felt no compunction to sentence a defendant if a case was not properly investigated. In an example from 1916, a charge against a criminal suspect was dropped after judges declared a mistrial when police officers and a village leader gave different accounts of who got to a scene of a crime first and what happened when they got there.[10]

For the police, then, crime was a practical problem. They needed to find ways to bypass webs of personal relationships and local politics. They also had to find proper methods for convincing judges in the kingdom's new, European-style courts of law that the men—and they were in large part men—accused of crimes were in fact guilty. The challenge facing the police, therefore, was connected to the solution: material evidence—the legal power to collect, compile, and record it and effective, convincing ways to display it in court. Without these things, criminals would continue, literally, to get away with murder. To wit, the adviser to the Ministry of Justice, Stewart Black, noted in 1903 that "the difficulty of obtaining proper evidence appears to be the chief reason [for low conviction rates]."[11] And in 1929, this sentiment is echoed in a police investigation manual by Phraya Manawaratchasewi, who writes that, based on statistics, the Thai police were arresting a very high number of criminals, but it was "unfortunate" that the evidence they obtained for each criminal was typically deficient, allowing defendants the opportunity to successfully contest charges against them in a court. The result was that criminals were simply not convicted.[12] It is this dilemma, this procedural and epistemological predicament, that shaped the new Thai police's path toward modernization, one that would lead them to adopt the visual practices that today dominate the legal system and mass media.

As Pridi noted in his talk, if the government was to find a solution to the seemingly intractable crime problem, it needed to look to the new disciplines that had taken Europe and America by storm. The scientific revolution that had already, at least in the minds of Pridi and other Siamese elites, transformed the countries of the West into modern nations could also revolutionize Siam. The appeal of these sciences, in turn, rested on the fact that they offered the police a set of what appeared to be convenient, clear methods and prefabricated, tangible objects that could be adopted wholesale. Lawson wrote in a report on the general conditions of the police in 1919 that even though ineptitude, corruption, and brutality plagued the kingdom's police force, most officers had a "generally good character" and were "as a whole . . . hard working, and able men, some of them pre-eminently so." He added that he was sure that his officers had "done as much with the hopeless material that they [had] to work with as any men could."[13] For Lawson, the tools with which they worked were bad, not the officers themselves. In another instance he wrote, "It may be said that 'It is a poor workman who finds fault with his tools.' That is quite true, but the best of workmen cannot turn out good work without any tools at all. Yet this is what is expected of the police."[14] For high-ranking police officers, foreign and Thai, adopting Western sciences meant providing the Thai police with the proper equipment; it entailed introducing things like statistics, photographs, and fingerprints. What they would find, though, is that these tools did not come ready to use. Instead, they demanded that people engage in a set of unfamiliar practices, ones that can be characterized as quintessentially visual. What follows is a brief history of four of these new practices and the classes of artifacts they generate.

Statistics

Luang Phraya Phetinthara, acting chief inspector for internal affairs of the Provincial Gendarmerie, wrote to Jao Phraya Yommarat on August 25, 1916, saying that the *banchi khadi* (list of cases) is very important as it allows people to know whether there has been an increase or decrease in crime.[15] That is, to see crime as a unified entity (as opposed to unconnected stories in local papers) with a past, present, and future required the introduction of numbers organized into tables, or the systematic production and visual deployment of statistics. In Europe, statistics had been applied to the understanding of crime since at least the 1820s. By the 1830s, they had helped change crime from an "individual act of will to a social phenomenon."[16] In Siam, comprehensive statistics on crime were not kept until the last years of Chulalongkorn's reign (r. 1868–1910). When the police began to compile numbers, they first surrounded them with text, in a narrative of sorts, just as I did in describing crime and conviction rates earlier. In fact, the text above is taken almost verbatim from a long report by Lawson from 1917. Prior to Lawson's report, A. J. A. Jardine, the British inspector general of Siam's Metropolitan Constabulary from 1890 to 1902, provided a similar story about incidents of crime in the kingdom's first-ever annual report on the Metropolitan Constabulary in 1898. What was novel in that report was that he included a statistical table of the kingdom's crime situation in addition to a narrative description. The following year, he did the same, only, in the 1899

Table 2.1. Incidents of Serious Crimes in Siam, 1908–1919

Year	*Homicides*	*Gang Robberies*	*Robberies*
1908–1909	429	281	310
1909–1910	658	598	347
1910–1911	661	709	303
1911–1912	859	707	346
1912–1913	1,052	610	296
1913–1914	1,218	701	345
1914–1915	1,201	691	448
1915–1916	1,222	612	365
1916–1917	1,139	668	404
1917–1918	1,299	653	405
1918–1919	1,493	963	559
Total	11,231	7,193	4,128

report, he included the numbers from the previous year, making it possible to compare and make judgments about the efficiency of the police at a glance. Jardine's annual police report, in other words, allowed officials to see crime as a single, coherent phenomenon that could be measured and analyzed. Beginning in about 1908, the police began tabulating the number and type of cases they processed in a systematic manner for the entire kingdom (as opposed to just Bangkok). By the late 1910s, the police were able to assemble tables like the one shown in Table 2.1. A complete table of crime statistics for the entire country could not have been compiled earlier than the 1910s because "the police simply did not keep any systematic records" before then.[17] David Bruce Johnston, writing about the rural economy during the late nineteenth century, added, "archival materials provide no usable statistical series" about the crime situation during the reign of Chulalongkorn; they simply did not exist.[18]

Before statistical tables, the state's knowledge about crime was derived from newspaper reports (like those described in Chapter 1), gossip, and tall tales—interesting but not comprehensive and hardly usable as proof in a court. Numbers and percentages in tables did more for the police and government officials than rumors, idle chatter, and news stories. They could be copied, distributed, managed, and presented to judges. They made conditions for entire districts, cities, regions, and indeed the entire "geo-body" of

Siam visible to officials in Bangkok.[19] While it is difficult to determine how accurate the statistical tables created by the police in the 1910s and 1920s are, they do show how new methods of conceptualizing crime resulted in the introduction of novel objects of information—here, statistical tables—which formed the basis for policy decisions made by elites in the Siamese government. That is, verifiable and thus "real" increases in crime could be used to justify increased policing efforts in and outside of the capital. Numbers in tables, printed on paper, have real-world effects simply because of their existence as material things within a bureaucracy, even if they are not accurate. Moreover, the tabulation of crime statistics in tables shows how the police, and their patrons in government, were beginning to see crime as a real object with formal properties.

Photographs

Perhaps the most celebrated form of visual evidence over the last 150 years has been the photograph. In 1839 in France, Louis Daguerre invented the daguerreotype, the name for images made through a chemical process involving the exposure of silver nitrate to light. In the 1850s, the daguerreotype was used primarily to create portraits for the middle classes of Europe. By the 1860s, mass-produced and portable photographs had become more widespread throughout Europe, especially as people traveled the colonies.[20] This popularity was made possible by the invention of the hand camera, fast-drying development techniques, and rolled film.[21] These advances also pushed the photograph into new realms like advertising, journalism, science, and the law.[22] By 1852, French lawyers were using daguerreotypes in court as evidence.[23] At the end of the 1850s, paper photos printed from negatives were common and were used in American courts, mostly in land disputes and forgery cases. In the 1870s, photos were used for proving identity in criminal cases.[24] The police were even quicker to use these technologies than the courts. As early as 1841, the French police began taking pictures of prisoners, and the British were photographing criminals by roughly the same time.[25] In 1858 in New York City, the police began putting up rogues' galleries at local police stations, a practice that spread quickly to Europe. In 1886, the head of the New York Police Department detective bureau even published a coffee-table book filled with photographs of criminals.[26]

A similar story can be told about the photograph's value and functionality in the Siamese justice system. The first camera was brought into the kingdom in July of 1845 by a French Roman Catholic priest named Jean-Baptiste François Louis Larnaudie at the request of Bishop Jean-Baptiste

Pallegoix, another French missionary in Siam. During the reigns of Mongkut (r. 1851–1868) and Chulalongkorn, photography spread as a hobby among the royal family and among wealthier urbanites. Most early photographs were portraits—primarily of the king and members of the royal family—and scenes of Bangkok. King Mongkut, for example, had photos of himself taken and sent to various heads of state in Europe. Photographs were, in other words, largely limited to commemorative purposes and use as postcards. Unlike the royals and urbanites, however, many Thais initially "were scared to have there [*sic*] picture taken, believing that doing so would shorten their life-span."[27]

As was the case in Europe and the United States, it did not take long for the camera's usefulness in criminal investigation to be noticed. In 1904, photos were taken of prisoners being released from jail. These photos were put in a file with their fingerprints in an effort to deal with the high rates of recidivism at the time.[28] As an investigative tool, photography took a little while longer to develop. Lawson wrote, in his police training manual from 1906, "Photography is used in police work for: 1. Preserving a record of habitual criminals. 2. Recording the appearance of an unknown person found dead. As a rule photography should not be used for showing the scene of a crime. A good plan is much better than photography for this purpose as a rule."[29] Lawson, then, did not see photographs as crucial for crime scene investigation; they were primarily a means for identifying known criminals. By 1917, however, Phra Sisena (given name Kit Katchachiwa), author of one of the first commercial manuals on criminal investigation in Siam, suggested that local officials in charge of crime prevention bring with them to investigations someone capable of taking photographs, as they might prove useful. He also stated that investigators should carry two "weapons": a camera and a pencil and paper.[30] A year later, a letter from Police Lieutenant General Phraya Athikonprakat, the commissioner of the Metropolitan Police from 1923 to 1929, cited the need for the police to have proper photographic equipment and recommended that they retain a full-time photographer.[31] This idea was reiterated in a letter to Jao Phraya Yommarat dated September 3, 1920, from Lawson, who seemed to have changed his mind on the function of photographs, as he recommended the creation of a new unit in the force that would include a photography section with adequate equipment and photographers. Lawson noted that suspects and prisoners were taken to privately owned shops to have their pictures taken and that photographic equipment had to be obtained and sent to crime scene investigations—a slow, inefficient process.[32] To address the issue, the government sent a man named Jaroen Purananda to Paris to study photographic techniques for criminal investigation in 1929.[33] After the *santiban* (Special Branch) was created in late 1932, photographs and other records could finally be made and kept in house. Manuals for police training after that invariably included sections on photographic techniques for criminal investigation.

The usefulness of photography as a tool for criminal investigation thus developed fairly rapidly over the first few years of the twentieth century, due in part to the perception that photographs provided an accurate representation of reality. In the early days of the twentieth century, this was not quite the case; some police officers regarded photographs with caution. Phra Sisena, despite his enthusiasm for the technology, noted in 1917 that while photographs "added weight" to witness testimony, investigators still had to exercise caution when using them. It was true, he stated, that photographs helped judges "see reality just as you [the investigator] have seen it."[34] But they did so because they captured a crime scene, a human being, or an object that existed at some specific location in the physical world. As such, photographs were only representations, not the actual thing being pictured. Phra Sisena therefore considered photographs as "second-level" evidence, as opposed to a piece of direct documentary evidence such as a contract with a signature:

> In some cases, photos of crime scenes are taken and presented to the court. These, like maps, are also second-level objects of evidence. The purpose of photographs is to provide the court an understanding of the conditions of a crime scene, how the defendant committed the crime in question, and how witnesses knew of the crime. It acts in combination with other evidence to give that evidence increased weight, which is very beneficial to a case. . . . Photographs that may be considered direct evidence are those taken of the actual criminal event or of something directly related to the criminal event. But because it is difficult to know in advance when a crime will occur it is not likely that one would be able to set up a camera in time to capture an actual criminal event.[35]

As such, photographs only increased the strength of a case when combined with other proofs, especially human testimony, and acted as a visual aid.

After World War II, a shift in the thinking on photographs begins to appear more clearly. Udom Latphli, a police officer writing in the early 1950s, tells readers in an article on police methods that photographs actually preserve a crime scene by stopping time at a specific moment. A week or two after a crime (or other event in question) has taken place, he writes, the crime scene will have changed. This could potentially lead to misunderstandings during an investigation. Photographs actually allow judges to return to the reality of the past many days after the fact.[36] Sanga Kittikhajon, an officer in the police science section and brother of military dictator Thanom Kittikhajon, repeats in his police training manual from 1953 the refrain about photographs merely being visual aids meant to help judges imagine a crime scene, but then he contradicts himself by noting that "the camera lens is able to capture various details in their entirety so that we [investigators] might be able to analyze these details in every respect as they appear in a photograph, just as if they were real."[37]

Sanga follows his statement up with several examples of the use of photography drawn from foreign police departments. In one murder case, a dead body was found in a room under the stairs in the victim's house. The investigating officer believed that the deceased had been killed in the living room. Unfortunately, he had no evidence to support this hunch. After photographs of the crime scene were developed, bloodstains on the carpet in the living room could be made out. The camera, noted Sanga, can thus see things in more detail than can the human eye.[38] He then describes a case from England in which a woman was found dead; her body sat on a park bench. There was a bullet wound in her right temple and her right arm lay hanging at her side. A pistol was on the ground just underneath the woman's right hand. Judging by the position of the body and the gun, officers felt that the woman's death was in all likelihood a suicide. Despite the availability of a seemingly straightforward explanation of death, officers took photos of the scene, perhaps out of habit. When these photos were developed and printed, one officer noticed that there was a bench across from where the woman's body was found. It had been raining, so the bench was wet, except for one small spot. This indicated to investigators that someone had been sitting nearby at the time of the woman's death, leading the police to suspect murder. Eventually they arrested the woman's lover, who turned out to be her killer.[39]

In a separate section of his manual, Sanga recommends taking photographs of clues found at a crime scene in order to preserve them. If a print of a bare foot is discovered, for example, an investigator should take a picture of it and then enlarge the resulting photograph to the size of a suspect's actual foot. The lines on the foot of the suspect and those that appear in the photo can then be compared. In cases where a print of a shoe is found, Sanga similarly instructs investigators to take photos of the shoe print and the suspect's shoe. He then tells investigators to develop and print both photographs to their "actual size" and compare them to see if they are in fact pictures of the same shoe. Similar instructions to take photographs and scrutinize them are given in cases where an officer needs to analyze marks left on surfaces like wood by tools such as saws and drill bits.[40] In another manual, Luang Bannasanprasit writes about how a police officer was convicted of beating a Chinese man (*jek*) in Chonburi province because he was by chance photographed holding a wooden staff just prior to the incident. A short time after the incident, a photograph of the weapon, the wooden stick, was taken. The two photographs were compared and it was concluded that the two sticks were in fact the same, leading to the conviction of the police officer.[41]

In all of these examples, it is the photograph that detectives and judges analyze, not the crime scene or the crime itself. The police and judges treat photographs as if they are the things they represent; they perform police work on visual representations, not the reality being captured. The focus of adjudication and detection is transferred to a visualization. So even though many of the early police manuals warned about the second-level, strictly representational status of photographs, they were, on occasion, perhaps unconsciously and unintentionally treated as if they were the thing they represented. By the 1950s, then, the photograph had quite clearly come to take on the status of "the real" in the criminal investigation process. This is not necessarily a negative development, but it is important to remember that photographs are ultimately material artifacts whose appearance, as will be demonstrated, is subject to forces located well outside science and the law, and these forces therefore have effects on the way modern criminal justice systems operate.

Fingerprints

The fingerprint is another tool of modern policing, used primarily to ensure that the right criminal is attached to the right crime. The two men generally credited with creating fingerprint identification are William Herschel and Henry Faulds.[42] Herschel, an officer in the British civil service in India, claimed to have invented the practice in 1858, but it may have been an old Bengali practice imported from China that he simply borrowed. Faulds, while working as a medical missionary in Japan, noticed fingerprints on pottery and published an article in 1880 about their potential uses in crime fighting. He later claimed to have solved a crime using fingerprints found at a crime scene, and went on to create a cataloging system by assigning names for each print type. At the same time, Francis Galton—half cousin to

Charles Darwin and a traveler, scientist, thinker, and the man who coined the term "eugenics"—was busy promoting the system in England with papers and books praising its merits. In France, too, fingerprint identification was becoming standard procedure for the police. Back in India, two men, Azizul Haque and Chandra Bose, devised their own system of cataloging prints, which was implemented in 1895.[43]

This same system from India made its way into Siam toward the end of Chulalongkorn's reign. Lawson, then commissioner of the Metropolitan Constabulary, claimed, "It was I who introduced the system to Siam. It was I who trained Johnson [the deputy chief of the Special Branch, a British national] who showed the method to HRH Prince Ratchaburi [Prince Rabi, minister of justice and half brother of King Chulalongkorn]. It was I who drew up and submitted to HRH the original rules for the identification of criminals. Also it was I who have trained the Police."[44] Lawson may have been exaggerating his accomplishments, however, as Prince Rabi gave a different account:

> About six years ago [about 1903], Lawson started the work from the system in use in India. He failed. I then with the assistance of a police officer started the work in Jail II and succeeded up to now. When it began the finger prints of those convicted in Bangkok, or rather those prisoners who were in Bangkok jails alone were taken. The head of the prisons wanted to extend the work, but he had not the where-with-all to start offices all over the Kingdom; so he sent some of his men to most jails in the provinces to teach them to take finger prints. His men could not teach the provincial jails how to classify the prints as the whole work was then in an experimental stage.[45]

In either case, the Fingerprint Bureau had existed since the late 1890s, when it was under the supervision of the Prisons Department of the Ministry of Metropolitan Government. A report by Lawson in 1919 noted that the bureau was started "20 years ago," putting its inception sometime around the year 1899.[46] He recommended moving the bureau to the Special Branch, which he helped establish in 1902.[47]

Before fingerprints were put into wide use, the police had no reliable, visible way of linking individuals with their crimes. In a letter dated March 7, 1909, Probationary Legal Adviser Henri Laurent wrote that in the area of Ubon, in what is now northeast Thailand, the examination of a defendant in an illegal gambling case revealed that "the Accused had been previously condemned to four years imprisonment for theft and had just been released from prison six months ago, without the Public Prosecutor saying anything about it."[48] Laurent then went on to note that this was due to the irregular use of fingerprint identification in the province. If criminals were not connected to their pasts, they would be free to repeat their offenses over and over again. This only began to change in the late 1910s. In 1918, Lawson reported that 16,998 prints were sent for search. From these, 4,691 identifications were made. Lawson wrote that while this showed good work, it also meant the recidivism rate was high, at least 30 percent.[49] The fingerprint thus helped the police place human agents within the criminal histories they were starting to create with photographs and statistics.

In addition to identifying criminals, fingerprints were used to keep tabs of the police themselves. Lawson wrote, "There is also a small finger-print bureau, containing the finger-prints of all men who have been dismissed or who have deserted the force, to which reference is made whenever a man is enlisted. The bureau for identification of criminals is kept up by the officials of the Ministry of Justice at the industrial prison."[50] This step was necessary because evidently many former criminals were trying to enlist. A fingerprint system was also used to track police officers' work routines, as members of the force had quickly developed a reputation for shirking their duties. Lawson, again, writes, "The constables leave their stations every night and visit the houses of the *kamnan* [subdistrict head], putting their thumbprints in a book kept at the *kamnan*'s house as a proof of their visit."[51] So, in addition to checking up on its subjects, the state had to monitor its own agents by placing them under surveillance.

Basil Thomson, a well-known British police officer and consultant to the Siamese government, recommended in 1929 that the Fingerprint Bureau be shifted to the investigative arm of the police once it was created, echoing Lawson almost thirty years later. The move finally happened in 1932, when the *santiban* was established. Division Three of the unit, the Police Science Section, was tasked with handling fingerprint identification, among other things.[52] The shift signaled that fingerprints could do more than serve as a check against recidivism. They were now officially classified as a crime-fighting tool for use in the criminal detection process. Accordingly, the first use of fingerprints in the investigation at the scene of a crime is said to have been by officers of the *santiban,* though I have found no examples.[53] In fact, it may have taken place earlier. Luang Phisitwithayakan, one of Siam's earliest and most prominent forensic police officers, claimed to have been the first to use a fingerprint produced at a crime scene investigation to apprehend a criminal. This would have been in the late 1920s.[54] In 1929, Luang Bannasanprasit wrote that he had once read about a case in a foreign country where investigators were able to use a chemical solution to make fingerprints at the scene of a crime visible. The detectives took photographs of these prints. Luang Bannasanprasit noted that he could not attest to whether this method actually worked. However, it did indicate for him that there were ways available for gaining prints from a crime scene.[55] From a slow and unclear introduction as a means to identify criminals, the fingerprint became a key visual tool for solving criminal mysteries.

The Report

While statistics allowed crime to be seen as a broad, regional, and historical phenomenon, photographs captured the likenesses of criminals and crime scenes, and fingerprints helped police identify suspected criminals, these new facts needed to be organized into a comprehensive framework to make sense and become usable. Another key practice—making detailed, standardized investigation reports—was adopted for this purpose. Written reports were tangible, material objects that did not change from day to day or falter depending on the memory of a witness. As such, they could be used at different points in the investigative process just as fingerprints and photographs could be. More importantly, reports could organize these other new artifacts so that in combination they could tell a story about the past. Prior to the turn of the century, police and other government officials tasked with crime prevention did not always make written reports as part of their investigation. One reason reports were not made was that police officers were often illiterate. In general, literacy rates were low in the early twentieth century, and one of the first lessons at the school for police constables (*rong rian phon trawen*) included instruction in the Thai alphabet and Thai numbers.[56] A letter from a British medical officer in 1915 regarding the operation of the police hospital states that the "police officers that volunteer to work at the hospital can't even read or write their own language."[57]

Some officers, however, did make lists. In 1877, King Chulalongkorn requested that officials of the "inner police" (*samut jao krom phra tamruat nai*) compile a list of names of bandits that had yet to be arrested or that had escaped. This list, he stated, could then be distributed to local leaders to facilitate arrest.[58] In the 1890s, Jao Phraya Surasakmontri made personal lists of suspected criminals to use in his manhunt campaigns in the central plains.[59] Similarly, a district head in Phasi Charoen in southwestern Bangkok told subdistrict heads and village leaders in 1907 to keep tabs on the behavior of the people in their areas. Should they find anyone with a history of unethical behavior, their name and address should be recorded.[60] The making of lists was possible in rural communities that were small and stable, and even in some urban neighborhoods where people knew one another as neighbors or from their interactions at markets or in other public spaces. As rapid urbanization and physical change gathered pace, however, this convenient situation could not be maintained, and it did not hold in non-Thai enclaves. In any case, the lists being made hardly informed anyone of exactly what crime had transpired, let alone how it unfolded. They referred to individuals in society, thus allowing for their capture, but they did not produce convictions; the connection between a captured suspect, a name on a list, and a crime still had to be determined.

Beginning around 1902, when Lawson became commissioner of the Metropolitan Constabulary, a system of recording criminal investigations was introduced. Describing how police should proceed in a case, Lawson wrote in 1909 that,

> on receiving any report [of a crime or other incident] whether made by a Police Officer or by anyone else, a short entry briefly stating the facts is made in the General Diary. The entry in the diary shows the hour and minute at which the report was made. If the report was of any offence, not being one of those offences of which I attach a list, concerning which the Police have been forbidden to take action, a report is then entered in foil and counterfoil in the complaint book. This report is made as nearly as possible in the exact words of the informant and is signed by him and by the Police clerk or officer who recorded the report.[61]

He explained further that

> the most important register kept in all police stations is the daily diary. In this register every occurrence of every sort that takes place within the station is entered, together with the movements on duty of every officer and constable attached to the station. Great importance is attached to the immediate entry of every occurrence in this diary, which forms a minutely accurate record of everything connected with crime and police since the institution of the force in the year 1897. The next most important register is the complaint book, in which are entered all complaints of a criminal nature made by the public. These complaints form a basis of all subsequent proceedings in the criminal court. The absconded offenders' register and

> the register of property seized by the police are also important registers found in every station. In addition to these there is a police manual, which is a guide for the use of officers and men on their departmental duties, and also in their duties under the various laws.[62]

In a subsequent letter to Stewart Black, a legal adviser to the Siamese government, Lawson would reiterate the need to make a diary entry, especially in complicated cases.[63] Training manuals for police and civilian officials from the period urged investigators to carry with them a pencil to take notes of what they had uncovered.[64] The practice of making crime scene investigation reports was already being carried out in other parts of the region, particularly those administered by the British. Police Officer Phra Wichaiprachaban, sent to Moulmein in British Burma to study police methods in 1922, reported that the police there were required to keep records on bandits and daily events in a "Village Crime Book."[65] Police investigation in the early twentieth century was thus becoming an exercise in report writing.

To be fair, the need to write down oral accounts of the past stretches back much further in time. For example, directions in the *Lak inthaphat*—a set of instructions to magistrates for processing cases that dates to the kingdom of Sukhothai (ca. 1240–1438), referred to in the *Phra ayakan laksana tralakan* (Laws for judges) of the Law of the Three Seals (1805 recension)—stress that when a disagreement takes place, the first step is to attempt to reach a negotiated consensus that eliminates the need to initiate a full trial. It was in situations where no compromise could be reached that a case was put to trial. When this occurred, witnesses would need to be called and their testimonies recorded in writing.[66] Sections in the *Phra ayakan laksana phayan* (Laws on evidence) and *Phra ayakan laksana rap fong* (Laws on accepting complaints) from the Three Seals Law also call for magistrates to write down the accounts of litigants and witnesses and compile them in a case summary (*samnuan*). It is this written case summary that judges then use as the basis of their deliberations.[67] The practice of entextualizing oral testimony is thus a conscious demand placed on officials by the criminal justice system. The first key shift in the late nineteenth and early twentieth centuries was that the ability and power to document crimes moved from local leaders and royal elites to the police (and, as I will show, a broad range of actors including fiction writers and news reporters). Second, the content of these logs began to include fingerprints, photographs, and maps—visual clues crafted by the police—in addition to human testimony. In other words, written testimony and other accounts of the past made by officers do not work in isolation as a self-evident record of the past. They exist in relation to other documents, including especially images, in a larger system of representations. This means that the interpretation of documents during an investigation and a trial takes place within a web of artifacts, a virtual world of paper-based objects. The seemingly uncomplicated relationship between the materialization of a clue and a past event is much more byzantine than surface appearances would indicate.

One additional point should be made here. The police notebooks and the records of criminal methods they contained were not creating an archive of "criminal types" per se. This view was common in places like England and Italy at the end of the nineteenth century, and it was one that Lawson might have concurred with: "The class of professional criminals in the Province of Bangkok is large. In the first place, the Chinese, who yearly enter the country in great numbers, contain amongst them a very considerable leavening of the professional criminal classes."[68] In Siam, however, anyone could break the law. According to local police and other officials, criminality depended on circumstance. Criminals, including several famous ones like Suea Fai of Suphanburi, could always "return" (*klap*) to being law-abiding citizens when the situation allowed for it.[69] So while the new forms that the police were filling out did include blank spaces for name, age, address, and physical description, these details were linked to other blanks that required police to describe what, when, and how something happened, rather than to descriptions of other criminals within a generalized category. The police were making event logs that told in as much detail as possible how a crime transpired. Modern police work has developed, therefore, as a process of defining and recording the past as images and text, linking the processes of detection and the organization of evidence with the production of history (or at least narrative fragments). Michel Foucault once noted that to police and to urbanize are one and the same.[70] It might be more accurate to say that to police is to document. It is through these documents that the police's intimate role in determining what a society may know about its own past becomes apparent.

The story of the introduction of these new objects of evidence might stop here, showing how high-ranking police officers and government officials modernized the criminal investigation process. But this is only part of the plot. The reality of criminal detection in Siam lagged far behind the aspirations and the orders of higher-ups in government. The practices of taking fingerprints, making tables, filling out forms, and snapping pictures remained terribly uneven well into the middle of the twentieth century. In a letter dated March 26, 1917, Luang Phraya Phetinthara, a Danish national, wrote to Jao Phraya Yommarat, the acting chief inspector of police, that not all police stations in Bangkok were keeping records. Some didn't even have a criminal record book (*banchi khadi aya*).[71] In another letter to Yommarat, this one dated August 25, 1916, he wrote that in Chiang Mai, police stations did not record cases properly, or at all, in some instances.[72] In the south, the police inspector of Phuket, F. T. E. Steiner, another Dane, lamented on November 3, 1916, that the police were not filling out their forms correctly. From April to August of 1916, he said, officers recorded 280 cases, while district administration officials listed 339, 59 more than the police, indicating that the police were not keeping accurate records.[73]

It was not until the late 1930s that it might safely be said that the police in many parts of the kingdom were producing criminal records, statistics, forms, and other documents properly, or at least regularly. By then, documentation had become so inculcated into the daily practices of the force that corruption and cover-ups required the manufacture of false documents or the alteration of "true" ones. As early as the mid-1910s, when the practice of documentation was just being introduced, police officers were aware of its potentially damning evidentiary power and had begun to intentionally mis-document events. Luang Phraya Phetinthara wrote that the provincial police were going out to inspect their assigned areas not to solve cases or prevent crime, but "only to make the record book look nice."[74] In another letter, this one from April 1916, the chief inspector of police wrote to Jao Phraya Yommarat that a clerk from the Forestry Department, the deputy district head of Amphoe Pong in Nan province, and a district office clerk went drinking and then started an argument at the local police station. This was not recorded in the station's record book. Neither was the theft of a box of books from an English envoy in July 1916. Moreover, judging from the record books, the police in districts Tha Pla, Amphoe Sa, and Phak Bo Wa did not catch a single criminal between April and November because there were none, an unlikely prospect at the time.[75] Many years later, after police officers from Kanchanaburi province assassinated Ari Liwira, one of the most prominent newspaper publishers in Thailand after World War II, Sirichai Krachangwong, head of the Kanchanaburi police, had pages 235 and 236 of the city's daily record book for March 8, 1953, the day of the murder, torn out and replaced with new pages with false information. The original pages were destroyed.[76] There are many reasons for this mis- or non-documentation. In part, police did not report incidents of crime to avoid having to go out to a crime scene and do work.[77] In some instances, they did not record things because they feared that the criminals would retaliate. In others, especially at the beginning of the police's shift to investigative activities, officers simply lacked the training to produce documents of any utility. It had become clear from the elites' focus on documents and material evidence and on the rank and file's concern with making the record books "look good" that, without proof on paper, courts have nothing to adjudicate. To prove whether or not something has happened and to describe how it has taken place in the criminal justice system being transplanted in Siam required paperwork.

TEACHING POLICE THE FACTS

As indicated by the difficulty in getting officers to properly document their work, and the slow and uneven introduction of fingerprint identification, crime scene photography, and statistical analysis, the police, especially those in the provinces, were only beginning to learn the trade of modern detection in the early part of the twentieth century. Fingerprints, photographs, and statistical tables were new types of information about crime, produced by transplanted practices for generating knowledge. They did not exist as discrete classes of fact in Siam before and thus had to be taught to the kingdom's detectives. Prior to the 1890 reform of the Metropolitan Constabulary, there was no police academy. Recruits were trained by senior officers in standing at attention, reading and writing numbers, fast walking, marching in a group, using a sword, and shooting guns.[78] Neither were many people being sent abroad to study the emerging field of criminology. One was sent before the turn of the nineteenth century. Another four were sent in 1912.[79] Jardine proposed a training school for the constabulary's new recruits and suggested that more experienced officers receive training one month a year. This proposal was approved in December 1897.[80] The police school finally opened in 1900 at Wat Phayurong in Thonburi province, just across the Chao Phraya River from Bangkok. This facility would be moved to a new location at Wat Saraphathum in Bangkok in 1908.[81] Another school, the *rong rian fuekhat nai muat* (school for police training), was located in Bangkok behind Captain Lawson's residence on Soi Sarasin, across from where Lumphini Park is today. There were ninety-five students in the first training session, which lasted six months. After the course, successful cadets were assigned to a station within the capital. Twenty-five people failed this first class.[82]

Like the Metropolitan Constabulary, the Provincial Gendarmerie did not at first have a school. Instead, men for the gendarmerie were drawn from the pool of soldiers already serving in the army.[83] It was not until 1903 that the gendarmerie opened a school, which they called the *rong rian nai roi tamruat phuthon* (provincial gendarmerie cadet academy). It was first located in Nakhon Ratchasima, 180 miles northeast of Bangkok, and then it moved to Nakhon Pathom, just west of the capital.[84]

As a result of the fractured nature of police training, cadets often lacked ability, basic skills, and knowledge in criminal investigation and relied excessively on force.[85] Some police were themselves criminals.[86] In fact, the gendarmerie had difficulty filling their ranks at first because the "Thai people at the time did not feel well disposed to join the police service, being under the misconception that it was no better than a body of watchmen."[87] It didn't help that officers received a very poor salary and risked being killed or injured on a daily basis. Conscription was later used as a method to address this problem. The practice began in 1905 and ended for the Metropolitan Constabulary in 1914 and for the Provincial Gendarmerie in 1918.[88] In 1915, the school for the gendarmerie was consolidated with the Metropolitan Police's officers' school in Bangkok and took the name *rong rian nai roi tamruat* (police cadet academy).[89]

When the Metropolitan Constabulary and the Provincial Gendarmerie and their schools were placed under the same ministry in 1915, there was also some rumbling for a change in the curriculum used to teach police recruits. It was thought that police training was too militaristic, as it followed the basic tenets of the army's training program, which focused on combat and drilling rather than investigation. Frequent complaints about the police's reliance on force only reinforced this perception.[90] In a letter to Jao Phraya Yommarat, Luang Phraya Phetinthara noted,

> When the new *krom tamruat* [police] is established, there will not be any suitable senior officers to be found. The *tamruat phuthon* [Provincial Gendarmerie] have schools for *nai phan* [lieutenants] and *nai sip* [sergeants] and there is also a school for *sarawat* [inspectors] at Nakhon Phathom but still, problems exist with police education. The basics of this education, the core classes, tests, teachers, etc. are still being revised. There is no clear system.[91]

Mom Jao Khamrop, the kingdom's first Siamese director-general of police, responded in a letter dated March 8, 1917, that changes to the training system for the police were not practical because they would be too expensive, and, in any case, the *nai sip* already received training. Moreover, he stated that officers of the *nai sip* rank did not need knowledge in criminal investigation because that was the duty of the district heads.[92] As noted in Chapter 1, people generally saw the police simply as the "muscle" for the district heads. In a separate note dated March 5, 1917, Luang Phraya Phetinthara expressed the opposite view, saying that investigation was in fact the police's most important duty.[93]

If the police were not learning how to investigate crime (that is, to materialize crime as texts and images), then what exactly were they doing in school? In their police school, Metropolitan Constabulary cadets attended lectures in the early 1910s that included topics such as how to maintain the confidentiality of issues brought to the police by the public, how to present work to ranking officers, how to explain orders, and how to set an example.[94] The training program for the constabulary took place over a year and was divided into three parts of four months each. The schedule of daily activities for students looked like this:

7:00 a.m.—Marching, drilling, weapons training
8:00 a.m.—Breakfast
10:00 a.m. to noon—Study of regulations and laws
Noon to 1:00 p.m.—Break
1:00 p.m. to 3:00 p.m.—Study of regulations and laws
3:00 p.m. to 4:00 p.m.—Break
4:00 p.m. to 5:00 p.m.—Marching, drilling, weapons training
5:30 p.m.—Dinner
7:00 p.m. to 8:00 p.m.—Study of regulations and laws
8:30 p.m.—Line-up and roll-call
9:00 p.m.—Sleep
Saturday—Rest[95]

Another document shows that the Metropolitan Police followed a physical training program that they based on the Thai army's basic training program of 1912. This included unarmed combat, swimming, marching, and salutes. It also included lessons on how to handle firearms, running long distances quickly for periods of not more than fifteen minutes, and basic exercise. Nonphysical studies included reading and writing the Thai alphabet and Thai numbers for those who could not read and write, improving the reading and writing levels of those who were already literate, basic vocabulary and royal language, first aid and health, rules, regulations, laws related to the Metropolitan Police of 1915, explanations of police disciplinary procedures, definitions of misdemeanors from the new criminal code (1908), *farang* (Caucasian) numbers, and methods to arrest people that make illegal liquor and opium.[96] This description of police training reiterates that at the beginning of the twentieth century, the Thai police knew very little about what was necessary for modern detection; the fingerprints and other forms of visual evidence they were being asked to produce were new to them.

This situation only began to change as the force began to emphasize investigative activities, first in Bangkok, then in the provinces. As changes continued, the police training curriculum began to include an increasing number of topics like law, locations of important places, how to be observant, and how to form hypotheses. Fingerprint identification, footprint casting, and the preservation of material clues from crime scenes were also introduced into the police training curriculum. It was explained, for example, that fingerprints could be used to identify people because no two had ever been shown to be the same, they remained unchanged from the age of four months to death, and they regenerate unchanged after injury.[97] In addition to courses in police school, training manuals for police investigation were also beginning to show up on the market. These manuals, written mostly by senior investigators, taught their readers what clues were, how to look for them, and stressed the importance of hard work and attention to detail. One such manual from 1929 taught its readers that most paper records, including receipts, contracts, and letters, as well as objects obtained from various locations, such as footprints, handprints, bullet casings, and even marks like scars or bruises left on a body—and the body itself—were all useful pieces of information that could be used later as evidence.[98] The police also put out their own magazine, *Tamruat* (Police), in an effort to spread information about modern police work to its officers. Articles in this magazine included instructions on how to interpret bloodstains, question witnesses, and conduct chemical analyses, as well as crime fiction and summaries of cases (mostly from other countries) in which detectives were able to solve complex cases by using physical clues left behind at a crime scene. That is, before the police could discover the facts "out there," they first had to know what constituted facts in the first place.

More crucially, along with introducing the use of fingerprints, photographs, and other types of evidence, training manuals and the police academy were teaching cadets that these new objects of evidence had a specific look to them and this look resulted from formalized techniques for production. Pictures of cadets learning to make fingerprints from *Thesaphiban*, for example, show students lined up at low wooden tables putting fingers to paper in an almost assembly-line manner (Figure 2.1). In Lawson's police manual, they are instructed on how to roll a fingertip from left to right with sufficient pressure and to fill the space allotted for each finger: "The proper way of taking finger-prints is as follows. A very thin layer of printer's ink is spread on the tin plate provided for the purpose. The ink is spread on with a roller. The right thumb is then placed on the tin and the point is impressed on the form at the top left hand corner [a sample form is attached in the magazine]. The fingers of righthand [*sic*] are then printed in turn."[99] When the bureau was still under the Prisons Department in 1910, a notice was issued for officials there to use white paper to record fingerprints.[100] Cadets were thus taught, after some trial and error, the correct color of paper and type and color of ink to use to make a print. In addition to being introduced to the unchanging lines on a fingertip, the police were learning how to make an aesthetically correct impression of them, one that could be analyzed by experts not present at a crime scene and thus useful as evidence in court. As Luang Phisitwithayakan warned, if a print did not conform to these formal rules, its status as proof would be undermined.[101]

The photograph, too, needed to conform to specific aesthetic rules to count in a court as evidence. As described earlier, when the photograph was first introduced into the criminal investigation process in Siam, it was seen as useful but still suspect, just as it was in Europe and America. It was

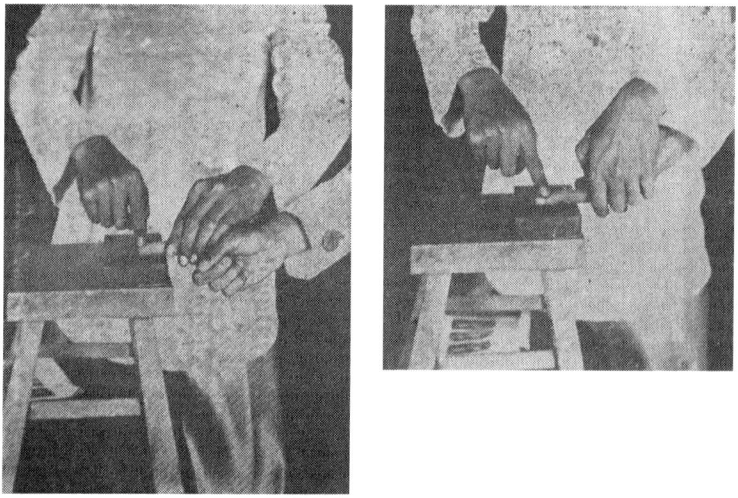

FIGURE 2.1. Police cadets learning to make fingerprints at police school, circa 1920. From *Thesaphiban* [Provincial administration journal].

"second-level" evidence, a perception stemming from the fact that it was a representation of something real in the world. In addition, Phra Sisena warned that photographs were vulnerable to manipulation. How a photograph looked depended on many factors, including weather conditions, lighting, and location, all of which made crime photography a difficult task. To complicate matters, there were techniques for taking photographs that made subjects appear close by when they were actually quite far away and vice versa.[102] To avoid taking misleading photographs, manuals stressed to investigators that they should try their best to produce them with as much detail and clarity as possible.[103] Early manuals on police investigation consistently included a section on how to properly take photographs for criminal investigation, complete with instructions on how to prevent distortion. In cases of murder, investigating officers were instructed by a manual published in 1935 to prevent people from entering the crime scene so that valuable evidence was not destroyed. The investigator was told to clear a crime scene of people and then check the floor around the body for traces of blood and footprints. Once the stage was set, a professional photographer was to take photos of the scene "as it was discovered."[104] The manual advised that dead bodies in particular should be photographed in the original position in which they were found. The same manual recommended that the photographer take pictures from as many angles as possible, to ensure that a complete image of the scene was preserved for later viewing.[105] Sanga includes similar instructions in his 1953 police manual, writing that crime scene photos should include one wide-angle shot from the "front" of the crime scene, one from the right, and one from the left. There should also be photos of the path leading to and away from the scene and a close-up of the entrance (for example, a door). For the interior of a crime scene, such as a bedroom, an investigator should take several photos from all angles so as to capture all details and provide useful material for subsequent analysis. Officers are then instructed to take a close-up of any dead body and of wounds and bloodstains. Problems that Sanga encountered often with crime scene photographs included images taken from "wrong" angles, bad lighting, and pictures that did not show the entire clue or object in question.[106] Thus, he included samples and instructions (taken directly from police manuals from the United States and Europe) on how to take a picture using the correct exposure and focal length (Figures 2.2, 2.3, 2.4, and 2.5). In other words, the photograph had to capture the crime scene as the criminal had left it. Yet, to achieve this naturalism, lighting and camera angle were stressed. All these rules were part of the development of a set of aesthetic principles, a "grammar of murder,"

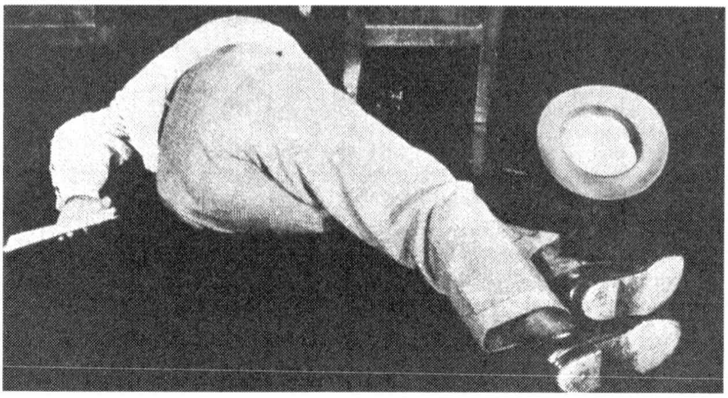

FIGURE 2.2. An example of a crime scene photo using incorrect exposure. From Sanga Kittikhajon, *Police Methods,* 1953.

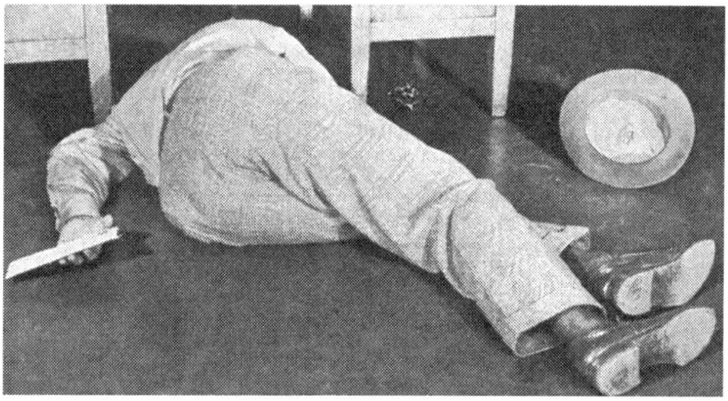

FIGURE 2.3. An example of a crime scene photo using correct exposure. From Sanga Kittikhajon, *Police Methods,* 1953.

that emerged to help distinguish crime scene photography as its own genre, distinct from portraiture or landscape photography.[107] They defined what a correct crime scene looked like. At a practical level, then, the scientific revolution that government officials attempted to bring to Siam had less to do with a sea change in the *mentalité* of the police than with the standardization of how to represent objects and past events visually.

There are three points to take from this discussion so far. First, the objects of evidence that the Thai police needed to solve a crime were not things that existed a priori, though they may seem that way today. The police are able now to search for and identify facts about crime and turn them into evidence visible in courts of law and the popular imagination, but this ability developed over time, through a conscious program of education of what

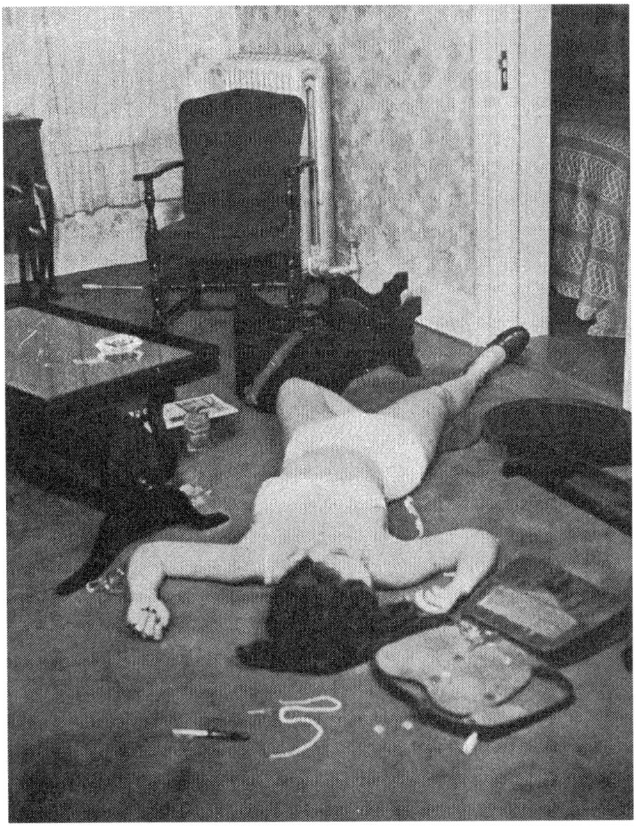

FIGURE 2.4. An example of a crime scene photo using incorrect focus (the depth of field is too narrow). From Sanga Kittikhajon, *Police Methods,* 1953.

facts about crime actually included. Fingerprints, footprints, blood stains, who to question, what to ask them, what to look for at a crime scene, what a crime scene was in the first place, what a criminal event was, and what an investigation of that event was were all introduced through practice and reinforced through routine. This means that before they could be seen as factual, the objects of evidence common today first had to go through a process of design.

Second, instructions on how to make prints and take photos may be understood as both aesthetic and epistemological considerations. The training and practice required for producing proper fingerprints and crime scene

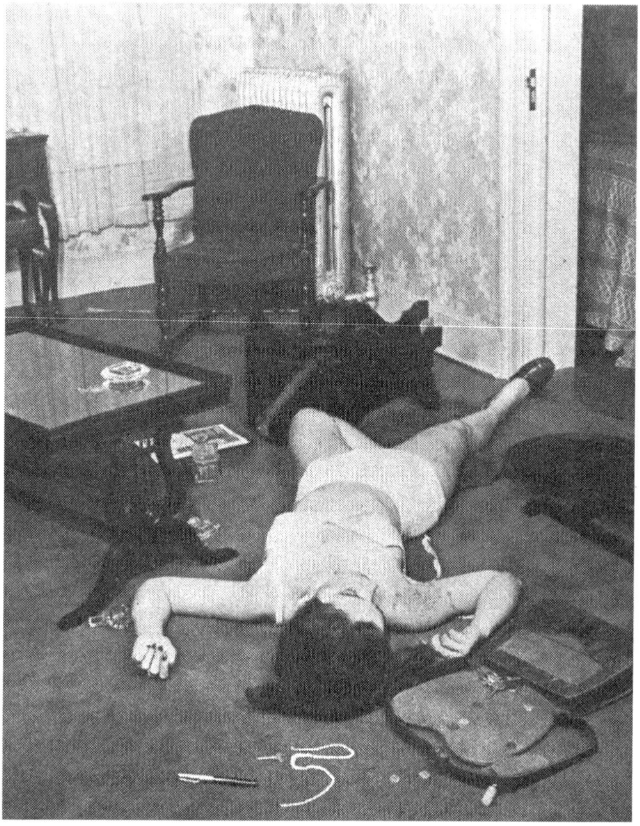

FIGURE 2.5. An example of a crime scene photo using correct focus (the depth of field is wider). From Sanga Kittikhajon, *Police Methods,* 1953.

photographs imply that making evidence, or capturing the likeness of something concrete, is a craft, one with clear, formal considerations. Requirements for color of ink and paper, camera angle, lighting, object (non) placement, and scale are all formal rules created to ensure the accuracy of the reproduction of a clue; aesthetic rules are needed to preserve an object's facticity as it goes through the production and presentation processes. Because these formal considerations developed over time, it can be argued that so, too, did the factuality of evidence. As the examples above show, the police over time began to treat their representations as if they were the objects being represented, and these formal considerations disappeared from view.

Third, the shift toward a paper-based mode of policing was the first step toward a new formalism in which the determination of how things should look became a key preoccupation of the state. Lawson, who saw quickly the potential for documentary mischief, issued definite rules for making changes in any record book: "Erasures are strictly prohibited in all Police documents of every kind. If an error in writing the document is made it should be neatly be crossed out and the correction written above it. All such corrections should be attested to by the writer's initials."[108] Erasing an entry from a record book, crossing out text, initialing an amendment, or any other alteration of a document is an operation that affects its appearance. By sanctioning some practices (crossing out and initialing) and banning others (erasing), Lawson was in effect telling his officers that correctly produced documents were ones that abided by specific formal rules of production. In other words, the facticity of even "nonvisual" texts has an aesthetic underpinning.

It took great effort on the part of people like Lawson, Jao Phraya Yommarat, and Luang Phraya Phetinthara to get their men in the habit of writing things down, taking photos, and drawing maps. Once that happened, proving that a crime took place became synonymous with making it visible in documents permeated by a tacit set of formal rules meant to ensure their stability and objectivity. The result was the birth of a new paper-based world whose efficacy rests upon a seemingly straightforward and relatively unassailable premise that police documents containing an account of the past, either as text or image, represent something real in the world. What underwrites this connection are aesthetic rules as much as anything inherent in the artifacts themselves. Lorraine Daston, a historian of science, has written that the common understanding today is that facts "are evidence *in potentia,*" that, when "mustered in an argument, deduced from a theory, or simply arranged in a pattern, they shed their proverbial obstinacy and help with the work of proof and disproof."[109] It is exactly this perceived obstinacy that gives facts value, frees them from corrupt local officials and hesitant witnesses, from human interference. The validity of material evidence, in other words, depends on its inertness as a real, physical object. What this chapter has illustrated is that the inertness of things like fingerprints and photographs of crime scenes is created in part through standardized procedures and aesthetic rules for representation. That is, modern legal evidence is produced by police officers going through the routines taught to them in school and described in textbooks about how to engage with the material world.

3

Criminal Mappings

At 12:10 p.m. on July 25, 1986, Captain Prayat Ngaongam of the Samut Prakan City police station received a dispatch over the police radio system. A man had found a dead body in Samae Forest, Samut Prakan province, just east of Bangkok. At 12:40 p.m., Prayat, Chief Inspector Thawisan Plengkham, Inspector Santi Phensut, Constable Phongdet Phetjaroen, and a few other officers, along with Wirawat Ditudomphot, a Samut Prakan City public health official, went to the location of the body, about fifty meters from Sukhumvit Road. The team noted various small trees and standing water on the ground. In the area near where the body lay, the water was about seventy centimeters deep. The body was that of a female wearing a blue-gray skirt with a pink, short-sleeved blouse tucked into it. Her head faced east, and her feet faced west. There wasn't anything, such as an identification card, that would help them determine her name. Prayat and the doctor performed an initial inspection of the body and found no scars or bruises. From the state of the body's decomposition, they estimated that the woman had been dead for about five days, and they began inspecting the area. They then took photographs of the body from several different angles before sending it to the police hospital in Bangkok.[1] Through an established routine, the police delineate a space—the crime scene—in the world and then use this space to establish the temporal limits of a criminal event (e.g., that the crime took place five days prior to the discovery of the body).

While the actions described above—a crime scene investigation—and the information they produce might be taken for granted today—images, made common by fiction, news, and real-crime television shows, of yellow tape and uniformed police officers with latex gloves searching for bullet casings or other objects spring to mind—they were hardly established practices in Siam in the early twentieth century. In 1919, Eric St. John Lawson estimated that in terms of actual criminal investigation, the district heads (*nai amphoe*) who were tasked with investigating crimes committed outside Bangkok only visited the location of the crime in about 5 percent of cases.[2] Much earlier he had written, "As a rule the *Amphur* [*sic*] does not visit the scene of a crime, and if he does, he goes away again immediately; nor has he, so far as I have seen, the faintest idea how to set about tracing an offender."[3] Recall also that the Provincial Gendarmerie did not leave its base camp more than once every four or five months, despite policies requiring it to conduct regular reconnaissance missions.[4] Space, according to the good captain, had not yet been connected to the detection of crime.[5] Sometime between Lawson's stint as police chief in the first decade of the twentieth century and the Sherry Ann Duncan investigation in the mid-1980s crime scene investigation had become a routine part of police practice. In this chapter, I describe how and show that, in the process, modern concepts about time and space became naturalized and were used to justify constant police surveillance and preemptive violence.

DELINEATING A SPACE

In 1906, Lawson compiled a manual for the Metropolitan Police based on one used by the English police. The book was mostly a collection of definitions and rules and regulations, not a "how-to" book for investigating crime. Curiously, Lawson does not give an explanation of what a crime scene is, despite his complaints about local officials not conducting investigations where a crime occurs.[6] Eleven years later, in perhaps the first manual on modern police investigation ever published commercially in Siam (1917), Phra Sisena (given name Kit Katchachiwa), a lawyer, one-time provincial prosecutor, former teacher at the school for military recruits (*rong rian nakrian nai roi*), and civil servant in the Ministry of Interior, describes a crime scene simply as a location where a crime happens.[7] Luang Phisitwithayakan, a prominent forensic police officer in the 1920s and 1930s and head of the first police science section (housed within the *santiban,* or Special Branch, after the 1932 revolution), gives more or less the same definition in his police investigation training manual published in 1935: a crime scene is the location where a crime or other event happens.[8] Subsequent manuals provide similarly tautological explanations. Sanga Kittikhajon writes in 1953 that a crime scene may be defined as "the area around which a crime as defined by law takes place."[9] In these manuals, the crime scene is a self-evident thing that exits a priori, a sort of geography that speaks for itself. All the police had to do was go there and inspect it.

Accordingly, the first thing an investigator is supposed to do after a crime takes place is to go to this self-evident crime scene. In an article on criminal investigation published after World War II, a police officer named Udom Latphli writes that the initial step in an investigation is to get to the location where it occurred.[10] Sanga also notes that in any criminal investigation, the officer in charge should get to the location of a crime as soon as possible.[11] More than two decades before either Udom or Sanga published their instructions to the police, Phra Sisena had given similar advice about the importance of going to a crime scene, telling his readers that doing so was in fact not a waste of time.[12] In 1935, Luang Phisitwithayakan let his readers know that crime scenes could take many forms: palaces, buildings rented to foreigners, houses of the middle class, floating houses, banks, shops, row houses, fancy restaurants, hostels or hotels, schools, places of entertainment, hospitals, government offices, and factories.[13] For each of these writers, criminal investigation was directly linked to specific sites, with place. Based on Lawson's estimate that only 5 percent of crimes outside Bangkok were investigated at the location where they occurred, merely listing specific locations and emphasizing the importance of inspecting them were already revolutionary steps in criminal investigation. They were the first part of a larger process linking policing to modern conceptions of space. For example, in 1929 Luang Bannasanprasit began his manual by stating that the successful suppression of crime rests with three important factors: the lead inspector or person in charge, his investigative methods (*withayakan*), and the specific conditions at the location of a crime.[14] He also listed the crime scene as one of the seven basic factors involved in a criminal investigation[15] and went on to describe the criminal investigation process as a whole using a spatial metaphor: "There are two ways to go about criminal investigation. One way is to draw a small circle. That is, one investigates the inside to discover the outside. The other is drawing a large circle, or investigating the outside to find the inside."[16] While he doesn't advocate one approach over the other, the point is that the modern criminal investigative process is conceptualized spatially, and this was being taught to police officers beginning in the early twentieth century.

A closer reading of the manuals shows what this emphasis on location meant in practice. Once investigators located the general area of a crime, they were instructed to determine its edges. Luang Phisitwithayakan suggests that investigating officers should try to ascertain where a perpetrator could have entered a particular area. Things that can tip a detective off include footprints, traces of mud, or gaps in a fence or row of flowers, since signs like these may indicate openings into a crime scene. He notes that a related and equally important aspect of the investigation of a crime scene is determining how and where the criminal made his exit. He therefore instructs his readers to scrutinize the outside of a dwelling or other structure where a crime has occurred. This inspection, he says, should include looking for footprints or any telltale tools (e.g., knives or metal bars) left behind by the perpetrator that can help determine his escape route. In describing the crime scene investigation report in another policing manual, Phraya Manawaratchasewi writes that while it is difficult to say what a crime scene report should look like, each one "should have some basic components including a description of the crime scene, the location were the criminal entered it, where he left it, locations where witnesses saw the criminal, and locations where evidence is found."[17] In other words, a crime scene has distinct entrances and exits, an inside and an outside, and topographical points of interest (e.g., locations where a criminal was seen or an object was located), and these are all determined during the process of investigation.

After investigators had determined the entrance and exit of a crime scene, they were told to clear the area and seal it off, especially in cases of murder.[18] The space of a crime, it turns out, is no place for amateurs. Luang Phisitwithayakan stated in a radio broadcast in 1934 that if a crime occurs, people should not meddle with the immediate area. Instead, they should simply report the incident to the police, whose job is to go to the site to look for things like footprints and fingerprints. Leaving a crime scene alone is the best way that people could help the authorities, he informed his listeners.[19] Sanga concurred, giving this ten-point list as a guide for crime scene investigations:

1. Get to the scene as soon as possible.
2. Once you get there, get rid of people that should not be there.
3. Make a plan of the site and take pictures.
4. Look for clues and evidence.
5. Preserve clues and evidence.
6. Some clues and evidence might be fake or left intentionally by the perpetrator.
7. Question people at the crime scene.
8. If there is a need to question people, do it immediately.
9. Protect the scene for future investigation if needed.
10. Record findings of investigation.[20]

In addition to getting to a crime scene and discerning its limits, then, an investigator must maintain its integrity by sectioning it off, clearing it out, and closing it down (as stipulated in steps 2 and 9). In doing so, the detective fashions a bounded space of crime in the physical world. Rather than being a self-evident thing, a crime scene is created in the physical world through a set of specific, routine practices.

After having established the extent of a crime scene and then separating it from its surroundings, an investigator has to conserve and transport it so that it may act as an investigative aid and as potential evidence in a trial. Objects like knives and guns can be physically moved to a police station and a courtroom.[21] Things like footprints and fingerprints are more difficult to transport, but, as the last chapter showed, techniques for their preservation have been developed. To capture and move a crime scene, investigators were instructed to make a map. Lawson stressed in 1906, "In all cases of violent crime a map of the scene should be drawn and attached to the case papers. The map need not be drawn to scale but the distances between different points on the map should be carefully paced and recorded."[22] He even goes as far as to say that maps are better than photographs in depicting the location of a crime.[23] In 1917, Phra Sisena suggested that "if a map or plan of the site can be made, then that would be useful to the investigation or in the adjudication of the case in court because it would allow judges to see reality as the investigator has seen it."[24] Similarly, Luang Phisitwithayakan writes that after inspecting a crime scene, a plan of the area should be made.[25] Luang Bannasanprasit also emphasized that maps should be produced and, furthermore, that they be "properly drawn."[26] Unfortunately, the pre–World War II manuals cited above only provide vague instructions without the benefit of any illustrations. Lawson, remember, did not even define what a crime scene was in his handbook. So how did anyone know what a "properly drawn" map looked like or how to produce one, especially since the maps people are familiar with now were not common in Siam during most of the nineteenth century? Thongchai Winichakul's discussion of the introduction of modern mapping techniques in Siam shows that, prior to the late nineteenth century, visual representations of the physical world were often illustrations featuring elements such as various deities and larger-than-life animals. In addition, many were composed in a linear fashion, suggesting a journey or movement through time.[27] There were also more abstract representations of space, like the *duang chata*. But both these types of representations were hardly the sort of map the reformed legal courts were looking for as part of a case file. As with photographs, fingerprints, tables, and reports, the conventions and procedures for making and evaluating crime scene maps required explanation and training. The police needed to see what a correct map was before they could produce one.

Luang Bannasanprasit begins his call for detectives to make proper maps by writing that ones "that have not been signed by their creator and that are not to scale are just estimates of no use."[28] From this, one begins to see that, for him, correctly produced maps adhered to a set of formal conventions like signatures and scale. Around the midcentury, police manuals began providing readers a more systematic treatment of how to correctly draw a crime scene map. Sanga, for example, does this in his book on criminal investigation from 1953. In it he writes that investigators should not include too much extraneous detail, as this will give a map a cluttered appearance and make it difficult to read later. The investigator should use a pencil first if he feels that he cannot produce a clean, neat map at the crime scene. He can make a copy in ink later, so long as the initial draft and the final one are identical. The map should be drawn on its own sheet of paper, not on the back or other part of another document. It needs to indicate the dimensions of the area covered, include a direction arrow, scale, and legend.[29] He then provides a few examples, taken directly from foreign police manuals. Figure 3.1 shows one of these. It is an image of a room in what appears to be a small studio apartment containing a sofa, chairs, a coffee table, and a dead man. To represent these objects, Sanga suggests the use of a standard set of symbols, of which he provides two pages of examples for things like trees, roads, and fences. He also suggests the use, when possible, of a rather cumbersome-looking apparatus, complete with collapsible legs and a mechanism comprising two bands or pieces of string, to help the officer maintain the map's proportions.[30] The examples he gives show the crime scene from a bird's-eye view. The space it depicts operates like an empty container in which objects are found. Aside from perhaps only some astrological diagrams, representations of space did not typically employ this sort of privileged, omniscient perspective. The crime scene map thus helped introduce a new way of picturing space as a discrete thing that could be isolated, recorded, transferred, enlarged or reduced, and then analyzed.

Prior to Sanga's book, one does find other examples of crime scene maps. One of the earliest instances is located in "Phu rai kha khon thi bang khun phrom" (Murder at Bang Khun Phrom), a fictional story from 1904 by King Vajiravudh, then still crown prince.[31] The story is a murder mystery adapted from Edgar Allan Poe's "The Murders in the Rue Morgue." A man named Thong-in is the story's detective, and his sidekick is named Pho Wat, the

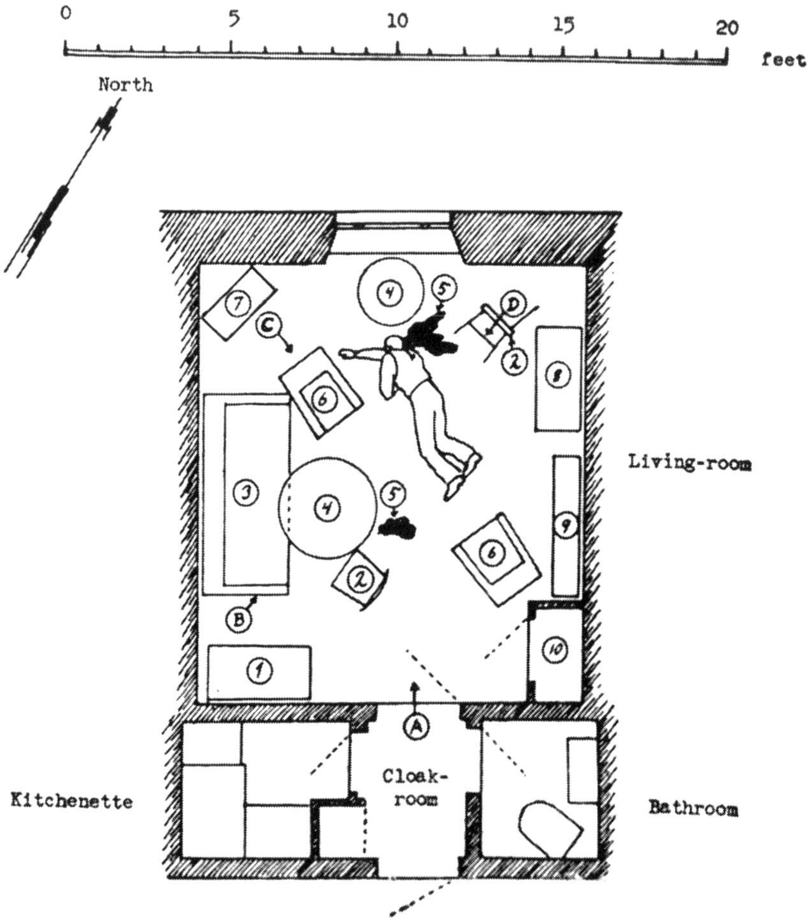

FIGURE 3.1. Example of a crime scene map. From Sanga Kittikhajon, *Police Methods,* 1953.

story's Watson figure and narrator. In the story there appears a plan of the room where a man named Rot is found dead (Figure 3.2). Pho Wat is the character that produces the plan. It, like Sanga's examples, presents the reader with an image of the room as seen from above, and it includes symbols that indicate where Rot's bed, table, chairs, and closet are situated. It also shows the location of the room's windows and doors, with indicators for where the murderer is likely to have entered (the window on the right side of the drawing, designated by an arrow) and where the dead body was found

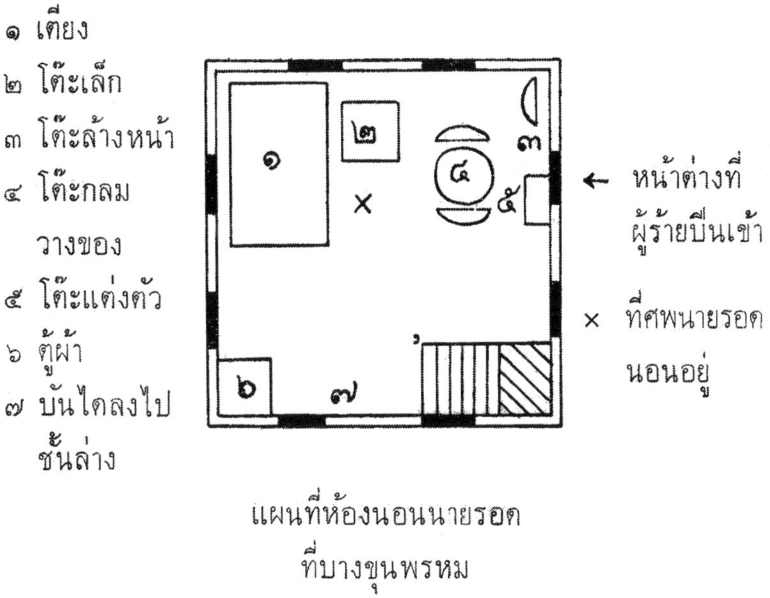

FIGURE 3.2. Fictional crime scene map. On the left is a legend indicating different furniture items in the room. On the right is an arrow indicating the window through which the culprit entered the room. The X stands for the location where the body of the victim, Nai Rot, was found. From Nai Kaeo and Nai Khwan [King Vajiravudh], "Phu rai kha khon thi bang khun phrom" (Murder at Bang Khun Phrom), in *Tales of Mr. Thong-in,* 1930.

(marked by an X).[32] These features—a bird's-eye perspective of a uniform, continuous space and symbols that stand for the physical elements that it contains—make Vajiravudh's fictional map different from earlier depictions of space. It matches more closely with subsequent examples of crime scene maps in police manuals like Sanga's. In another translated story, "Khwam phajon phai khong soe roboet beden paowen" (The adventures of Sir Robert Baden-Powell), a similar type of map can be found (Figure 3.3).[33] The story, published in serial form in the military journal *Senasueksa lae phae witthayasat* (Military studies and the spread of science) in 1921, is a translation of *My Adventures as a Spy,* an autobiographical introduction to spy craft by Lieutenant-General Sir Robert Baden-Powell, originally published in English in 1915.[34] The English version of the story contains a map drawn by Baden-Powell (Figure 3.4). One can see from these two examples that the conventions for mapping (and the conceptions about space that they

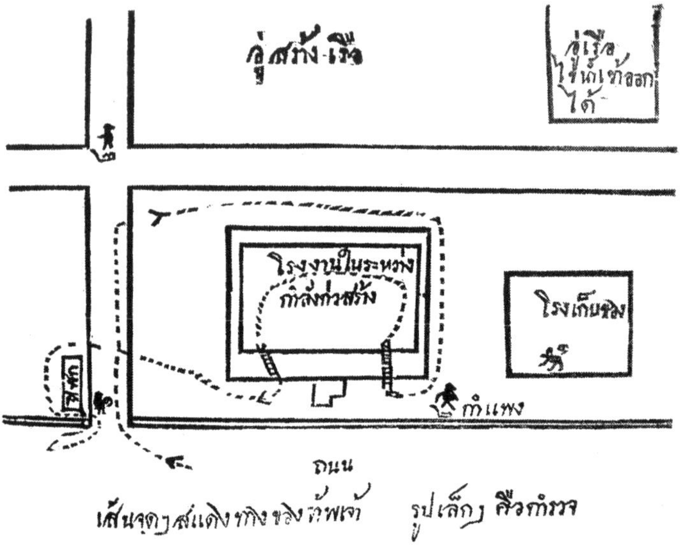

FIGURE 3.3. A map showing the route used by Baden-Powell to evade the police in "Khwam phajon phai khong soe roboet beden paowen" (The adventures of Sir Robert Baden-Powell), a translation of *My Adventures as a Spy* by Baden-Powell, 1921.

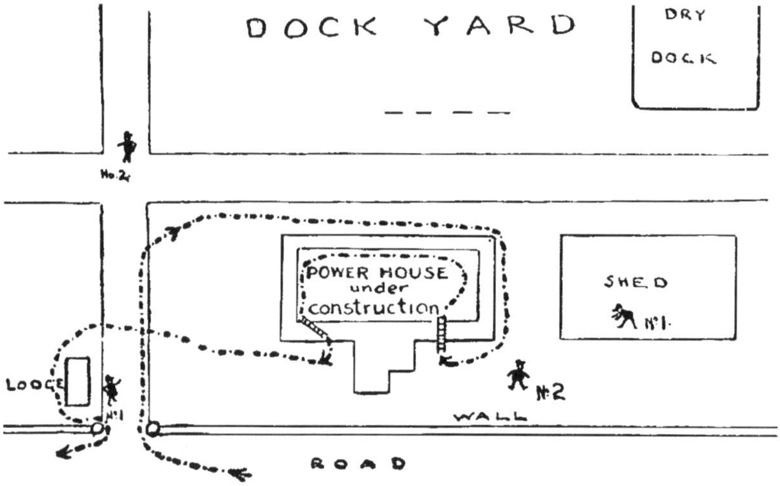

FIGURE 3.4. The map as it appears in Baden-Powell's *My Adventures as a Spy*, 1915.

represent) were transplanted more or less directly into vernacular fiction, just as they were into police manuals.

It was not long after the detective stories of Vajiravudh and others appeared that police training manuals began to recommend that investigators make plans of the area where a crime occurs. Drawing maps, for example, was part of the training program proposed by Prince Paribatra in 1928 for officers of the soon-to-be-established *tamruat phuthon klang* (Central Investigation Division),[35] and fairly standard-looking maps of crime scenes begin to appear in police case files by the late 1920s. At first, maps were not necessarily seen as having to be mimetically accurate. They were simply schematic representations to aid police officers in solving a case. Lawson, as mentioned above, wrote in 1906 that scale was not necessary. Meanwhile, Luang Bannasanprasit noted,

> Even though a map or plan is made on paper and marked with letters, it is not to be considered documentary evidence [*phayan ekkasan*]. It is to be considered material evidence [*phayan wathu*] and because maps preserve [*jamlong*] the characteristics of a location where an event happens it is not that location itself. This implies that there is a real crime scene that is better. For this reason, a map is second-level evidence.[36]

The view that maps were schematic shows that their status as true representations of the world was still unsettled in the early days of police reform, and it was not until midcentury that the map was more or less regularized and accepted as part of normal police practice. In short, ideas about what a crime scene was, what to do when investigating one, and what its map might (or ought to) look like entered the kingdom through the transnational phenomenon of crime fiction at the same time that it entered through professional training.

The idea that fiction might inform professional practice should not be dismissed as a frivolous claim. In Europe during the late nineteenth century, practitioners of legal medicine and forensic science read and loved Sir Arthur Conan Doyle's Sherlock Holmes stories: "Real-life investigators found the character [Holmes] fascinating. [Forensic doctor Jean Alexandre Eugene] Lacassagne's disciple Edmond Locard said what in part motivated his career choice, aside from his mentor, was the Sherlock Holmes stories."[37] Serious academic journals even published articles analyzing the methods employed by Holmes. Of course, the reaction of real-life practitioners was not always positive: "Lacassagne admired the work of Conan Doyle, but he, like his colleagues, had reservations about Holmes's methods and the misleading impression they gave to the public."[38] Holmes worked fast and was always sure. Real-life investigations took time, and Lacassagne made it a point to always remain uncertain till the end of an investigation. Nevertheless, Lacassagne and others remained fascinated by Holmes and his stories. In Siam, police officers and other government officials were also enchanted with the Holmes character, as well as with other fictional detectives. Some of King Vajiravudh's Thong-in stories were adaptations of Doyle's mysteries, and the name of his Thong-in character is likely a play on the name Dupin, Poe's detective figure in "The Murders in the Rue Morgue." In addition, periodicals in the early twentieth century regularly published translations of the Holmes series and fiction by Agatha Christie, Sax Rohmer, Robert Barr, and others. The popularity of detective fiction in the late 1890s was so great that Phraya Samosonsaphakan, the author of a series of detective stories in *Wachirayan,* the journal of the Royal Wachirayan Library, complained that the journal could not keep up with requests for more because there were not enough skilled writers who could actually produce them.[39] The demand came from a small group of new bourgeois Bangkokians comprising petty aristocrats, merchants with ties to the Siamese elite, and members of the growing government bureaucracy, military and police officials included. In fact, early military and police journals all contained translated crime fiction and crime reports from overseas. Like "The Adventures of Sir Baden-Powell," Luang Saranupraphan's *Phrae dam* (Black satin), the kingdom's first indigenous crime novel, appeared in *Senasueksa lae phae withayasat,* a military journal read by army officers and literate urbanites.[40] In addition to reading crime fiction, Siam's new detectives were watching foreign films, which had become a popular pastime in the early twentieth century. Phra Phinit Chonkhadi, a prominent police officer during much of the twentieth century, talks about how in the 1920s, he and his fellow police detectives would pass scraps of paper to each other in darkened movie theaters and used code names just as he saw detectives do in the foreign films that were beginning to flood Bangkok.[41] A long editorial piece in the newspaper *Krungthep deli me* (Daily mail) from 1912 talks about how the kingdom's new plainclothes detectives went around mimicking the detectives they saw in popular films. They wore sunglasses and made themselves conspicuous as detectives rather than blending into their environment, defeating the purpose of being undercover.[42] So while no single, concrete link—aside from the striking resemblance, in terms of drawing conventions that included symbols, perspective, and subject matter, between the example of a crime scene map in Sanga's manual and the map from King Vajiravudh's detective story—can be made between artifacts of fiction and those of police practices, it is quite reasonable to conclude that ideas about how a representation of a crime scene should look (and how to investigate it) have origins in two epistemological realms: fiction and fact. Ideas about how to represent space entered the kingdom through a number of channels, some clearly cultural, as opposed to being purely scientific. These ideas were then institutionalized as standard police routine and their products became an inconspicuous part of the visual culture of criminal justice.

This point is important when thinking about beliefs commonly expressed by police reformers about maps (e.g., that they help judges see reality as an investigator has). Rather than neutral and objective representations of space, maps, as Michael Lynch writes, "are systematic drawings . . . made by hand or reproduced from engravings" that "aid identification and classification by isolating or targeting 'essential details' " like a river, a house, or, in the case of this discussion, the location of a dead body. Through the deployment of "a variety of conventions for isolating and delineating" relevant features, one can discard "gratuitous details." Assumptions about what qualities are relevant in a crime scene, about the qualities of space in general, are therefore made and imbedded in a map of a space created during the criminal investigation process.[43] By analogy, and to paraphrase Lynch, things like scale, or the distance between points (e.g., ten feet versus one hundred feet), "presumes something about the movement and territory" of a criminal and a crime in a "non-discursive" manner. Suppositions, sometimes not at all scientific, about the space and time of crime are thus "built into the graphic."[44] This means that the visual basis of legal decision making in the modern criminal process is saturated with preconceptions (here, about the nature of space) not immediately apparent in the same way that human bias might be in witness testimony. When the police delimit a territory in the earth with their yellow tape and make a drawing of that space, they are really performing a modern ritual in which they inscribe in the world and then on paper theories about the natural world that they may not be completely conscious of. Mapping may therefore be thought of as a systematic way of tapping information "out there" and presenting it as a coherent, unbiased illustration of that information, but it is also a practice that helps naturalize sometimes unspoken beliefs about space in a visual manner.

KEEPING TIME

There is a goal to the practice of conducting a crime scene investigation beyond simply making a map, and that is to tell a story about the past in order to solve a crime. To do this, detectives must mine the crime scene for clues. Phra Sisena's manual tells the reader that within a crime scene an investigator should look for footprints, especially those made in mud because they can be preserved. In addition, he reminds investigators to look for bloodstains or anything that a criminal may have left behind.[45] Luang Bannasanprasit includes a long section in his 1929 manual describing things to keep an eye out for, such as bullet casings and documents.[46] Luang Phisitwithayakan explains to his readers similarly that they ought to be looking out for things like weapons that may have been touched by a perpetrator and thus carry his fingerprints. He then instructs investigators to check for lines of dust or other minutiae that might indicate something has been moved or is out of place.[47] If a criminal has dropped any of his tools, it is imperative that police do not let anyone touch them. Moreover, even the police must be careful in handling them so as not to destroy any possible identifying traces that the criminal may have left on them.[48] Phraya Manawaratchasewi writes, "Little things that might not seem important may come back later and prove to be critical bits of evidence. Therefore, investigators must check everything and record every detail. Even a single grain of powder can be an important piece of evidence."[49] Sanga, too, points to the importance of looking for potentially telling objects—from dead people to scraps of paper—in a crime scene.[50] In fact, he writes that the entire purpose of investigating a crime scene is to discover "clues, evidence, and facts."[51] Within a delimited and sealed space of crime, otherwise meaningless objects become potentially meaningful signs.

The importance of these objects is twofold. First, they can help the police identify telltale characteristics of a culprit. Openings into crime scenes become markers that detectives can use to interpret the skill level of a robber. Luang Phisitwithayakan teaches his readers that holes in doors, ceilings, floors, or walls show that the perpetrator has a relatively high level of skill or experience. Criminals with less ability tend to create awkward openings, such as by drilling a hole too close to a bolt. Second, and more importantly, objects in a crime scene can potentially reveal to investigators information about a sequence of past events. The bloodstains, footprints, and other material clues that investigators are asked to look for allow skilled detectives to deduce things like the path taken by a perpetrator and whether he may have dragged his victim's body or was injured during a struggle.[52] Bruises or other markings on dead bodies help doctors determine how a fight may have taken place, while the trajectory of a bullet through a body tells investigators the relative positions of a victim and his assailant at the time of a shooting. Luang Phisitwithayakan, in a foreword to a translation of a case report from England, says that detailed reports that describe clues like these are a key aid in investigating crime because they help the police put together an image of a crime scene as it appeared when the crime took place.[53] Tire tracks in the street reveal the make of the car, its speed, and its direction; smudges on tabletops potentially provide incriminating fingerprints; stains on a cup or in a bowl can expose to an officer what a dead man drank or ate just before death, and so on. Clues found in the process of delimiting a crime scene help investigators cobble together a picture about the past, which then aids them in solving a crime and theoretically bring a guilty party to justice.

While tying criminal investigation to specific places and the objects in those spaces would seem to indicate at first blush that modern detectives have prioritized space over other aspects of the past, including time, it becomes apparent upon closer inspection that in fact the goal of the exercise is creating a narrative; the purpose of distilling a bounded space from a broader field is to make a story about the past possible. As Thongchai has shown with his study of modern mapping and nationalist history for Thailand, this was the case with the kingdom's national historiography. The Siam that existed on maps made before the late nineteenth century was located only in the Chao Phraya River basin and the upper Malay Peninsula. It stretched north to about Sukhothai and eastward to the mountains of Khorat. The south was a fluctuating set of sovereignties and lordships. In short, the kingdoms of Lanna, Laos, and Cambodia were not part of Siam. Mapping made borders suddenly appear where they did not previously exist and provided evidence of the nation's territorial claims against the British and the French. The body of the Thai nation "was being created literally on paper."[54] It was this iconic representation of the nation that produced what Thongchai calls a "geo-body," and it is the image of this geo-body as a single, continuous, and discrete entity that makes the history of modern Thailand conceivable. Once an object—here, the Thai nation—is depicted on paper, it can be projected back into time and given a biography—or, in the case of Siam, a national history.[55] The past of the nation is not so much an illusion, then, as a conceptual possibility enabled by a particular practice of visual representation. Even though Luang Bannasanprasit spoke of criminal investigation in spatial terms, as the drawing of a large or a small circle, he ended his discussion by tying geography to a temporal understanding of crime: "Both methods involve investigation over three temporal dimensions: during the crime, after the crime, and before the crime."[56] An investigator should think about his job as a historian might about the past: What did the culprit do after the crime? What about before it? What actions constituted the crime as it took place? The identification and separation of a crime scene from other spaces is in fact a process of marking time, of making history.

That people think of life's events, including crime, in terms of a three-part temporal structure such as that described by Luang Bannasanprasit may seem mundane, but this concept of time, like its modern spatial counterpart, is neither natural nor timeless, and its implications for police practice can be deadly serious when systematized as part of the criminal justice system, as it has been in Thailand over the course of the past hundred years. In the early part of the twentieth century, two similar terms existed for investigation: *suep suan* and *tai suan* (now *sop suan*). Phra Sisena wrote in his 1917 manual that no law existed that defined *suep suan*.[57] So he tried to define the activities of *suep suan* and *tai suan* based on personal experience, telling his readers that criminal investigation can be thought of as having two temporally organized parts, a "beginning" (the pre-crime period) and an "end" (the post-crime period), both of which need to be scrutinized.[58] The beginning, for an investigator, involves looking for evidence before someone actually commits a crime. This is important, reminds Phra Sisena, since many crimes require forethought, planning, and preparation. He describes a situation where before A kills B, A expresses dissatisfaction with B to C. A then borrows a knife from C and goes to stake out B's house before actually stabbing B. Phra Sisena says that this shows that a crime begins before the criminal act itself (e.g., the putting of a knife into another person's body). Phra Sisena also tells investigators that after a crime takes place, a criminal may attempt to cover up his actions. This means that the police must look for signs after a crime has taken place that will help uncover the true identity of a culprit. So, for example, A might have blood on his clothes or on his knife, act funny, run and hide, or tell someone about his action.[59] It follows logically that the temporal and legally actionable limits of an investigation should be set well before and after the criminal act to be useful in court.

After World War II, the idea that crime has a prehistory (and is thus preventable) became even more prevalent. Sanga writes that because criminals plan their activities, investigation must be conducted *constantly,* not just after a crime takes place. He extends the time of criminal detection out indefinitely: "When no crime has taken place, an investigator should be out observing local conditions and the behavior of people, making lists of names and behaviors of trouble makers [*khon phan gaerae*] and then recording it all or making statistical tables that can be used in the future."[60] The effect of this particular temporal structure (or narrative form) of criminal investigation, of a *potential* criminality requiring constant detection, cannot be overstated. During his time as head of the police, Phao Sriyanond justified the assassination of suspected criminals on the basis that they *intended* to commit crimes (which could then be rationalized in some cases by the fact that they had previously committed a crime or were on a watch list). A proposal by the head of the government's Science Department in 1959 to castrate criminals to prevent future crimes and Sanga's suggestion, cited earlier, to sterilize them are also indicative of this thinking.[61] So is Thaksin Shinawatra's 2003 war on drugs, in which the police committed over 2,200 extrajudicial killings. In one instance, four ethnic Hmong men were killed, and, according to official sources, "none of the victims had a previous record of drug-related activity. The police summarily classified their murders [aptly, in light of this discussion] as 'cut-off killings.'"[62] Just in case. The state creates and co-opts a prehistory of crime and then uses it to justify the need to engage in constant surveillance as well as the use of preemptive, deadly force.

A final point to note is that the separation between the two processes, *suep suan* and *sop suan,* was never all that clear, even to the police themselves. For example, Luang Bannasanprasit wrote in the 1920s that a detective's work could be categorized into two parts, *suep suan* and *tai suan.* While he admitted that the two were difficult to separate, he did say that *suep suan* was simply the gathering of information and did not involve recording in writing any findings, while *tai suan* involved documenting evidence, such as the testimony of witnesses and suspects, for use in a criminal trial. The simple definition of *suep suan,* he wrote, is "the search for the truth, and for evidence that proves that truth [*khwam pen jing*]." He based his definition on the *Tamra pokkhrong lem 1* (Manual for administration, volume 1), which states that *suep suan* is the practice of asking for information about a crime in the area where the crime took place. Information is not recorded on paper in this process. He added that while anyone could *suep suan,* only authorized officials could *tai suan* since it involved the exercise of specific state powers, including calling witnesses, making people take oaths, and recording signatures. These, he said, were official legal functions.[63] After World War II, some police officers gave more specific descriptions about the two activities. Sanga wrote, "according to the definition in the criminal procedural code [*pramuan kotmai withi phijarana khwam aya*], *suep suan* is the search for facts [*kho thet jing*] and evidence [*lak than*] conducted by a civilian official or a police officer as part of his responsibility to maintain peace and order and for discovering the details of wrong-doings." *Sop suan* (previously *tai suan*), according to the Criminal Procedure Code, meant "the consideration of evidence and other activities according to the law that officers conduct related to wrong-doings in order to know facts or to prove something so as to bring a suspect to trial and be sentenced." He concluded, therefore, that, "*suep suan* is part of *sop suan*. The main difference is this: *suep suan* is the first step of the *sop suan* process that can be conducted by civilian or police officials but *sop suan* must be conducted by specific officials of the police's *sop suan* section."[64] The unclear distinction between the two functions remains today, and there are officers that do not agree with separating them since they are closely related.[65] What is clear from this ambiguity is that the division between the two processes, between a pre-crime and a post-crime period, is not self-evident. The narrative structure of crime, which closely resembles that of the detective story, that now informs police investigations is not natural. Instead, the police have come to understand crimes as such by giving particular events spatial dimensions (inside and outside, entrance and exit) that then reveal temporal ones (before, during, after). The consequence is that state agents are now able to rationalize the use of preventative force as a normal response to the natural order of things.

Of course, not every case gets the same spatial treatment. Most crimes, violent or otherwise, never lead to the full-scale crime scene investigation, complete with advanced chemical analyses, that television shows lead one to imagine as universal. In 1929, Phraya Manawaratchasewi wrote, "the crime scene investigation report is an important part of criminal investigation, but mostly investigators only conduct a crime scene investigation in important cases."[66] In these important instances, perhaps the bloodiest crimes or the ones with direct national, political significance, the police do in fact mark out spaces of crime in the real world through the criminal investigation routine to reveal a story about the past. Early in the morning on March 4, 1949, for example, Police Major General Luang Samridh of the Royal Thai Police Department summoned Captain Yongyudh Damrongchai to Paruksawan Palace, temporary police headquarters during the state of emergency prevailing in the capital at the time.[67] Luang Samridh explained to Yongyudh that a police escort transporting four former parliament ministers loyal to exiled prime minister Pridi Phanomyong had come under attack in a predawn assault. Pridi's followers had hoped to spring the four former ministers from police captivity, he said. In the ensuing gun battle, the four ministers were killed. Luang Samridh ordered Yongyudh to join the investigation at the Central Hospital, where the bodies had been taken. That was at about 5:00 a.m.[68]

Perhaps because of his training in modern police investigation, when Yongyudh's work was done at the hospital, he went to the location of the incident: Phrachathipat Highway (Phahonyothin Road), between kilometer posts 14 and 15, past the Saphan Khwai Bridge. It was noon or so by the time he got there. There were no houses on either side of the road (in 1949), and the area was deserted. He saw patches of blood on the western side of road. The biggest were about six inches long, but there were not many of them. Some were thick, some thin, and some had flowed down the side of the road. He saw about forty bullet casings on the ground, an almost equal number were lying on each side of the road. The grass on the eastern side of the road, just off the asphalt surface, had been disturbed as if human feet had trampled it, while the grass on the western side of the road was smeared with mud patches from the asphalt down to the bottom of the ditch. Certain parts of the grass bore impressions as if something heavy had been placed on them. He noticed footprints in the half-dried mud bed of the ditch on the western side of the road. The footprints were few in some places, but at other locations huge patches could be found. There were altogether about ten such areas. Each covered an area of about one square meter. No trace of footprints was present in the paddy field beyond the edge of the ditch. On the eastern side of the road there was also a paddy field, but the whole area was dry and bore no peculiar markings.[69] Yongyudh spoke with the people that lived near the highway. Some had heard gunshots. None dared come out to look.[70] As in the Sherry Ann case, early crime fiction, and early police manuals, a police investigation turned an otherwise ordinary space, here a stretch of nondescript highway, into a crime scene: a medium containing objects of information crucial to the police's mission. This space is subsequently bound, sometimes quite literally, and given over to specialists, including the police detective and the forensic expert (*phu chiao chan*), to read for information that will allow them to revisit the past and solve a crime. Much like a ritual space carved out by sacred stones or other markers, the crime scene is sectioned off from the ordinary world and turned into a charmed site with the potential to help police detectives, as modern-day diviners, discern the past and explain a criminal mystery.[71]

CHRONOTOPE OF CRIME

The previous sections have shown how government officials and high-ranking police officers worked hard to change the way that the state's detectives went about investigating crime, though the development of new methods of representing space and conceptualizing time based on practices borrowed from the United States and various countries in Europe. Their efforts have in most instances proved successful, to sometimes deadly effect. It might be tempting to conclude from this discussion that modern conceptions regarding the geography and temporal structure of crime, and of the physical world more broadly, have successfully replaced older beliefs. In important ways this is true. Prior to the introduction of modern mapping, the *traiphum* (three-worlds cosmology), as contained in the *Traiphum phra ruang* (Three worlds according to King Ruang), guided the way people in Siam thought about their physical world: "The Thai spiritual culture is based on the Buddhist teachings promoted in this work [the *Traiphum phra ruang*], which embodies not only the ordinary people's attitudes but also those of the ruling class." Moreover, "Many artistic works in the fields of architecture, painting, and sculpture of Thailand were produced with inspiration derived from the Traibhumikatha's structure and descriptions."[72] It is regarded, in short, as one of the most important literary works in Thailand and has shaped the thinking of Thais of all stripes. In brief, the *traiphum* describes the three realms of the cosmos and the forms of existence that each contains. The first realm is that of the five senses, the *kamaloka*. The second is the corporeal world of the sixteen celestial grades, the *rupaloka*. The third is the incorporeal world or *arupaloka,* where the senses are "no longer operative."[73] Humans live in the *kamaloka,* the realm of the five senses. This realm consists of several landmasses and bodies of water. The main landmass, or continent, is the *chomputhawip,* which comprises *machimprathet* (an area that corresponds to central India) and *patchantaprathet* (an area that corresponds to India's borderlands).[74] At the center of the *chomputhawip* is Mount Meru, the highest point of the continent and the center of the realm. Architectural evidence indicates that the concept of space contained in the *traiphum* did reflect the geography that the Thais in the fifteenth through the eighteenth centuries knew and believed to be true. The cities they built exhibited a layout that tallied with the image of the *chomputhawip.* Typically a centrally located stupa stood for Mount Meru, and pools of water acted as the oceans. Mount Meru is also the conceptual center of the *duang chata,* itself a diagram of the cosmos. Likewise, temple murals often depict a heaven or hell realm from the *traiphum.*

Over time people began to question and make adjustments to the geography of the *traiphum.* Historian of Thailand Nidhi Eoseewong explains that increased interaction with Europeans and Americans over the course of the nineteenth century forced Thais to rethink older conceptions of space, and this was reflected in the way the cosmos was represented. The early nineteenth-century text *Nang nophamat* (Lady Nophamat) is an example. In the story, there are landmasses called *chomputhawip* and *patchantaprathet,* and islands around another landmass called *singhonprathet.* What is important for Nidhi is that the version of the cosmos contained in *Nang nophamat* has no center, no Mount Meru. *Chomputhawip* is just one territory among many.[75] A similar shift in the Siamese conception of space is seen in Rama I's (r. 1782–1809) recension of the *traiphum* story, called the *Traiphum lokawinitchai.* In Rama I's version, the center of the universe moves from Mount Meru to the Throne of Enlightenment, "in line with new beliefs about the king which early Bangkok monarchs wished to stress."[76] Tony Day and Craig J. Reynolds write that one of the innovations of Rama I's recension is the reorganization of the order in which various worlds were presented in the text, not from low to high as before, but beginning with the middle level of mankind.[77] The *Traiphum lokawinitchai* thus places mankind at its starting point. This reordering of the cosmos and the myths that came with it, Nidhi says, legitimized the status and power of elites and the king. Another text, Chaophraya Thipakorawong's *Sadaeng kitchanukit* (On diverse subjects), written in 1865 and published in 1867, explains that the world is not flat, with Mount Meru at its center, because "evidence" revealed it to be round. Nidhi concludes, "In the early Bangkok period [ca. 1782–1855], the divergence between theory and reality became even more glaring."[78] By the late eighteenth century, the notion of space contained in the *traiphum* therefore "upheld a truth without any reference to the real world."[79] In political terms, this gradual disassociation of representation and referent, artifact and idea, meant that there was no cosmological basis for the existence of a *chakravartin* (universal ruler): "in *Nang nophamat* the universal ruler has no role, for the text describes a world which has more than one great state, and the various countries are subject to no single, superior universal force."[80] Because of this change, Nidhi believes that *Nang nophamat* is the first literary work in Siam to ignore the theory that other states were merely tributaries to

Siam. An entire political system, based on a supposedly true mapping of the world, was slowly losing that which gave it power—fidelity to an external reality.

Despite the disappearance of the world it once stood for, forms of the three-worlds cosmology live on stubbornly today. The *duang chata* is based on the geography contained in an astrologer's manual called the *tamra phrommachat,* known colloquially as the *tamra mo du* (fortuneteller's manual). This geography is derived from the one in the *traiphum* and is now widespread in Thailand, with different editions of the *phrommachat* published by various publishing houses.[81] There are even interactive versions online. The *tamra phrommachat* tells readers that the surface of the world lies mostly flat. There are peaks and promontories, but not many, and space in every *thesa* (realm or place) and each *kala* (time period) comprises mysterious powers and hidden or unseen forces. *Phaya nak* (naga, or serpent beings), for instance, live under the surface of the world and can be used to determine the positioning and timing of human affairs. One is instructed to build a house or plant a crop in the ground according to the direction of the *nak*'s scales. In addition, each day of the week and various time periods have a *phi* (spirit) or *thewada* (deity) associated with them, while time has a cardinal direction (*thit thang*).[82] These entities have effects on daily activities, so threshing rice, cutting a tree, or building a house should be carried out according to the characteristics of each *kala* and *thesa* if one is to expect good fortune.[83] Space and time in this rendition of the cosmos are quite literally alive. Astrologers who understand this and master the peculiar characteristics of the cosmography can help humans predict their futures and recover their pasts. The basic cosmological order of the kingdom has changed, as convincingly shown by scholars like Nidhi and Thongchai, but the continued popularity of alternative conceptions of space like those contained in the *phrommachat* indicates that the spaces of modern mapping and older cosmologies now exist side by side.

In practical terms, the simultaneous existence and validity of distinctly different geographies leads to apparent contradictions. David Engel's work on modernization and legal consciousness in Thailand shows that many Thais see causality in cases of bodily injury in terms of a host of actors and forces, many of which are supernatural. He writes, "fortune and misfortune arise primarily because of destiny, karma, ghosts, and spirits."[84] One of Engel's informants noted that the causes of her being hit by a car while trying to save a child in a stroller included negligence on the part of the driver and herself, the fortunes (*khro*) of both the driver and herself; her karma from past lives; a ghost that lived in a mango tree near the incident; the unluckiness of the space, in which unfortunate things regularly happened; and past acts of sexual impropriety in her village for which an ancestor spirit was now punishing residents. The driver of the car involved in the accident claimed that a ghost was pushing his vehicle at the time of the crash. In this example, at least one party saw the causes of the accident in terms of geography (e.g., a mango tree, an ancestral village, a fated location at which previous accidents had occurred), and, as with space in the *phrommachat,* this geography is alive and imbued with an agency over human affairs. One can imagine, however, that if the case described by Engel were to go to court, the scene of the accident would be mapped in a way that could not capture either of the litigants' notions of the forces at work in the accident. The map in the court case would probably indicate roads nearby, the mango tree, and any other structures in the vicinity. It might also have symbolic representations to indicate the direction of the car, the locations of the two litigants, and perhaps an X or other mark to show where the car hit its victim. It is unlikely the map would contain any inscriptions to represent the ghost in the mango tree, ancestor spirits, fate, or karma. It is also quite possible that whatever the outcome of the trial, the litigants would have claimed that the judgment reflected the workings of one or more of these supernatural agents. Space has always been connected with crime and other events, though not in the way Lawson had in mind. The modern maps that police officials wanted the rank and file to produce simply could not, and still don't, represent various aspects of the world many Thais (and, to be fair, many others) see as being real. As such, people toggle between modes of representing the real world as a matter of necessity.

Mikhail Bakhtin, writing about space and time in modern literature, notes, "In the literary artistic chronotope, spatial and temporal indicators are fused into one carefully thought-out, concrete whole. Time, as it were, thickens, takes on flesh, becomes artistically visible, likewise, space becomes charged and responsive to the movements of time, plot and history. This intersection of axes and fusion of indicators characterizes the artistic chronotope."[85] More simply, a chronotope is a concept used in literary criticism to describe how configurations of time and space are represented in novels. If one views the visualizations of space and time in the *traiphum* and in crime scene maps as two different but simultaneously existing chronotopes, then it is possible to see modernity as a genre of description as much as a historical era, a mind-set, or an evolutionary stage of society. When the police introduced the new visual practices of investigation to the country during the early twentieth century, they added a new way to articulate space to already existing conventions. These older methods for making visualizations were not completely replaced, and today their legacy continues to influence how people imagine and interact with the physical world.

4

Murder, Reenacted

A curious thing began appearing in the daily papers and weekly and monthly magazines of Thailand during the early 1950s. The *Phim thai rai duean* of April 1954 contains two photos of Liang Muangphrae in which he demonstrates to the police, at the scene of the crime, how he shot and killed his lover. In one, Liang looms behind a stand-in for his victim while holding a gun. He is about to shoot (Figure 4.1). In another, he stands over his lover's dead body (Figure 4.2). Dozens of spectators are at the scene of the crime. The police, the captions explain, are there to take photos for their records. In July 1956, Nin Saisaat appears on the pages of *Phim thai bueang lang khao,* showing how he cut a man named Phrom in the neck with a long machete, as police officers take notes for their files (Figure 4.3). In April 1957, three men show up in *Phim thai rai pak,* letting readers know how they derailed a train in order to rob its passengers (Figure 4.4). Since their first appearance, images like these—of criminals in action—and the stories of crime and investigation that accompany them have been prominent in the Thai press, gaining popularity well before reality television shows like *Cops* and dramas like *CSI* became pop culture phenomena around the world.

Photographs of reenactments like the ones presented here are still produced by the police as part of the criminal investigation process in Thailand. The performances of violence they depict typically take place after a suspect has confessed to a crime. Like maps, which are generally meant to be representations of real spaces in the world, the reenactment of a crime after a confession is seen as a representation of a real criminal event from the past. Photographs of the reenactment capture this past, thus providing a material object in which history is stored. The photographs, carrying with them the epistemological weight of fact, can then be transported and used as proof in police reports and trials. The pictures of people acting out crimes, therefore, perform a critical function in the operation of modern Thailand's legal

FIGURES 4.1 AND 4.2. Photographs of a reenactment of a confession. These two photographs show a man named Liang Muangphrae demonstrating how he shot his lover as the police and an audience watch. From Suthep Muanprasitthiwet, "Jot mai rak chok lueat" [Bloody love letter], *Phim thai rai duean* [Thailand in print monthly] (April 1954): 8.

FIGURE 4.3. Photograph of a man named Nin Saisaat showing the police how he cut the neck of another man. From S. Photiriang, "Pit pak phayan aek" [Silencing the star witness], *Phim thai bueang lang khao* [Thailand in print: Behind the news] (July 1956, 1st half): 10.

system, which requires, in part, material objects to make judgments about the past, guilt, and innocence. As Carlo Ginzburg writes, material evidence (or physical clues) act as "traces" that lead to the comprehension of a "deeper, otherwise unattainable reality."[1] For him, the practice of making inferences from these traces turns them into evidence for historians.[2] Along similar lines, Robin Collingwood writes that historical "evidence is a medium—a window to reality (a past one)."[3] And Carl Becker, a Cornell professor of history at the time of Siam's police reforms, stated in a presentation in 1931 that the present depends on knowledge of things "said and done in the past and distant places."[4] This knowledge, in turn, is embodied in what he called "the artificial extension of memory," that is, in material objects such as images and texts.[5] For police detectives, material objects act similarly, opening a

FIGURE 4.4. Photograph showing three suspects demonstrating how they derailed a train in order to rob its passengers. From Chalothon [pseud.], "Plon 617" [Plundering 617], *Phim thai rai pak* [Thailand in print biweekly] (April 1957, 2nd half): 21.

window to the past for investigators. Indeed, the artifacts of evidence introduced to Siam at the turn of the nineteenth century and produced by the police today on a routine basis seemingly allow the criminal past to travel through time, thereby allowing modern systems of law to function.

The problem in applying this understanding of visual evidence to the reenactment is that photographs of people demonstrating their alleged crimes do not necessarily connect the past to the present. Instead, as the Sherry Ann example shows, they tie a *simulation* of the past to an image of that simulation, creating a self-referencing artifact into which "real" history disappears. Meanwhile, the mass media, in its push to present increasingly realistic and detailed reports on criminal investigation, has aided and abetted the police in naturalizing mechanically reproduced images of crime as factual reproductions of the past through years of exposure. By the 1950s, echoes of crime and violence had in Thai law and mass media become more distinct than the initial sound. In this chapter, I piece together the history of the reenactment, beginning with an account of its first appearance as a legal innovation of mid-twentieth-century vintage. I then trace its rise in the vernacular press from the 1920s to the 1950s and 1960s before closing with a discussion of the broader sociocultural function of this peculiar legal and media fiction.

ORIGINS OF AN IDIOM: THE ROLE OF LAW

The beginnings of the reenactment in Siam are not altogether clear, but it seems to have emerged in the late 1920s: "Crime re-enactment was first introduced in Thailand in 1929, based on the British system of criminal behavioral study and analysis. The Police Department at that time noted that criminals were basically cunning and would not confess unless there was solid evidence against them."[6] The year 1929 is also given in a Thammasat University master's of law thesis on the criminal process from 2007, and this is repeated in an interview of retired police officers conducted by a *Bangkok Post* reporter in 2008.[7] Perhaps it is not a coincidence, then, that, in his manual published in 1929, Luang Bannasanprasit mentions the practice of taking a suspect to a scene of a crime to point out the location and explain how a crime took place. He notes that this is a good method for criminal investigation since any person that did not commit the crime would not be able to accurately point out its location or explain the incident properly.[8] In 1933, Luang Phisitwithayakan wrote, "We have only just started the practice of recording the behaviors of criminals and the process has not yet been refined enough to fulfill its intentions,"[9] which he said were to "know the details of the way a criminal operates."[10] Twenty years later, Phao Sriyanond, then director-general of the police, wrote that he was taught the practice by the previous director-general, Luang Chattrakankokhon, who told him that it was taken from New Scotland Yard, home of the most famous police force in the world. He added that the practice had been imported to Thailand some twenty-five years earlier, making the year of origin around 1929.[11]

If 1929 is indeed the year that the practice was introduced to Thailand, then it is possible that a foreign adviser to the Thai police or perhaps Siamese students studying criminology overseas during the 1920s brought the reenactment technique to the kingdom. It was in that period that police detectives and medical doctors involved in police work promoted a practice involving crime scene reconstructions in Europe. Investigators in France, for example, tried to re-create crimes as a way to help solve mysterious cases (but not as a demonstration of a confession) as early as the 1880s, and it was during the early twentieth century that the Thai prince Wongnirachon

Thewakul studied criminal investigation in Paris under the direction of the (in)famous British police detective Basil Thomson and the well-regarded Swedish criminologist Harry Soderman.[12] Wongnirachon, who may have been exposed to the idea of crime scene reconstruction while studying, returned to Siam in 1929 to head the new detective police (*tamruat phuban*), which had a section for maintaining criminal records, including something the police referred to as the *phaen prathutsakam*. This is the term the police and the general public now use to refer to the reenactment of a crime after confession (as depicted in Figures 4.1–4.4). It was, however, initially coined for a procedure for categorizing criminal methods, one altogether different from the ones that appear as photographs in today's news. That practice is known in English as the modus operandi.

The modus operandi technique was developed by Major General Sir Llewellyn W. Atcherley, an inspector with the Royal British Police, in the first decades of the twentieth century. It was then refined by August Vollmer, chief of police of Berkeley, California, between 1909 and 1923. Vollmer wrote that no "orderly system of classifying the professional criminal's methods of operation was used in any police department in this country [the United States] or in England until the Modus Operandi System devised by Major L.W. Atcherley, N.V.O. West Riding of Yorkshire Constabulary, was adopted by some of the English police organizations."[13] Vollmer would go on to become a key figure behind the push to professionalize the police in the United States.[14] Professionalization at that time meant organized training, a system of standard examinations, and routine investigative procedures based on the use of scientific methods and new technology. Chief among these methods, Vollmer hoped, would be the modus operandi technique, which he justified by saying, "large accumulations [of photos] almost destroyed the usefulness of photographic files, as it is a tiresome and often a confusing task for the victim of thieves to view all of the pictures [presented to them]."[15] The indexical function of images was turning out to be more problematic than anticipated. Vollmer's modus operandi technique was therefore meant to counter the problems of visual systems of criminal detection rather than serve as an example of one.

When the modus operandi procedure was first introduced in the West, some objected to it as being too "theoretical," but others saw it as "early evidence of Vollmer's interest in the use of scientific techniques to solve crime problems."[16] What was scientific about the system was the attempt to categorize criminal acts according to a standard set of variables such as location type, tools used, time of day, characteristics of victim, and so forth. It was a way of making a specific, historical event a general, repeatable type. Accordingly, Vollmer's revised system consisted of the following categories: A—Crime, B—Person or Property Attacked, C—How Attacked, D—With What Attacked or Means of Attack, E—Time of Attack, F—Object of Attack, G—By Whom Attacked, H—Nationality of Attackers, I—Color and Number of Attackers, J—Individual Characteristics of Attack or Trademark. Each category had its own subtypes, which were numbered. A crime in Vollmer's modus operandi system looked, literally, like this:

A	B	C	D	E	F	G	H	I	J
3	152	10	9	49	4	61	60	15	5

This "formula," as Vollmer called it, translates to: "a robbery (A-3) was committed. The victim, a night watchman (B-152) was held up (C-10) at the point of a revolver (D-9) Saturday evening at 10:15 (E-49) and his watch (F-4) and money taken. The robber was dressed like a laborer (G-61) and had an Irish accent (H-60). He was alone (I-15) and was very deliberate and cool (J-5)."[17] What Vollmer, and Atcherley before him, had in mind, then, was not the visual representation of crime that the Thai police employ today, the one that the press regularly splash on their front pages and that helped the provincial court in Samut Prakan link four men to the murder of Sherry Ann Duncan. What they were creating was a predicative classification system that could be used to help identify criminals through their habits.

In the human sciences, the urge to quantify information, to generalize through the creation of various typologies, had been present in Europe since at least the eighteenth century. Ginzburg calls the focus on general types, as opposed to individual cases, "the Galileian [*sic*] paradigm" of knowledge production because it analyzes objects and categories rather than humans and specific incidents.[18] In the area of criminal investigation, the Galilean paradigm began to exert an influence at the end of the nineteenth century, when phrenology and anthropometry came to prominence. These methods, most often associated with the Italian school of criminology and its most well-known representative, Cesare Lombroso, were attempts to rethink crime and its investigation through the identification of broad, recurring phenomena. Thus, some criminologists sought to classify criminals into categories according to physical attributes such as head size and facial features. At the same time, researchers in Europe were trying to substantiate the idea that races exist as real, biologically distinct categories by identifying and mapping blood types; the entire human species could be expressed as a numerical index and then ranked accordingly. Attempts to determine criminal types has been written about, and denounced, elsewhere. The point here is that the modus operandi system was part of a larger movement to understand the natural world in terms of ideal types, a return, of sorts, to the classical notion in Western intellectual history that abstract forms are truer than their manifestations in the world. Along with the human body, the police were also targeting human actions and historical events, particularly the ones that unfolded in the modern world's new geography of crime, for this sort of formalization.

The case of Si Ui, a child murderer from the late 1950s, illustrates how this trend in thinking, the Galilean paradigm, translated into practice through the crime scene reconstruction, or modus operandi, practice. Si Ui, a Chinese national, was arrested in 1958 for the murder of a child in Rayong province in eastern Thailand. The murder became a hot news item because of the sensational way in which he killed his victim. He cut open the torso of the child in order to remove and eat his heart and liver. Si Ui confessed to the crime in Rayong and to two similar murders from previous years, one in Bangkok and one in Nakhon Pathom province, but there was no direct evidence linking him to those cases.[19] In an interview about the murders with *Phim thai rai wan*, the head of the police's Modus Operandi Section (*phanaek phaen prathutsakam*) of the police's Science Section admitted to being confused as to why he had not yet received orders to conduct a modus operandi reconstruction for the murder in Rayong. He said that in an important case like this one, his officers should be sent to the scene of the crime to collect evidence and conduct a modus operandi reconstruction. Since the police had already performed and recorded modus operandi reenactments for the other two murders, these could be tested (*thot sop*) against each other to determine whether the killer in each case was the same person. A modus operandi test would show, for example, details like whether the children's chests were "cut from bottom up or top down." He added that in the first case, the victim's genitals were cut completely off, but in the second case, the girl's genitals were only mutilated with a knife. By comparing specifics like these, the police would know "instantly" if the killers in each of the cases were the same person.[20] The reenactment, whether a modus operandi or a crime scene reconstruction, was, therefore, not originally intended to act as evidence in trials per se. Instead, the information produced by reconstructions is kept in the police's Criminal Records Office (*kong thabian prawat atchayakam*) as a sort of archive of crime and violence that could help the police identify criminal agents. Like Atcherley and Vollmer's modus operandi technique, crime scene reconstructions are performed without suspects. They are a catalog of effects without agents, patterns without explanations. A demonstration of a confession reverses this logic. It begins with a suspect-actor and ends by showing the effects of his actions on history.

So how did a quantitative system for classification and prediction introduced before World War II become a visual tool for historical representation only twenty-five or so years afterward? In terms of legislation, there was no standard operating procedure with relation to the modus operandi system when it was introduced. The practice was not codified in the kingdom's laws, as no mention of it was made in the Criminal Procedure Code of 1935, which replaced parts of the kingdom's previous code of law (known now as the Law of the Three Seals). In fact, what the police, the press, and the public commonly called the *phaen prathutsakam* is today a separate practice that developed over years of trial and error as a response by the police to the procedural demands of the judicial system. The first sign of the reenactment of a crime as proof of a confession, as opposed to the modus operandi and the crime scene reconstruction, does not appear until 1938. In that year, a *san dika* (Supreme Court) decision (number 901/2482) made reference to evidence provided by the police in a criminal trial indicating that they had taken a suspect to the scene of a crime to verify his confession. Exactly where and why the police started doing this is not clear. In its decision, however, the court does state that a suspect's ability to point to the location of a crime did not by itself constitute sufficient proof of guilt. Furthermore, confessions by themselves were not adequate evidence of wrongdoing because they could have been coerced or given falsely. The problem for the police and prosecutors was that the testimony of a suspect obtained during a police investigation was only acceptable for comparison with testimony given during the trial stage of a case.[21] Testimony gained during a police investigation by itself was and is still not enough to gain a conviction (*long thot*).[22] A confession made to the police is instead treated as hearsay evidence (*kham thoi kham bok lao*), while a confession made by a defendant during trial counts as direct evidence. The distinction is due, again, to the court's concern about the use of force by the police to extract an admission of guilt. The police, meanwhile, worry that a suspect may retract his confession, even if given voluntarily initially, during the trial stage by saying that he was coerced or forced (*thuk bangkhap*). It was therefore necessary to find a standard (*matrakan*) way to prove that a suspect's confession was both accurate and voluntary.[23]

The Thai police seemed to settle on a solution to their dilemma in 1948, when the reenactment of a suspect's testimony was officially made part of Thai police procedures. Specifically, police rules now stated that if a suspect confessed to a serious crime, officers should "take the suspect to the crime scene and *demonstrate* [*sadaeng*] what transpired."[24] In 1954, the police issued a new set of operating rules (*nangsue rabiap kan tamruat kiao kae khadi lem 1*) that maintained and elaborated on the practice. Section 10, item 261 of the 1954 rulebook states,

> If a suspect confesses voluntarily then have the suspect tell the story of his wrongdoing [*lao rung kratham phit*] and listen to the details. Then record in writing the statement of the suspect in detail. The officer is to also record in brief the cause and effect of the crime. The practice is required because even if a suspect confesses, it is not enough as the suspect may deny the confession during the trial stage of a case. Therefore, one must ask oneself regarding the suspect's confession whether there is any other evidence to corroborate it. If the case is a serious one [*khadi ukchakan,* a capital offense] or one that has a penalty of ten or more years imprisonment or is a case with weak evidence, then the officer in charge should have the suspect point out the crime scene and make a plan of the location [*tham phaenthi sangkhaep*] for the suspect to confirm. If a photo can be taken of the scene then this is even better.[25]

The 1954 rules also state that a suspect may be asked to show the police step by step and in detail how he committed his crime while at the crime scene.[26] The public ritual of a suspect acting out the past therefore emerged slowly after the year typically given (1929) for its first appearance in Thailand. The 1954 regulations have since been superseded, but the police still view a suspect's voluntary confession that aids in the solving of a case as an important form of evidence (of noncoercion as much as the veracity of testimony) in the trial process. The reenactment therefore remains in the books: "When a suspect confesses let the officer in charge of the *sop suan* process [the investigation and questioning that takes place after a crime] take the suspect to point out the location of the crime and record the suspect pointing out the location of the crime with a map for evidence. The suspect must sign off on the plan of the crime scene."[27] For the police and judges, then, a suspect's performance of a crime developed as a method to confirm the veracity and voluntary nature of a confession. It was a tactic for visual representation not originally intended as a criminal investigation tool in the same way that the modus operandi technique and its close cousin, the crime scene reconstruction, were. The latter two evolved specifically as detective practices that would help police determine how a crime was committed and alert investigators to potential correspondences between separate but similar crimes.

Despite their distinct aims, crime scene reconstructions and reenactments of confessions have over time become confused with one another. The number of different but similar names used to refer to both practices, including *kan tham phaen prathutsakam prakop kham rap saraphap* (demonstration of criminal acts in support of a confession), *kan nam chi thi koet het prakop kham rap saraphap* (pointing out the location of an event in support of a confession), and just *phaen prathutsakam* (modus operandi or crime scene reconstruction), illustrate the overlap. Even the police get the two practices mixed up and use the different terms more or less interchangeably. A retired former head of the Criminal Investigation Bureau of the Thai police noted with some consternation, for example, that the two were indeed different procedures, but that mostly people simply called the reenactment of a confession the *phaen prathutsakam*.[28] Meanwhile, two authors of a study on incidents of lynching, mob violence, and other forms of extralegal social retribution that sometimes occur during a public reenactment indicated that the police see the practice of demonstrating a crime at its location after a confession as a basic investigative procedure that was believed to be a vital aid in the search for facts in the *sop suan* process.[29] This, of course, is the intended function of a crime scene reconstruction, not the reenactment of a confession. For the most part, then, the two practices have come to be one in the legal system and in the public imagination, confusing scientific policing with legal formalism and in the process creating a new social ritual and media spectacle.

ORIGINS OF AN IDIOM: THE ROLE OF MASS MEDIA

Once the police had come up with a way to bring a criminal act to life, by taking a suspect to a crime scene to act out his crime, the next step was to capture the process and present it to the court. Judges, who are not at the demonstration, require some form of evidence. Here I cite Ginzburg again, who notes that the term "evidence" is from *evidentia,* which means "the ability to make a topic evident, palpable, or vivid. It is the translation of the Greek word *enargeia,* a word used to praise historians, poets and painters for their ability to conjure absent realities belonging either to the past or to fiction."[30] Clearly, Atcherley and Vollmer's modus operandi formula did not make the crime it described "palpable." And while the demonstration of a confession may have been quite vivid for the police and any onlookers present at the performance, judges never saw it firsthand, just as they never saw a fingerprint or a dead body at a crime scene. Like other types of evidence that had to be captured, transported, and presented, so, too, did the reenactment of a crime by suspects. The immediate answer was the map or sketch of the crime scene, as noted in the police regulations above. Then came the photograph, which could provide better, more illustrative evidence of the reenactment. The police argued and the courts accepted that if a suspect was willing to act out his testimony, have that demonstration recorded, and then put his signature on that recording, the resulting image would show not only that the confession is accurate, but that no coercion was involved in procuring it.

As with crime scene maps, statistics, and fingerprints, images of reenactments were a new class of legal fact, a novel form of information, when they first appeared in the kingdom. Ideas about what they were supposed to look like developed over time, under the influence of agents not typically considered part of the law, including the press and commercial photographers, as the following examples show. From the earliest introduction of photography to police work, officers, lawyers, and others were doing more than simply putting names to faces and attempting to capture what the location of a crime looked like. They were employing photos to create pictorial narratives of crime. In the police documents for a murder investigation from 1929, for example, there are eight photos of various locations, numbered sequentially, adorned with symbols such as arrows and dashed lines and short captions describing from beginning to end how the suspect approached his victim's house via a nearby market, killed him, and then attempted to escape.[31] This type of pictorial storyboard was developed to help judges presiding over criminal trials visualize a crime, and it thus facilitated conviction. So, by the early decades the twentieth century, the Thai police were already beginning to work with images in ways that helped them create knowledge about the past. As with their other new tool, the crime scene map, the police used photos to conjure the criminal past into existence and then asked this apparition to help divine the truth.

The case of Bunpheng *hip lek* ("Iron Trunk" Bunpheng) is another early instance of the use of photography to construct an image of crime. In this example, however, the commercial photographers did the visualizing, not agents of the law. In 1918, a man named Bunpheng murdered a woman named Prik, put her body in a metal trunk, and disposed of the trunk in the Chao Phraya River, which runs through Bangkok. Bunpheng was an orphan from the countryside who had moved to the capital and been ordained as a Buddhist monk in the mid-1910s. In due course, he became attracted to a young woman who worshiped at the monastery, Wat Suthat, where he was resident. He decided to marry her. However, the woman's bride price was too high for Bunpheng. Desperate to raise the money, he murdered and robbed Prik, a woman he had gotten to know through the gambling circle based in his *kuti* (monks' quarters). Unfortunately for Bunpheng, the trunk containing his victim surfaced and was discovered. Upon investigation, the police discovered a letter that Bunpheng had written asking that Prik meet him so that he might return some money that he had borrowed earlier. By the time the police started looking for Bunpheng, he had disrobed and married the woman of his affection. In his possession were items belonging to Prik. The police arrested him and he was subsequently tried, sentenced to death, and beheaded in public.[32] The case proved such a sensation that various photography shops produced picture cards for sale that showed different aspects of the crime. One photography shop called Chailak printed photos of Bunpheng and sold them as a sort of memento of the case. The photo card had the title "The Secret in the Floating Iron Trunk" (*Khwam lap nai hip lek loi nam*). Another photo card contained two pictures on the same cardboard stock, with the title "Office of Pheng, Phan, Charat, Charoen. The Mystery in the Case of the Important Iron Trunk, the Story of Miss Prik" (Figure 4.5). One of the photos showed a picture of Bunpheng being escorted by police officers. The other showed the trunk in which he put Prik's body. Below the second picture was the caption "King's evidence includes this iron trunk that was used to hold the body of Miss Prik."[33] Yet another photo card shows a portrait of Prik. Though not exactly reenactments, some of these pictures show the trunk Bunpheng used to store his victim's dismembered body placed on the trishaw he used to transport it to the river for disposal. I do not know whether the police or the photographer had the trunk placed in the trishaw for effect, whether it was part of an early modus operandi

FIGURE 4.5. "Iron Trunk" Bunpheng photo card. The picture on the left shows the rickshaw and trunk Bunpheng used to carry his victim. From Anek Nawigamune, *Criminals in the Past,* 1995.

procedure, or whether it was simply chance. What is clear is that criminal investigation, mass media, and commercial interests were connected from the earliest stages of the development of the criminal justice system in Thailand by photography. The police, in conjunction with the commercial media, developed a way to represent the simulated past through the technology of the photograph.

Over time, the relationship between the police and the media became closer and more complex, and the importance of photographic (and now video) technology increased. As the vernacular press worked to shape its identity and stake a claim in the social, cultural, and political life of the kingdom, it turned increasingly to crime stories and policing. Since the earliest years of the press, crime stories had been common. They were, however, typically only short and pithy snippets about crime. The *Bangkok Times,* a well-known English-language daily from the late nineteenth century, for example, published reports that included one- or two-paragraph summaries of minor skirmishes, arguments, thefts, police news, and road accidents. On July 8, 1898, a short, untitled report tells of a Chinese man named Lae going to the market in Hua Lamphong district and beating another Chinese man unconscious. When the beaten man regained his senses, Lae beat him again, this time to death. No one attempted to stop the fight.[34] In another story, the *Bangkok Times* reported that in May 1898 an Indian constable in Bangrak district returned to the police station there after his shift. The station's chief inspector noticed that the Indian's turban was missing. After a bit of questioning, the inspector discovered that someone had stolen the turban from the constable's head after he had fallen asleep on duty.[35] The examples cited in Chapter 1 demonstrate that the vernacular press adopted a similar approach to presenting crime news.

Around the late 1920s, the crime story began to occupy a more central role in the news, reflecting global trends. It is at this point that the vernacular press also took on a new purpose and a new look. Papers like the *Bangkok Daily Mail,* edited by the American Andrew Freeman, deliberately chose sensational news (*khao tunten*) for their front pages.[36] The appearance of the *Bangkok Daily Mail* also began to change as its layout went from one of "staid British sheets" with "lifeless headlines like black clay pigeons waiting to be shot" that reminded Freeman of "tombstone epitaphs" to one with a bolder style of large letters and catchy phrases.[37] Freeman was one of the first editors to begin printing headlines in extra-large script to draw the eyes (*khao sadut ta*) of readers.[38] When he completed the paper's makeover, he proudly described it as "a saucy little sheet with its pictures and piquant headlines."[39] Prince Sawasti, the paper's royal patron, reportedly said to Freeman, "I never realized that there was so much news in Bangkok until I read your American headlines."[40]

That Freeman spearheaded the *Daily Mail*'s makeover may not have been coincidence. In his native America, the press in the 1920s went through an era of change that saw consolidation of ownership, polarization of readership, and tabloidization in form and content. In New York City in 1920 there were eleven dailies. In 1930, there were only seven, but two were picture tabloids and one of them, the *Daily News,* was the nation's largest paper. These new tabloids, in turn, featured "a steady fare of murder, startling photos of crime scenes, and courtroom drama." It was an era in which "murder seemed, to many eyes, to rise phenomenally in the post–World War One years," "organized crime seemed to link the glamorous world of celebrities to that of criminality," and "yellow journalism seemed to experience a resurgence." Scholars now estimate there were "many times more crime stories [in the 1920s] than in the 1890s."[41] The changes in the *Daily Mail* of Bangkok, and in the vernacular press more broadly, echoed those seen in New York papers, and the phenomenon went hand in hand with the police reforms of the early twentieth century that have been discussed so far.

In addition to shifting crime to center stage and employing large, bold typeface for headlines and occasionally outlandish captions, both the *Bangkok Daily Mail* and the *Krungthep deli me* ushered in the use of news photos. Most of these appeared on the front page and pictured events like royal parades, meetings of foreign dignitaries, social events, and even interesting scenery. Many were purchased from international photo services. Freeman noted that he got many of his prints, which included pictures of "movie actresses, skyscrapers, [and] street scenes of New York," sent in by "photographic syndicates."[42] It was not until the late 1920s that local photographers were employed seriously by the burgeoning publishing industry.[43] And it was no coincidence that Siam's first photojournalist, Chuang Midet, worked for the *Daily Mail.* The use of a local photographer meant that pictures in the paper could now showcase a wide range of images, including those of criminals, victims, and police officers (Figures 4.6, 4.7, and 4.8). If a *Daily Mail* reporter got wind of a crime, for example, Chuang or another photographer could go to the crime scene and take a picture. Freeman recalls this exchange in the newsroom:

> "That was Chuang [Midet] at headquarters [the central police station]," he [*Daily Mail* staff person] says. "He's got a story about a murder up at Wat Saket." "My God," I say, "who'd have the energy to commit murder in this heat? Wat Saket? A temple, isn't it? Let Nakorn take the story and tell Pleng to hurry up there and get some pictures."[44]

This is the way that photographs of criminals (and the police) made their way into Siamese newspapers. In fact, the press employed their own crime photographers before the police did.[45] During the late 1920s, the form and content of the vernacular press went through a significant makeover. In terms of appearance, publishers began to move from the staid, text-based broadsheet to the more dynamic tabloid style of newspaper familiar today. Headlines became more prominent and eye catching. Photographs added spice and intensified the feeling of the news' realism. In addition, advertisements, which took up the entire cover page of some periodicals, were pushed in between the covers, and new sections were created for specific types of content like entertainment, sports, and, of course, the crime story.

After World War II, the emphasis on sensational crime news intensified, and the relationship between the press and the police grew more intimate. One observer noted that during the late 1920s and early 1930s a reporter's duty was simply to wait around a police station or a courthouse for

FIGURE 4.6. Images of notorious criminals began to appear in newspapers in the early 1920s. This one shows the famous bandit Suea Thai, who is also mentioned in Siam's first indigenous crime novel, *Phrae dam* [Black satin], from 1922. From *Sayam ratsadon* [Siam citizen], July 23, 1921.

news.[46] In the mid-1950s, when reenactments emerged in the mass media, this was still the case. Thawon Suwan, a reporter with the *Daily Mail* in these years, wrote later that when he went to work as a reporter for the paper, getting stories meant establishing a close relationship with the police.[47] On his first day on the job, he went with his partner, Chaloem, to the Phathumwan police station to introduce himself to the *sip waen* (sergeant). He asked if there was any news. The *sip waen* replied, "There's nothing." This would be the same response he would give throughout the beginning of Thawon's time with the *Daily Mail*. Thawon and Chaloem then went to the police station in the Phaya Thai district, where it looked like there might have been

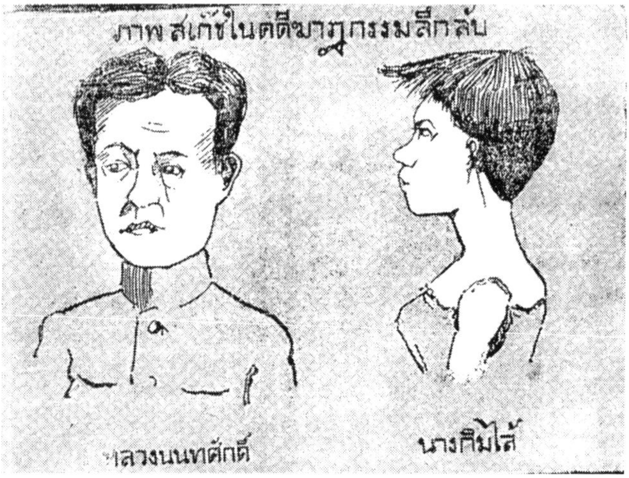

FIGURE 4.7. A drawing of Kim Lai, a woman accused of murdering her husband, who is also pictured. From *Sayam ratsadon,* May 7, 1921.

oja. who killed Nai Yim, of Bang Brom Samud Songgram, will soon suffer the extreme penalty for his act. 2.—Ai ntenced to death for the murder of Nai Morn, of Bang Ta Muang, Kanchanaburi. 3.—Ai Soon Hee, of Nong Kanak. the price for the killing of Nai Prong. 4.—Convicts of Changvad Rajburi.

FIGURE 4.8. Photographs of criminals. From *Bangkok Daily Mail,* September 28, 1928.

an auto accident and a fight. They asked if they could look at the daily blotter in which the police logged incoming cases. The *samian waen* (clerk) replied, "You can't, its government [*ratchakan*] business. People without any legitimate reasons are prohibited from seeing it."[48] Later, though, as he became close to the *samian* at each station, Thawon was able to look into the daily logs. He only had to be careful not to let the station's chief inspector (*sarawat*) or deputy chief inspector (*rong sarawat*) see him peeking at the book. Sometimes the *sip waen* would even call into the paper's office to let them know of breaking news. According to Thawon, this happened after the police had read some positive reports about themselves in a case reported by another reporter at the *Daily Mail*. The police at Phaya Thai station, he notes, were especially open to working with reporters. In one case that took place around 1951 (he can't recall the actual date), a police officer named Captain Kamon Chanowan even invited Thawon to accompany him on a mission to arrest a bandit (*suea*) on the outskirts of Bangkok, which he did.[49]

From these examples, it can be argued that the police in the early twentieth century were still primarily going about their routines as a matter of professional duty. The press would report on their activities and occasionally take photos of them. As the nature of the media and the technologies for representation changed, so did the relationship between the police and the press. In 1998, a *Far Eastern Economic Review* article described a drug bust in Suphanburi province that was intentionally conducted under "the gaze of scores of reporters and cameramen" to promote the government's war on drugs.[50] Despite the "glare of media publicity," the police apparently felt no qualms about shooting (off camera but within earshot) six handcuffed suspects dead. Sanoh Thienthong, then minister of interior, said soon afterward, without elaborating, that the suspects deserved to die. In this instance, the media is the key audience and motivation for the police's show of force. As the twentieth century progressed, policing became more performative. Suspects, too, became part of the performance as they were co-opted by the police to star in reenactments. In some cases, the suspects themselves requested that the media be part of the process. In 2009, Siripong Kanchananiwit, a forty-year-old taxi driver, showed up at a local television station and claimed that he had shot and killed a Thai woman and her half-Japanese son in the back of his taxicab. He said that he had murdered them after a heated argument over the fact that he refused to assassinate the woman's Japanese husband as they had previously discussed. Siripong rebuffed attempts by the police to talk unless they ensured the presence of the media, with cameras running. This may not be too surprising, as David Engel, in his study of legal consciousness in Thailand, has shown that many of his interviewees "expressed the opinion that justice could be obtained through the media. Both Pongsak and Jaemjai [two of Engel's informants] gave examples of unfair or corrupt behavior that they addressed by notifying newspapers and television reporters. They assumed that the media, rather than the legal system, offer a few individuals the possibility of achieving justice."[51] Images, both still photographs and video footage, of Siripong's reenactment show the police directing the scene, telling the suspect to look into the camera (Figure 4.9). A statement by a former head of the Central Investigation Bureau (*kong sop suan klang*) explains this directorship. He claims that the police sometimes try to make the suspect smile into the camera to indicate that that he or she has voluntarily agreed to participate in the reenactment.[52] It has also been suggested anecdotally that some photographers will occasionally spice up a crime scene, say, by hiking up the skirt on a female murder victim, before taking a photograph. In reenactments, the past is as comfortably

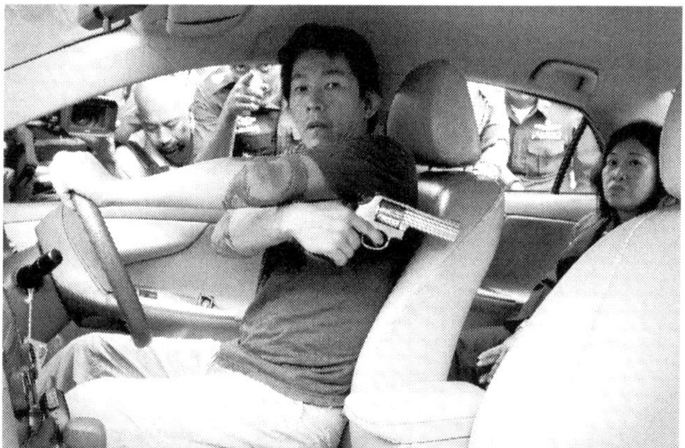

FIGURE 4.9. An image from the reenactment of a confession by Siripong Kanchananiwit. Siripong confessed to having killed a woman and her son in the back of his taxicab. Note the police officer standing outside the driver's side window giving Siripong directions to look into the camera. Photograph courtesy of Nation Multimedia Group. The photo appeared on the *Khom chat luek* [Sharp, clear, deep] website on October 14, 2009, http://www.komchadluek.net/media/img/size1/2009/10/14/9ag9bbefa89dabgaehh5e.

transparent and doubt free as it is saucy. The demand for crime stories in the vernacular press therefore helped shape the form of both police evidence and what is now mass media.

To get stories about crime, the press relies on the police, who had by the 1950s institutionalized a series of imported investigative practices that included fingerprint identification, crime scene photography, statistics, chemical analyses, and reenactments. The press took the objects that these new practices generated and used them to fill the demands of their own evolving forms. The police, meanwhile, had come to rely on the press to help justify their existence and the violence they employed as a matter of routine.[53] By the middle of the 1950s, when reenactments started appearing on the front pages of local papers, the police were already in a close and complicated relationship with the print media. The press needed the police to provide them information about crimes, while the police wanted good publicity and also were happy to control the news. The result was a sometimes antagonistic, sometimes friendly relationship.[54] It also helped that crime news, though there existed some concern for its potentially negative impact on society, was seen as more apolitical than reports about ministers, policies, and the army. According to one account, Kamphon Wacharaphon, editor of the kingdom's best-selling daily in the 1960s (*Thai rat*), said, after the police burned down his office and damaged his printing presses in the late 1950s, that his new paper would "not have political news. We will report news about crime. This will be the paper's foundation. It's safe. There will be a bit of politics here and there."[55] Crime stories, because they were not subject to the same scrutiny as political news was throughout the middle of the twentieth century, flourished and became a major part of the kingdom's mass media. Today, the crime news report is the primary link between the police and the press, providing a form through which the mass media exerts an influence on the visual culture of the law.

THE FUNCTION OF FICTIONS

Underlying the prominence of the reenactment, whether as a demonstration of a confession or as a crime scene reconstruction, in the media and the criminal process is the idea that the practice and its image prove or reflect something—the voluntary nature of a confession or the accuracy of testimony about the event. It also helps the police make sense of the material objects they have been taught to gather as evidence. The epistemological purpose of a reenactment, in other words, is to bring together or compile evidence (*ruap ruam phayan lakthan*), as the full names for the practices associated with recording a demonstration of a confession indicate. The term *prakop* in both *kan tham phaen prathutsakam prakop kham rap saraphap* (demonstration of criminal acts in support of a confession) and *kan nam chi thi koet het prakop kham rap saraphap* (pointing out the location of an event in support of a confession) literally means "to assemble or compile." In other words, it stitches together facts that already exist. The two authors of the lynching study cited earlier note that the police they spoke to generally agree with this understanding of the practice and its output.[56] Similarly, the retired officers interviewed for the *Bangkok Post* article mentioned above state that a reenactment is useful since it enables investigators to retrace the steps they took to solve a case and helps determine whether the information they have collected is enough to prove the guilt or innocence of the suspect.[57] The prevailing notion is therefore that knowledge about crime (and the past) exists in the world and the reenactment helps organize that knowledge, makes facts comprehensible as such. This conception means that for many the reenactment is a relatively passive act that merely captures preexisting information and makes it portable and presentable. A reenactment, like a crime scene photo or a map, does not theoretically alter the fabric of space and time; it merely makes both visible to the present.

The idea that the reenactment practice and its artifacts are strictly representational would not be a major problem if they operated more like the fingerprint or photographs of dead bodies or preserved objects at crime scenes. The status of reenactments as reproductions of facts is not so clear-cut, however, even if they might be treated the same, epistemologically speaking, as other types of material evidence. I earlier compared the reenactment to real-crime television shows and crime dramas. Real-crime shows like America's *Cops* may be considered documentary in that they are journalistic recordings of police work as it happens, including investigations, confrontations with suspects, and the moment of arrest. Similarly, CCTV footage or videos captured on mobile phones sometimes show crimes as they take place. These sorts of recordings might be seen as true or unmediated representations of actual events, "first-level" evidence, in the language of the early police manuals. Crime dramas, however, employ actors to play fictional characters committing imagined crimes. In some instances, actors act out real crimes, those that actually happened, as in dramatic adaptations of historical events. Both types of crime drama are generally considered fictional, either completely imagined or a not-quite-true account of an event from the real world. With reenactments, suspects play themselves after having confessed, at least theoretically, to a crime. They act out their own pasts for the benefit of the police and the press.[58] And despite the fact that reenactments often take place in the actual locations where a crime or particular event is believed to have happened, and with many elements of the original occurrence replicated, they occupy an epistemological space that is neither clearly documentary, as in real-crime television, nor completely imaginary, as in television dramas.[59]

A set of photographs published in the daily *Thai rat* in 1961 illustrates the semi-fictional, semi-factual nature of reenactment photographs vividly. The first shows a murder suspect (and reenactor) behind bars (Figure 4.10). Another photo from the same reenactment shows the body of the murder victim, a woman known as Duan Jai, accompanied by the headline "Police Don't Believe It Was Rape!" (Figure 4.11) A third photo was published after the case against the suspect pictured fell apart. A question mark is placed over his face, indicating that the real murderer's identity remains unknown (Figure 4.12). What these images remind their viewers is that a photograph of a reenactment is a record of a hypothesis about the past, not history as it

FIGURE 4.10. Photograph of a reenactment of the murder of a woman named Duan Jai. A photograph of the suspect is published next to the photograph of the reenactment in which he is shown stabbing his victim. From *Thai rat,* 1961.

FIGURE 4.11. Another photograph of the reenactment of the murder of Duan Jai in 1961. The headline of the article reads, "Police Don't Believe It Was Rape!" From *Thai rat,* 1961.

FIGURE 4.12. This collage from the front page of *Thai rat* again shows the reenactment of Duan Jai's murder, but with a question mark over the face of the suspect, indicating some doubt over the identity of the real perpetrator. From *Thai rat,* 1961.

happened or a material object like a gun or knife. Thus, the application of formal rules to "fix" the facticity of a reenactment does little to ensure its fidelity to any external reality in the same way the rules for fingerprints, photos, and maps are supposed to do. In a way, then, reenactments may be likened to the solutions of fictional crimes found in detective stories, in that they are revelations "not exposed to tests against an outside reality."[60] The truth about the past, the validity of a photo of a reenactment, is internal to the narrative the police put together about a particular crime. In this way they cannot be proved false except, as in the cases of Sherry Ann Duncan and Duan Jai, through their replacement by another simulation.

More than just the capture of an external reality, the reenactment is a recording of an educated guess that "can help in the discovery of clues or make sense of existing material evidence [*phayan waetlom*] related to the case."[61] On this point, officers are very clear in their manuals; the purpose of standardized forms, the appeals to be observant, the statistics, the lists and reports, and the modus operandi technique were all meant to help police detectives make hypotheses, or educated guesses, about the past. Phra Sisena, for example, did not believe that fortune-tellers or people with alleged magical powers could solve crimes. He noted, "Only the hypotheses [*sannitthithan*] and the rationale of an investigator matter" in solving crimes.[62] Luang Phisitwithayakan writes similarly that people reading about how detectives in other countries are able to solve mysterious cases must think that they have some sort of magical power. This is not the case, he assures his readers. They are humans who expend great effort and pay attention to details. What detectives in other countries do that is different from what they do in Siam is to form hypotheses and then prove them with evidence. This, he says, is their only "magic."[63] Similarly, Sanga writes, "this data [on people's habits] is useful in making hypotheses, which can then be tested through the search and consideration of facts and evidence."[64] It's no coincidence that all three see the practice of hypothesis making and testing (i.e., the scientific method) as the antithesis of magic. Modernizing the criminal process by replacing existing, "magical" systems of detection (e.g., divination) with other, more efficacious ones was one of the goals of police reform. Methods of visual representation based on the newest technologies available embodied objectivity and rationality for many Thai government officials involved with the development of the Thai police. That a particular method allowed them to visualize and test hypotheses was all the more reason to support the practice.

Part of the power of the reenactment, therefore, stems from the fact that it facilitates the acceptance of circumstantial evidence, of allowing guesses, in court, even if a defendant refuses to accept the charges against him. That is, the reenactment allows for previously excluded objects to become part of a broader narrative about a specific case, one that would not be possible without reenacting the crime in the first place. The case of the three men derailing a train in 1957 (Figure 4.4) illustrates this. The police took the suspects to conduct a reenactment after their confessions. This allowed the officer in charge to test a hypothesis he had that the culprits stole railway maintenance tools from a rail yard and took them to the scene of the crime for use. The officer guessed this because tools used to lay train tracks (or remove them) are not simply found in local markets. The three suspects began their reenactment by showing the police the location near a bridge crossing the Nan River where they sat together to plan out their heist. They then showed the police how they removed the bolts and screws of the train tracks using a *chalaeng* and a *kunjae pak tai* (both are essentially heavy-duty wrenches for laying train tracks). Afterward, the three suspects took the officers to the place where they hid themselves to wait for a train to pass, and then they showed them the path they used to escape into the forest. Throughout the process, the police took photos of the crime scene (*banthuek phap sathanthi koet het*). They also made a map, which was included in the news story. During the reenactment, the police were able to locate the *chalaeng* and the *kunjae pak tai* used in the heist. It turned out that the officer's hypothesis that the three accomplices took the tools to the site without the knowledge of the railway foreman was correct.[65]

The reenactment thus confirms existing truths even as it helps to construct new ones. It is a tool as much as a representational practice, shared by the state and society, that performs multiple functions for the police, judges, suspects, and communities affected by violence. The reenactment of a confession does not generalize or put specific crimes into categories, nor does it make the particular universal. Instead, it maintains history's specificity by recreating it, albeit under controlled conditions. When the order to demonstrate a confession met with the scientific techniques of capturing and recording facts about the past, a new artifact of evidence emerged that, unlike Atcherley's numerical system, could create an event and simultaneously prove that that event took place, all in a single picture. It is this generative aspect that makes photos of reenactments powerful and that demands scholars acknowledge them as more than representations.

Represent. Diagram. Proof. In the end, what does the reenactment really do beyond satisfying a few technical demands of the criminal process? Why do suspects participate in a spectacle of public self-incrimination, and why does Thai society continue to accept the practice as an integral part of their legal system and their public sphere? When asked, some note that, for suspects, reenacting a confession is desirable because it can result in a reduced sentence. It shows that the suspect is willing to cooperate with the state and also that the suspect, in some cases, is repentant. The concept of a confession as an indicator of contrition may make sense in that "negative karma" (*bap*) built up from bad deeds "can be canceled if the wronged party grants forgiveness."[66] The idea of public confession and forgiveness may also be related to the need to maintain harmony at the local level, especially in rural areas or small, tightly knit communities where unresolved conflicts can destabilize important social relationships. Thailand, particularly Bangkok, is not a village anymore. Yet, a consensus remains that the reenactment provides a public benefit (*prayot satharana*). A retired criminal court judge interviewed about the practice explains this when he notes that, in addition to proving that a confession is voluntary, a reenactment allows the public the opportunity to participate in the criminal justice process. The presence of the public at a reenactment aids the suspect because having a group of eyewitnesses protects against the suspect being manipulated by the police during the process. The judge goes on to state that, unless the timing of an event is crucial to the confession, reenactments are usually performed in the daytime so that the public can be present.[67] The public must also be present at these events so that they can have the opportunity to indicate whether the demonstration of the confession is accurate. After all, some of the onlookers may have knowledge of the crime.[68] The accuracy of a reenactment is guaranteed by the presence of an audience. In Thailand, where criminal trials do not have juries, this becomes especially important. Criminal investigation, as it plays out in the mass media, is a social activity. So is the criminal trial. Nowhere is this more clear than with the reenactment, which serves as the revelatory ending of a public murder mystery as well as a ritual that mediates relationships between individuals (as suspects and victims) and institutions of the state like the police, who play the part of the prescient detective arriving at the scene of a crime to shed light on the darkness created by modernity's long shadow, to return order to the public life of the kingdom.

5

History of Conspiracy

On the morning of June 9, 1946, young King Ananda Mahidol was found dead in his bedchamber with a single gunshot wound to the forehead. He had no known enemies, had not apparently quarreled with anyone prior to his death, and there were no third-party witnesses present when the fatal bullet was fired. Preliminary investigations indicated an accident, but this did not stop public speculation about the cause of death. The government put together a special investigative committee consisting of "senior court justices, the speaker of the house, the president of the senate, three high-ranking princes, three representatives of the armed forces, and two others" to look into the situation.[1] Police investigators and medical doctors assigned to the case used forensic techniques to analyze the gun found lying on the bed next to the king, a bullet and a bullet casing discovered at the scene, and the king's body to produce various facts that they could use to string together a narrative about how events might have unfolded on that fateful morning. In October, the committee announced that the death of King Ananda was likely an accident, but the pronouncement did not conclusively rule out the possibility of either suicide or murder. All the while, wild stories about the king's death surfaced and spread, both in the press and through informal chatter. In an attempt to get a handle on the situation, Pridi Phanomyong, then prime minister, declared a state of emergency and banned press reports about the king's death.

The unsatisfying official explanation and the moves by the government to censor the media created an atmosphere of mystery, which then spawned suspicion and triggered increased public speculation. In many instances, public conjecture is innocuous, but in a situation involving possible regicide, idle talk became tinged with dark, ominous overtones. Alexander MacDonald, the first editor of the *Bangkok Post,* wrote the following passage about the day the news of King Ananda's death broke:

> By afternoon the atmosphere of tragedy had become surcharged with suspicion. It came coiling evilly in. The hushed tones of bereavement changed to dark whisperings. Something more is behind this tragic matter, one whispered tentatively to another. There is wickedness here. Death could not have come by the hand of our gentle King. Someone. Someone. There were plotters. Someone ambitious, someone vengeful, someone afraid. This was no accident—our gentle monarch slain. The whispers grew sullen, became an insistent chorus. This was *murder!*[2]

He adds,

> The change [in the country's mood] was particularly apparent in politics. What had been a good-humored scramble for places of power, a *sanuk* [fun] game, like schoolboys playing King of the Hill, was becoming now a grim struggle for political survival. The first ugly whispers that the King's death had been part of a political plot had begun to be heard. The rumor spread. Politicians out to unseat the Pridi government began to inject the poison into their campaign speeches. The opposition press took it up. Innuendoes, outright charges were made. There was talk of a republican plot to overthrow the monarchy. Pridi's own name and the murder rumor began to be linked. Politics suddenly had become a dirty, deadly game.[3]

This, then, was a markedly different sort of crime story compared to the sensational ones that began to appear almost daily in the press after the war. In many of those cases, an unexplained death would initiate a police investigation in which officers of the law would deploy the detective practices and administrative routines described in the preceding chapters. This implementation is expected to generate, if all goes well, an explanation of who killed the victim and why. The resulting account more often than not takes the form of a story, a closed narrative complete with villains, heroes, and victims. The vernacular media then makes the story public in newspapers and broadcast news. The investigation into the king's death, however, did not produce such a story; there was no satisfying ending, no ready culprit available to confess and engage in a public reenactment. Instead, the case spawned a narrative of a less definitive type: a conspiracy theory.

As a single extraordinary event in which limited and conflicting information was made available at the time to ordinary citizens, the flowering of conspiracy theories in the public imagination makes sense. Yet, a quick look at the way the press and the public often discuss politics today indicates that something more was, and is, going on. Indeed, recent political turmoil in Thailand has been a hotbed for conspiracy theories. Taxi drivers, office workers, old "Thai hands," and others are all quick to speak of secret agreements, the hidden influence of various members of the government, a particular general or politician, and large-scale plots against the nation. As recently as 2011, an opinion piece entitled "It's a Good Time to Be a Conspiracy Theorist" appeared in the *Nation* in which the author discussed conspiracy theories related to border conflicts between the Thai and the Cambodian governments.[4] In 2010, not long after the military had forcibly cleared antigovernment protesters from the streets of Bangkok, a columnist in the *Bangkok Post* noted and bemoaned the tendency for Thais to see politics through the lens of conspiracy theories.[5] In 1994, the *Far Eastern Economic Review* published a report on the unexplained bomb attacks in the southern town of Hat Yai that highlighted the widespread idea that they were part of a larger conspiracy against the government: "Groups of teachers, businessmen and bankers in the south have suggested that a Bangkok-based movement intent on toppling the government is instigating and financing many of the attacks, which are carried out by the separatist guerillas."[6] A quick search on the electronic database ProQuest using the keywords "conspiracy theory Thailand" generates 733 results. The database even provides a small bar chart that shows a dramatic spike in the number of hits for these words beginning in the 1990s, an increase that is sustained to the present.[7] The belief that there is more than meets the eye, that what can be seen in the realm of politics and power is an effect of the maneuverings of powerful, hidden agents, did not simply go away, even years after the king's death. Instead, Thais of all stripes continue to search for the "real" truth behind the visible reality of everyday life. So, rather than merely being a passing moment as a response to the untimely and unexpected death of the king, conspiracy theory, as a governing rubric or narrative architecture, endures to shape the way in which Thais interpret current events.

In this chapter I argue that the development of this unfortunate situation, of an entrenched cynicism and general air of suspicion, is linked directly to post–World War II trends in international politics and economics—the development and spread of transnational networks of people, technologies, and money to fight Communism—and the brutal deployment of physical force by competing agents of the Thai state. These agents subsequently needed, partly because of the existence of a vibrant vernacular press, a way to justify the political violence they so regularly employed. Reference to mysterious and ill-intentioned figures materialized as an expedient and ingenious method of obfuscation and denial. In this light, conspiracy theories can be seen at once as a convenient and potent way for people, from factory workers and street vendors to doctors and professors, to make sense of the violence and inequity of modern life and as a technique of modern statecraft in response to (and taking advantage of) international capitalism and technological modernity. Since the end of World War II, conspiracy theories have been the dominant model for understanding and articulating power, agency, and history in modern Thailand.

THE POLICE AFTER WORLD WAR II

People looking for the truth that existed behind the scenes in the early 1950s would have had a difficult time avoiding the conclusion that it resided somewhere in the file cabinets, desk drawers, and hallways of the new police headquarters at Pathumwan in central Bangkok. Compared to the image of the inept, comical figure of the late nineteenth and early twentieth centuries, the police of the post–World War II period were much more menacing, in large part because the 1950s saw police power bolstered by the aid of the U.S. government, ostensibly to counter a rising Communist threat. Between 1950 and 1970, the U.S. government's aid to Thailand totaled $580 million in gross obligations. In terms of allocation over that same period, the police benefited handsomely. J. Alexander Caldwell, former special assistant to the director of the United States Operations Mission (USOM), wrote that "aid to the police and closely related programs amounted to 19% of net accruals, transportation received 17%, health and sanitation 12%, education 8%, industry and mining 8%, the Office of Accelerated Rural Development 7%, community development, social welfare and housing 5%, public administration 2%, labor 1%, and general and miscellaneous 14%."[8] In November 1950, a separate credit bill was pushed through the Thai parliament for 48 million baht, of which 26 million was earmarked for the police.[9] In a report on USOM support to the Thai police, Theodore J. Curtis, an administrative officer in the Office of Public Safety, wrote that "at the end of FY-1973, the United States Government had completed nearly sixteen years of assistance to the Thai National Police Department (TNPD) and related internal security activities." Funding levels increased dramatically in 1965, when there was a "marked increase in subversive activity in the Northeast." U.S. dollar amounts totaled $6.4 million in 1965, $13.1 million in 1966, and then $18.5 million in 1967. Aid began to decline in 1968, falling to $13.3 million in 1968, $7.4 million in 1969, $6.1 million in 1970, $5.3 million in 1971, $4.7 million in 1972, and $4.7 million in 1973.[10] Curtis adds, "From FY-1957 through FY-1973, the US support to these projects has totalled $91.4 million . . . in obligated funds. This has been matched by about $54 million . . . baht equivalent in special funds from the Royal Thai Government (RTG), plus the regular TNPD budget has been increased by approximately 12% per year, from $5.6 million . . . baht equivalent in 1957 to $95 million in 1973."[11] A separate report from 1970 published in the *New York Times* indicates that the United States sent a total of $2.2 billion in economic and military assistance to Thailand between 1949 and 1969 and invested another $702 million to construct military bases in the kingdom. The report also estimates that the American presence injected about $200 million a year into the Thai economy.[12]

This American monetary aid allowed the Thai police to grow in number and also in capability and firepower. In 1951, a *New York Times* article reported that the "police force, which has the job of maintaining internal order, is armed with such equipment as armored cars, Bren guns and mortars" and they "outnumbered their counterparts in the Army, Navy, and Air Force combined. Out of a total armed force strength of about 85,000, the police accounted for about 40,000. The Army was estimated to have about 30,000 soldiers. The Air Force 4,000. The Navy 8,000."[13] Curtis' report indicated that in 1965, there were approximately 51,000 people in the police force. In 1973, the number reached 82,316. Their target was to reach 90,000 people by 1975.[14] Of the entire force, the Border Patrol Police numbered 10,500 men in 1973. Curtis called it "the primary security force of the TNPD."[15] The Provincial Police had 46,000 men. This was a significant increase from the 26,000 they had in 1966. By 1973, they had built 662 *amphoe* (district) police stations in the country.[16] In the capital, the Metropolitan Police had 7,400 men covering 1,550 square kilometers with a population of over 3.3 million, running operations over forty-nine precincts, seven subprecincts, and 136 kiosks throughout the city.[17] Today the police number over 200,000 (including administrative staff), a far cry from the 3,900 or so that Eric St. John Lawson had under his supervision in the early twentieth century.[18] So while Daniel Fineman, in his detailed account of Thai-U.S. relations in the Cold War period, writes that "Thailand of 1950 was still no police state," one might reasonably argue that it quickly became one under the auspices of the notorious police director-general Phao Sriyanond, who oversaw the creation of several new police units, including an armored car division for border areas, a paratroopers unit, a firefighting police, a riverboat police, a police radio division, an air police, and a dog-assisted police.[19]

In a separate study, Mizutani Yasuhiro concludes similarly that the Thai police did not become a major force in society, especially in the provinces, until the 1950s, with the aid of the Americans.[20]

To complement the police's increased numbers and enhanced firepower, Phao, as any good police chief might, promoted the adoption of the most current knowledge-production techniques and stressed scientific methods. On this topic, it is worth citing him at length. He wrote in 1953 that when he started work in the Police Department he was perplexed because it was a "big department, the basis for the administration of the country, yet the police cadet academy [*rong rian nai roi tamruat*] was in a state of confusion, being shifted here and there." He asked several high-ranking officers if there was a textbook for the police. The answer he got was "policing isn't a single discipline [*wicha tamruat nan mai chai sat*]. The police have to know many things: military studies, law, science, and medicine, and they have to be observant." Phao retorted, "Exactly, so is there a text book?" The answer then changed to yes, but he was told the book was not very good. Phao followed up by asking whether they have textbooks in other countries. The answer was again yes. "So why not translate them?" he asked. The reply given was that there was no one to do the translation. Moreover, "we [the Thai police] lack the equipment others have."[21] Phao went on to write that he noticed that police officers often expressed the need to beat suspects to obtain information. He collected the materials used to train cadets to see if the use of physical force was something actually taught to them. It was not. He then looked through the materials more closely and saw that they were full of laws and royal decrees. He thought this was fine in general, but the lack of content on how to conduct an actual police investigation was concerning. There was a bit in the texts on "military studies that instructed students how to fight, kill, and cut, but nothing relevant to police work, like how to deal with criminals in a village, in a house, or in other places they might actually be." Instructions on topics such as the prevention of the use of force in the investigation process and how to deal with suspects were almost nonexistent. He discovered that officers basically did what they wanted on a case-by-case basis and there was little cooperation between them. For example, he noted that some investigators kept lists of criminals but they did not share them. Phao concludes by saying that there had been no change in police practices in fifty years.[22]

In 1952, Phao created a new school for police investigation (*rong rian suep suan sop suan*).[23] The *Bangkok Post* reported that the first detection course given to government officials at the Administration School, in Wang

Suan Sunandha, began in 1954. Twenty *amphoe* (district-level) officials, forty-two provincial policemen, and eight army officers attended the course, which Phao said "would make them less dependent on informers, who are not always reliable."[24] Regional training schools were set up as well. A communications department (*kong suesan*) was created in 1952 with a call center to take complaints and receive reports of cases from the general population. Police officers were also sent overseas to see other police departments operate, and Phao hired British advisers to work with officers in Thailand.[25] One of the officers who went overseas was Somkit Santhunsing of the Thai police's identification bureau. He visited police forces in Japan, the United States, England, France, Switzerland, Holland, Italy, and West Germany. Of the need for a new science lab he wrote, "The Thai police are still quite far behind [*la lang mak*] other police in the world [in terms of scientific policing]." He added that the drive to improve scientific policing was necessary for the country to progress (*jaroen*) since those countries that already enjoyed the fruits of modernization were the ones that relied on scientific methods. This fact is illustrated, he said, by how scientific methods in combination with the latest tools help people in other societies discover the truth (*khwam jing*) and promote justice (*yuttitham*).[26] Moreover, the existing science section (*kong withayakan*) was being overworked. Their average case load in the early 1950s was "14 cases a day or 450 cases a month or 4500 cases a year with only seven experts to handle them all. So one expert handles 771 cases per year or two cases a day."[27]

For all these reasons, Phao wanted to establish a new science lab for the police, similar to the one they had in the United States. The Thai police, however, "had no qualified people and no equipment. The existing identification bureau [*phanaek phisut lakthan*] was based on the Institute of Police Science at Lausanne University, which was the model that Luang Phisitwithayakan created about 20 years ago."[28] It was only with the aid of the United States that the Thai police's crime lab eventually caught up with international standards, but that was not until the early 1960s. Curtis writes, "The Scientific Investigation Laboratory was supported from 1958 to 1962 with commodities, participant training opportunities in the US, and other training classes in Thailand. The RTG [Royal Thai Government] constructed a new building to house the laboratory and USOM provided equipment. The capability of this unit was considered adequate in 1962."[29] In late 1959, the police even got a mobile crime lab from the Public Safety Division of the USOM in Thailand. The lab was an ordinary-looking delivery van on the outside, but inside it was "equipped with all the necessary aids for dealing with on-the-spot detection work," including

> a complete dark room where film taken at the scene of a crime can be developed, printed and enlarged. There was also a police tape recorder with two four-hour spools and interception devices. Another section of the van housed a well-stocked chemical laboratory, complete with apparatus and glassware. Other features included a lie detector, a model finger print camera, and a finger print filing cabinet; a kit for making blood tests, and a kit for casting plaster of Paris models of tire or foot prints. To complete the picture, there was a library of crime laboratory books.[30]

In terms of technical assistance, the United States had fifty-two technicians working in the Thai police department during the peak of USOM support in 1967. In 1973, thirty-five of these positions remained. More importantly, Curtis notes with pride, eighty-three former USOM trainees had moved into top-level command positions, making up 26 percent of the police's command staff.[31] Americans and their protégés were thus penetrating the top echelons of the police, just as the police were expanding into the countryside and beefing up their military capabilities. Curtis concludes, "During the past 15 years of USOM assistance, the TNPD has made outstanding progress in its development into a modern, viable police institution. Compared with the police in most developing countries, the TNPD is a relatively experienced, professional organziation, able to perform its assigned mission of maintaining law and order and helping to meet the threats of the insurgency."[32] The head of the Central Investigation Bureau at the time compared the police under Phao to someone that had "just woken up from a long slumber. It [the police] is now progressing and improving."[33]

BRAVE NEW WORLD

If these moves by Phao to improve the kingdom's police force seem similar to those the government pursued in the early twentieth century, that's because they are. Both sets of reforms were attempts to transform the way the police went about their business by equipping them with new tools and practices. The latest international methods and technology were to replace outdated local processes. New equipment, restructured training centers teaching up-to-date core subjects, foreign advisers, and scientific techniques were all seen as a way to keep up with international standards and aid in the delivery of justice through the law. Just as in the early twentieth century, government officials in the post–World War II period could justify strengthening the force with the fact that there was simply a lot going on that needed policing. When Field Marshal Phibun Songkhram returned to power in 1948, the kingdom was in the middle of one of the most tumultuous periods in its short history. Following World War II, the country experienced widespread shortages in most categories of basic goods, including cloth, oil, gasoline, sugar, and salt. The minister of parliament from Saraburi province wrote that the oxen population there had suffered a critical decline, recovery from which would require no less than seven years. This decline was caused by the wartime food shortage that led people to kill draft animals for meat.[34] These shortages caused prices for consumer goods to rise precipitously. A study by the Committee to Consider the Economic Situation after the War puts inflation at anywhere between 436 and 1,446 percent.[35] Alleged price gouging by Chinese merchants, especially in commodities like gold, did not help the situation.[36] Rampant corruption and inefficiency in state-owned enterprises and the civil service only made matters worse. "Irregularities" in rice exports, for example, were common with shipments sent to the British via Malaya in exchange for cloth and cooking oil.[37] From these conditions of economic crisis and corruption came a rise in radical labor unionism, which led to "a wave of strikes among the big work-forces in the railways, port, rice mills, cement company, soap factories, and tobacco factory."[38] Not surprisingly, Thailand saw an increase in petty and violent crimes in the years after World War II. Thai historian Chalong Soontravanich writes, "Crime and violence spread throughout the country, becoming a national crisis and the subject of frequent parliamentary debates during the 1940s and 1950s."[39] Chris Baker and Pasuk Phongpaichit call the period between 1944 and 1951 "one of the most violent and critical in modern Thai history."[40] This rise in crime was attributable in part to the sudden availability of small arms, whose supply had been previously monopolized by the military and police: "Thousands of automatic pistols, submachine guns, hand grenades, grenade launchers, and all kinds of explosives, were almost freely circulating around the country" in the years after World War II.[41] Another historian, Christopher Goscha, writes of the 1950s, "Buying arms in Thailand was as easy as buying beer."[42]

While most armed crimes were associated with banditry, robbery, plunder, or other "personal crimes," just as they were at the turn of the nineteenth century, criminal violence in the post–World War II period was not confined to crimes between private citizens, and this is one key difference between the two periods of police reform. Police and other state agents adopted increasingly brutal methods for carrying out vendettas and silencing political opponents. In 1944, Wanit Pananon, a close aid to Phibun in the early 1940s, was suddenly arrested on charges of gold profiteering. He subsequently and mysteriously died in prison. Another notable case was the murder of two defense lawyers and several defense witnesses in the 1948 trial of three men accused in the death of King Ananda. In 1949, the police arrested four men, all ministers prior to Phibun's return to power in 1948, and assassinated them on a highway in northern Bangkok as they were ostensibly being transported from one prison to another. In December 1952, Tiang Sirikhan, former minister of parliament from Sakon Nakhon, and four others were murdered, their bodies burned. In 1953, Ari Liwira, publisher of several popular newspapers and magazines and a prominent critic of the government, was shot dead outside his beach house in Hua Hin. In 1954, Phon Malithong, another former minister, was killed "mafia style"—his body was tied to concrete posts and dumped into the Chao Phraya River.[43] Also in 1954, Haji Sulong, prominent leader from the Islamic south, and his son disappeared without a trace after having been requested to report to the provincial police station in Songkhla. In the same period, the police also killed Banchongsak Chippensuk, a former police officer himself, in Lampang in northern Thailand. Banchongsak was accused of being a "Pridi accomplice" and was shot and killed at his house while "resisting arrest."[44] His real "crime" was intercepting and investigating opium shipments that Phao profited from. Chuan Rotchanawiphat, editor of *Thammathipat,* who "had been writing harshly of government corruption, singling out for special attack a graft-ridden agency known as the Food Drive Organization which was supposed to cut down living costs," was gunned down on the way home from work. MacDonald writes,

> Pedaling home on his bicycle one evening, [Chuan] had just passed Sanuk Palace when a black sedan drove up behind him. The snout of a submachine gun was stuck out of the window and a quick splash of bullets felled the editor. The car sped on. The whole town knew that someone had been hired to kill Nai Chuen [*sic*]; newspapermen knew the police constable who did it, but the case of the editor's murder was never brought to court. The Police Department had orders to forget about it.[45]

Suri Thongwanit, editor of *Siang thai,* "which published a racy account of the arrest of a Siamese colonel's daughter by customs men in Manila for smuggling diamonds out of Siam," was also shot. Suri "had also [like Chuan] just finished his day's newspaper chores. He was getting into his jeep when a bullet caught him from behind. It didn't quite kill him. It tore through the back of his neck and came out in the front part of his face, but he was taken to hospital quickly enough to make repairs."[46] In all, the police killed at least twenty well-known public figures between 1944 and 1957.[47] In each of these cases, there are echoes of the crimes experienced in Siam during the late nineteenth and early twentieth centuries, as in many instances the identities of the murderers were known. In the 1950s and 1960s, however, the killers were well-armed and dangerous agents of the state rather than bandits that local headmen and villagers protected from the central government. As a result, these and many other cases remained without resolution for years. Some still have yet to be officially solved.[48]

For their part, the police either claimed that they had no knowledge of the murders being committed or that some nonpolice agent was behind the violence. Many members of the public, and, in some cases, members of the police themselves, were skeptical of this stance, knowing full well that Phao's men were often the culprits. In the case of the murder of the four former ministers, for example, the police publicly blamed Malayan bandits who allegedly attempted to free the prisoners, though no one believed this. One officer recalled a telling conversation that took place at Phalap Phalachai police station immediately after the incident occurred. According to his testimony, an officer named Luang Phichit told another officer named Iam Panthudej that the four ministers had just been shot and killed by Malayan terrorists. Iam responded by laughing and remarking, "that is an old trick."[49] Another officer, one that was at the scene of the crime when it occurred, noted that when he saw a paper report that the four ministers had been shot by Malayan bandits, he "did not believe the newspaper report because [he] knew that the gunfire came from in front of the car carrying the four accused."[50] In the 1944 death of Wanit Pananon while imprisoned, the government stated that the death was a suicide and even released a copy of his handwritten suicide note, though most of it was illegible. This led to speculation as to the real cause of his death.[51] In the disappearance of Haji Sulong and his son, the police claimed they got lost on the way to the police station. The suspicion is, however, that both men were abducted and killed by the police.[52] In the Ari Liwira murder, the police suggested after a summary investigation that the culprit was an unidentified gunman.[53] In his defining study of Field Marshal Sarit Thanarat and politics in the late 1950s, Thak Chaloemtiarana writes, "While the violent tactics of the police were well known and talked about, those actions were condemned only at the gossip level. Official investigation was impossible, for the crimes were committed by the police themselves."[54] That the police were behind the spate of political murders can therefore be called a public secret, something people know but cannot talk about openly, for very real, very threatening reasons.

Another, equally important, difference between the early twentieth-century police reforms and those of the 1950s was that a network of covert relations among politicians, businessmen, police officers, and Americans living in Thailand helped fuel the post–World War II buildup. This network existed in addition to the overt flows of monetary and technological aid from the United States outlined above. Fineman describes a special committee set up in 1950 by Willis Bird, an Office of Strategic Services (OSS) officer during World War II who "rapidly sank roots in the country." Using his connections, Bird organized "a secret committee of leading military and political figures to develop an anticommunist strategy and, more important, lobby the United States for increased military assistance."[55] The cabal, which was called the Naresuan Committee, included Phao, the army generals Sarit Thanarat and Phin Chunhawan, air force chief Fuen Ronnaphakat, and Sitthi Savetsila, who would serve as foreign minister from 1980 to 1990. It was during the early 1950s, too, that the CIA established a presence in the kingdom, primarily accomplished through their funding of the development of the police's criminal investigation department. By 1953, there were two hundred CIA advisers in the country whose mission was to train the police. The Naresuan Committee enjoyed close relations with the CIA and both operated clandestinely, often keeping Phibun's government in the dark as to their movements. To facilitate the committee's covert work, Bird and an associate from his OSS days, Paul Helliwell, established a dummy operation called Sea Supply to act as a cover. By 1951, Sea Supply was receiving arms from the United States, and, by April of that year, they had opened a camp in Lopburi, outside of Bangkok, to train the Thai police in counterinsurgency tactics.[56] Of American aid programs, both covert and overt, Fineman writes,

> In effect, the assistance programs initiated in 1950 and 1951 created a series of multilevel patron-client relationships between the Thais and the Americans. On one level, the United States acted as patron of the state as a whole. American economic aid benefited the entire state apparatus, including the civilian bureaucracy. On another level, the United States took on the

> military in particular as American clients. . . . On yet another level, the United States functioned as patron to individual leaders. . . . From this domestic perspective, the United States was now working within the Thai political system and assuming the top positions in the patronage networks of Phao and Phibun.[57]

The international relationships that drove the growth and helped justify the murderous tactics of the Thai police during the Cold War were, in other words, directly connected to various and complicated local networks taking hold of and reshaping political and economic life in Thailand. These networks are best described by Fred Riggs in his foundational study on the Thai bureaucracy, *Thailand: The Modernization of a Bureaucratic Polity.*[58] In it he argues that political conflict in Thailand in the 1950s and 1960s stemmed from intense competition between individuals for seats in the cabinet, which facilitated control over the kingdom's bureaucratic machine and thus created avenues for amassing private wealth. This observation is borne out by contemporary reports on the government under Phibun in 1952, one of which had a sub-headline that reads, "Military Chiefs Who Dominate Cabinet Vie for Profit from Corrupt Administration."[59] The article notes that "army, air corps and police force commanders all occupy Cabinet posts in the new regime. Of twenty ministers, only four are civilians."[60] To gain an upper hand in the struggle, army and police officers formed alliances, cliques, and coalitions, which then determined the fault lines for political conflict. In the early 1950s, the two most prominent cliques were ones presided over by army officers—Phin and Phao in one circle and Sarit Thanarat, Thanom Kittikhajon, and Praphat Jarusathien in another. Once in the cabinet, clever and ambitious individuals from each of these cliques could assign friends and retainers to positions in various departments and ministries and thus derive benefits from the inflow of foreign aid and international capital. The following section from Riggs describes one example of how the process worked:

> [The Ministry of Agriculture] contains departments concerned with agriculture, rice, fisheries, forestry, animal husbandry, and irrigation. We find that [Army General] Phin was a member of ten boards [of private companies] and [Police Captain] Lamai [Udthayananon] a member of twenty. One of these firms manufactured gunny bags, which were sold to rice millers on a compulsory basis by legally requiring that a minimum percentage of the bags used for rice exports be of domestic manufacture, despite the higher

> cost and lower quality of domestic as compared with imported bags. Another concern manufactured plywood, taking advantage of strict limitations by the Forestry Department governing all commercial exploitation of Thai lumber resources. A third firm manufactured matches. Several warehousing companies took advantage of governmental programs to stabilize rice prices. Sugar companies were designed to exploit the government's policies for the expansion of sugar production. Another firm specialized in the sale of salted fish, presumably taking advantage of special services from the Fisheries Department. The Farmers Bank was on the list, a beneficiary of public funds for agricultural development. Shipping and insurance firms were able to take advantage of governmental programs intended to spur trade in agricultural products.[61]

Phin and Lamai were not alone in their pursuit of wealth through politics. Phao, despite his public anti-Communist stance, began to expand his commercial contacts with pro-Communist Chinese merchants and had by the early 1950s become "involved in the opium trade, gold-selling, rail, transport, banking, and trucking" to such an extent that his business interests "penetrated almost every commercial sector in the country, legal or otherwise."[62] Phao even tried to buy Ari Liwira's Siam Phanitchayakan publishing empire before having him killed.[63] Another high-ranking police officer, Phra Phinit Chonkhadi, the head of the unit tasked with determining the cause of King Ananda's death, was part of a group that brought Pepsi Cola to Thailand.[64] Sarit, meanwhile, used the early 1950s to enrich himself personally; records made public after his death indicate he may have amassed a personal fortune of over 2.8 billion baht in assets.[65] In short, it was through relationships with the largely Chinese business community that the many high-ranking police (and army) officers were able to build up substantial personal fortunes. On one hand, bureaucrats sustained themselves and their many bad habits by exploiting Chinese businesses. On the other, the Chinese had incentive to establish ties with leading government officials to conduct their businesses safely. Government officials provided protection from arrest and harassment in return for benefits, while ethnic Chinese-owned companies could secure government contracts made possible by aid from the United States in its fight against Communism.[66] So alongside the first set of competing alliances within the bureaucracy was a less visible clutch of relationships that linked predominantly Chinese businessmen to political elites. Both, in turn, were joined to the international system of exchange created by the American anti-Communism campaign.

Conditions in the kingdom after World War II were therefore just as, if not more, crime-ridden and chaotic when compared to those of the late nineteenth and early twentieth centuries. However, the unsatisfying solution in the case of the death of King Ananda, the high-profile political murders that took place after 1945, and the encroachment of new global networks of exchange and influence meant that the growing power of the police could no longer be seen as solely a positive, or even benign, modernizing trend. Instead, the rate and character of growth of the police in the 1950s is symptomatic of the Thai bureaucratic elite's various economic entanglements rather than a straightforward reflection of the police's concern with serving and protecting Thai subjects. It also means that the Cold War world that Thais found themselves in was distinct from the one of the reform period (1890s–1920s) in that the structure of the Thai state could no longer be imagined in the ways it had been before. The political and economic situation during the Cold War was not one typified by a unified state rationally expanding its control into the provinces, consolidating the authority of Bangkok, as Chulalongkorn's government had been. Instead, the state during the 1950s and 1960s was a fragmented organism whose parts were often at odds with each other, working secretly against one another.[67] The absolute monarchy had been replaced by bureaucratic elites in 1932, and this bureaucracy, both military and civilian, became tied after World War II to Cold War capitalism. The period saw the creation of social formations of cultural and knowledge production that were significantly different from those that existed in the early twentieth century: far-flung transnational networks, expanding and contracting, with overlapping lines of money, people, ideologies, and objects, reshaped what were once local affairs and reassembled them as modern.

THE DARK HAND OF INFLUENCE

To explain the violent events that defined history during the Cold War years and the expansive, seemingly unknowable, network of people, money, power, and weapons behind them, the state and its subjects required a new vocabulary, a different social narrative, through which to articulate and interpret the unprecedented and unsettling era of turmoil. Not coincidentally, it was during this period that two peculiar, and generally unremarked, developments related to the meteoric rise of sensational crime news in the vernacular press took place. First, publishing houses began to produce new weekly and monthly news magazines with titles that included the phrase *bueang lang* (behind the scenes or inside story), like *Phim thai bueang lang khao* [*Phim thai* behind the news], *Phim thai lang khao sapada* [*Phim thai* behind the news weekly], *Deli nio bueang lang khao* [*Daily News* behind the news], and *Deli me bueang lang khao* [*Daily Mail* behind the news]. These magazines featured analysis and investigative reports about current events, mostly crimes. Their front covers often featured color photos of attractive women, and their contents included a mix of in-depth news reports, short stories, editorials, political commentary, and social news. Claiming to provide the story behind the story, these news magazines offered a common vehicle of dissemination for a variety of content, but more importantly, they cemented in the public imagination the notion that behind the headlines and the seemingly straightforward factual descriptions of everyday, ordinary events lurked more interesting tales that could best be told through in-depth analysis and opinion pieces. There *was* a truth behind the violence, both state and private, rapidly engulfing the country. It just required some investigating to discover. The problem became, however, that any accurate explanation often pointed to people in positions of power, including police officers and local officials. Explanations of these events by agents of the state and reportage on them in the press by reporters therefore required a bit of finesse.

One early example of this delicate situation is found in the murder investigation for the death of Ari Liwira. Ari's publishing company was the "most successful newspaper organization in the country. Ari's leftist *Sayam nikon* was reported to control the market in every town in the military strategic northeast, and his *Phim thai* possibly enjoyed the largest circulation in the country."[68] On March 9, 1953, at just after 9:00 a.m., a plainclothes police officer shot Ari dead at his beachside retreat in Hua Hin, a quiet coastal town about three hours by car south of Bangkok. Ari had just finished taking a walk along the seashore. When he reached his bungalow he saw his maid, Chanthana Yimcharoen, in the yard washing clothes. She was talking to a man Ari did not recognize. As Ari approached, the man turned to him and said that "Rong Maitri" (Police Lieutenant Colonel Maitri Banyen), a police officer and a friend, was coming to town and would like his help in finding a place to stay. The two men then walked out of the yard through a gate in the compound's fence, where a second stranger stood waiting. This man drew a pistol and with great calm shot Ari three times. Both strangers then got into a jeep that had been waiting for them nearby and left the scene. Ari died ten minutes later, with his wife by his side.[69]

The news of the assassination spread quickly through the press. The story appeared on the front pages of Ari's company's flagship dailies, *Phim thai* and *Sayam nikon,* those of his competitors like the *Deli me* (no relation to the *Bangkok Daily Mail* of the 1920s and 1930s), and also that of the English-language *Bangkok Post.* It remained there for several days as officials conducted their investigation. The case was, after all, one that hit close to home for many journalists. One reporter for the *Deli me* described the murder of Ari as "news that shook the soul of the publishing world."[70] The staff at another popular paper from the period, Kamphon Wacharaphon's *Khao phap rai wan,* echoed the sentiment, saying the murder left them "shaken."[71] The day after the murder, Phao Sriyanond announced to reporters that five policemen from the province of Kanchanaburi had been detained on suspicion of being involved in the assassination, and he reassured everyone that the police would get to the bottom of things.[72] A few days later, Sirichai Krachangwong, police superintendent of Kanchanaburi, defended his men, saying that all five had exhibited "one-hundred percent good conduct" over the years; they did not drink liquor and were "afraid of ghosts."[73] Phao then put Deputy Police Chief Phra Phinit Chonkhadi, a man accustomed to dealing with high-profile cases, in charge of the investigation.[74] By month's end, Phinit announced that the police's inquiry indicated that a mysterious "sixth man," a hired gunman, had assassinated Ari, and that the police were now looking for this person. He added that the motive in the murder was not political, but was related to Ari's "personal business" involving women.[75] Here the police, as representatives of the state, conjured a phantom "sixth man" for the press to materialize as news in the daily papers. The recourse to a fabricated agent of history was a deliberate tactic of obfuscation similar to the ones engaged in after the assassination of the four former ministers in 1949 (i.e., Malayan bandits as the culprits) and so many others during the period.

This leads directly to the second, related development of the period. Not long after the police's "sixth man" appeared, a series of other new criminal agents, including third hands (*mue thi sam*), dark hands (*mue muet*), and people of influence (*phu mi ithiphon*), began to surface in the news. And like the police's "sixth man," these agents existed as shadowy figures working behind the scenes, rarely being named directly. They referred to specters more than anyone real. The ambiguity of their existence and furtiveness of their identity meant that they were often the subjects of gossip and rumor, materializing only in newsprint and later on television. One can trace the origins of these new historical actors primarily to the mid-1950s.[76] The most common was probably the *anthaphan* (social delinquent), but the one that most captured the imagination was what would later become known as the *jao pho* [godfather]. The story of Kangwan Wiranan is illustrative. It was Kangwan whom *Phim thai* dubbed the king of bandits (*racha jon*) in 1954 in a feature piece entitled *Racha jon haeng lum nam mae klong* (Bandit king of the Mae Klong basin). The author notes that Kangwan, unlike other bandits at the time, did not himself engage in the dirty work of robbing and killing. Rather, he had others, including *anthaphan*-like elements, do this for him. And because other criminal bosses would later adopt Kangwan's hands-off approach, he would become known as the kingdom's first *jao pho*.[77] Kangwan was a new criminal figure precisely because, unlike other bandits at the time, he stayed behind the scenes, directing a masterpiece of intimidation, racketeering, and death. Another figure that people began to speak of on a regular basis was the highly ambiguous person of influence. Political scientist Viengrat Nethipho combed through political and crime news reports from 1957 through the end of the 1960s and found that terms like *ithiphon* (influence) or *phuak ithiphon* (influential group), as well as *phu ying yai* and *phu kwang khwang* (both roughly mean "big man"), began to appear with regularity in the news during the late 1950s.[78] These persons of influence appeared commonly in stories about illicit economies, including opium and marijuana trade, prostitution, and illegal logging, which were becoming increasingly common as Cold War capitalism restructured Thai society. Rarely were the owners of the illegal operations or their counterparts within the state apparatus named. In 1960, for example, a judge in Chonburi was killed, but no clear explanation was given as to why. It was only reported that the police had questioned a man referred to as *sia* Jio.[79] In this story, the term *ithiphon* was used to refer to otherwise unnamable figures in positions of authority or with the potential to exact terror on their enemies.[80] After the end of Sarit period in 1963, stories of murder—and there were many—continued to appear, and they continued to regularly employ the term *phu mi ithiphon*. As before, news reports of violence and corruption did not name the individuals believed to be behind a particular crime, even if the person was someone the general public already knew or thought they knew.

A series of stories that appeared between March and October of 1973 in the newspaper *Thai rat* about two connected cases, one a mass murder–suicide and the other a murder of a village volunteer, provides another example of how the term is used. Using the terms *klum ithiphon* (influential group) or *jom ithiphon* (influential boss), the reports gestured frequently to the involvement of a provincial governor in the deaths and to his complicity in a terror campaign to keep an illegal logging concern from public scrutiny. Headlines over three weeks in March featured a variation on the term "influential person" at least six times.[81] The term would be used again later in the year to indicate that someone in a position of power was intimidating potential witnesses in the case. Over the course of the seven months, this influential person and his retainers haunted the front pages of the nation's consciousness in a fabulous tale of corruption and violence.

Stories about *suea,* or the simpler, almost quaint social bandit of the imagined past, were still popular throughout the 1950s. In fact, Thak calls the 1950s the "heyday of the *suea,*"[82] and they often appeared in the weeklies, dailies, and popular fiction of the period. MacDonald writes, "At the time, reports of banditry in the kingdom were becoming routine copy for the *Post.* Out in the country bandit gangs were taking over whole areas. Yao's [Sunthinoon, a *Bangkok Post* reporter] ordeal had to do with two of these *khon suea,* or 'tiger men,' named Suea Kaeo and Suea Thanom."[83] The two were brothers from Kanchanaburi who had made a fortune from robbery. They had decided to retire and celebrate by holding a two-day feast. They even sent out engraved invitations to their followers, government officials, and the press. At the event, undercover police officers shot Suea Kaeo through the head, triggering a gun battle that ended with the police burning down the bandits' house. The next morning, the police arrested several officials and others for cooperating with the bandits. Even these older types of bandits, however, were becoming tied to a larger system of crime that was driven by political and economic trends well beyond their control. The type of industries (e.g., logging for export), the capital (from international markets and foreign aid), and the actors (government bureaucrats, foreign capitalists, and local crime bosses) involved in post–World War II crime attest to this. Alongside the exciting, if soon to be anachronistic, tales of bandits and gunfights, then, were an increasing number of reports about murders related to the struggle for territory or commercial profits, often involving powerful agents of the state, just like the cases described above. In reporting these stories, the press opined simply that there were problems or personal grudges between intimates or business partners, invoking phrases like "men of influence." Government officials and the popular press thus kept pace with shifts in economics and politics that were taking place during the Cold War by innovating ways to explain and report state-related violence.

Beginning in the 1950s, a space behind the visible, *bueang lang,* opened up in the modern discourse of power and politics, and into that space went all the human agents of violence and power that could not be named. Of course, the notion that visible reality is an effect of hidden forces is not new. Gods, spirits, ghosts, and other beings have long been seen by people in Thailand, as well as by those of the West, to have a hand in determining the worldly affairs of men and women. For many Thais, these spirits and deities are all entities that interact with humans and even exist, per the *traiphum* cosmology, in realms that form a continuum with the one that humans occupy. Moreover, supernatural beings can for the most part be named (e.g., Indra, Brahma, *praet* [hungry ghost], and various *phi* [ghosts]).[84] The mostly invisible force, karma, also has a very potent effect on the way human affairs play out. Unlike supernatural beings, however, karma is a phenomenon that is arguably more manageable since it, if understood as the relationship between an individual's actions and thoughts and real-world outcomes, may be controlled in many ways—do good things, receive good things (*tham di dai di*). There is nothing menacing about its operation, as its logic is transparent. The socioeconomic changes that began in the 1950s meant that powerful, unnamable human actors, including military generals, police officers, godfathers, and wealthy entrepreneurs who sought to control parts of the state or the economy for their own benefit, joined these older supernatural beings and cosmic forces "behind the scenes."

CONSPIRACY THEORY AS STATECRAFT

A conspiracy theory, writes Mark Fenster, stems from "the conviction that a secret, omnipotent individual or group covertly controls the political and social order or some part thereof."[85] This certainly fits the description of Cold War Thailand that I have presented so far: men of influence were portrayed as lurking everywhere behind the scenes during a particularly violent period of Thai history. Take the following news stories. The *New York Times* reported in 1953 how Phibun claimed that a "Communist-inspired plot to overthrow the Government" was behind increasing social unrest and political tension in the country. The report added, "The police said incriminating documents had been seized." No details were given about the documents or the alleged plot. The sub-headline of the article read, "Former Officers, Government Officials among Accused—Vietminh Hand Seen."[86] The subtitle here, and indeed each of the examples from the American press below, shows that, like conventions for making crime scene maps and photographs, conspiracy theories and the hidden hands behind them are transnational phenomena. Less than a year later, the *Los Angeles Times* reported, "Naval authorities [in Thailand] have seized a suspected key underground conspirator and four bags of documents which police say may unlock the full story of subversive conspiracies against Thailand." This suspect was Thongyen Halilamian, "reputed close associate of Pridi Phanomyong."[87] The government had sought him since the abortive coup of February 1948. In 1957, Phibun "charged . . . that 'Leftist-inclined opposition parties' were engineering a plot to partition Thailand."[88] A 1965 news article notes, "The chief of Thailand's Criminal Investigation Department said that a border police patrol discovered a secret terrorist camp deep in the jungle in Ubon Province."[89] In 1976, another article reports that the military regime that violently crushed student demonstrators on October 6 of that same year claimed to be fighting a "red conspiracy," and that "Police General Srisuk Mahintorathep, announcing a tightened curfew, said it [the curfew] was to guard against terrorist attacks predicted by vague intelligence reports."[90] Casual readers of the news between the 1950s and the 1970s would have had good reason to conclude that subversive elements were conspiring to destroy the Thai nation.[91]

Academic literature on conspiracy theory typically points its finger at groups of suspicious-minded, discontented individuals. The American Right during the Cold War years, for example, believed that America had "been largely taken away from them and their kind" and were thus "determined to try to repossess it and to prevent the final destructive act of subversion" being planned by their enemies. What was worse, writes Richard Hofstadter in his now classic essay "The Paranoid Style in American Politics," the conspirators plotting the destruction of the old order, of national security and independence, were "major statesmen who are at the very centers of American power. . . . The modern radical right finds conspiracy to be betrayal from on high." Furthermore, "decisive events" in a conspiracy theorist's mind "are not taken as part of the stream of history, but as the consequences of someone's will." In the United States during the 1950s and 1960s, for the right wing, this someone was the state. Hofstadter adds,

> The situation becomes worse when the representatives of a particular social interest—perhaps because of the very unrealistic and unrealizable nature of its demands—are shut out of the political process. Having no access to political bargaining or the making of decisions, they find their original conception that the world of power is sinister and malicious fully confirmed. They see only the consequences of power—and this through distorting lenses—and have no chance to observe its actual machinery.[92]

For these believers, history is a broad plot against them.

There are similarities between the United States of the 1950s and the Thailand of the immediate post–World War II period in that the self-identified dispossessed and the most active purveyors of conspiracy theory included primarily conservative elements of the Right. Unlike the United States, however, one finds in Thailand that these conspiracy theorists were agents of the state rather than individuals excluded from the halls of power. The people claiming the existence of conspiracies in the 1950s included Phibun, military and police officers, and members of the royalist old guard. That this final group would be attracted to conspiracy theory makes particular sense in Thailand since, as Thongchai Winichakul has argued, the aristocratic elite developed a marked sense of victimhood from the traumatic encounters of the colonial period, particularly after the Franco-Siamese war of 1893, during which the French navy blockaded the mouth of the Chao Phraya and cut Bangkok off from seaborne communications. In the aftermath of the skirmishes, the French negotiated a treaty that gave them control of territory on the eastern side of the Mekong River, a concession the Siamese elite saw as a mortal loss to the national "geo-body."[93] The years leading up to the revolution of 1932, which saw attacks on the monarchy in the vernacular press, are likely to have only aggravated the elites' feelings of victimhood. Conspiracy theories thus provided for this group a seemingly accurate way of representing historical events, similar to the way that it did for the American Right during the 1950s and 1960s.

If viewed in this light, conspiracy theory was never just a spontaneous and natural fit to describe the situation Thailand found itself in after World War II. It was a deliberate program of misrepresentation, and the peculiar occurrences that took place in the aftermath of King Ananda's death may therefore be seen as signaling the beginning of a significant shift in way the bureaucratic elite went about fighting for supremacy. A man shouted in a movie theater that Pridi killed the king. The man, it turns out, was allegedly hired by politicians of the Democrat Party to do so.[94] Meanwhile, a few well-placed individuals were telling officials at the French Embassy in Bangkok that the king had been shot in the back, therefore ruling out suicide.[95] Later, a woman came forward saying that she overhead two royal pages talking about how Pridi had sent someone to kill the king.[96] Historical events like the death of the king, when presented in a framework of conspiracy theory, reveal a furtive, wicked truth that can only be determined through the interpretation of otherwise disconnected signs. In a mystery novel, detectives search for and use clues to help them solve a crime, in the process bringing the reader to narrative closure. In the conspiracy theories being concocted in postwar Thailand, however, clues like the ones being scattered around Bangkok in the 1950s did not solve any real mystery. They only helped discredit one's political competitors and justify the use of force. Conspiracy theory has developed in Thailand, therefore, as a way of understanding history as well as a strategy of elites against their enemies, real and perceived. It is a multifunctional tool of statecraft.

Conspiracy theories, however, are hard to control and are therefore a dangerous technique for the state to use. A short op-ed piece from a 1958 issue of the *Bangkok Post* reads,

> Bangkok periodically is filled with rumors, and this is one of those periods. There are rumors of plots against the Government, of Government-Military-Police plans to arrest National Assemblymen and journalists, and of various other startling things. There are even counter-rumors by accused persons that the original rumors were really started by the seeming targets of the rumors so as to make the accused look like wicked rumormongers. It gets very devious at times.[97]

In another example, when John Peurifoy, the U.S. ambassador to Thailand, died in car crash in 1955, Phibun and some officials in Washington, D.C., became suspicious of Phao. Fineman writes,

> On August 12, while Peurifoy was driving his two sons back from a paratrooper display at the PARU camp, a truck ran into his robin's-egg-blue Thunderbird, killing Peurifoy and his son, Daniel. Although the circumstances of the accident indicated no foul play, the Phibun camp, having seen the handiwork of Phao's hired killers time and again in the past, immediately assumed police involvement. Apparently, the CIA also had its worries at first.[98]

In this case, even some government officials did not believe that the death of a diplomat could be a mere accident. Under conditions like this, facts quickly become lost, fugitives in a world of the unspeakable, one full of secrecy and intrigue.

The key aspect of conspiracy theories that allows them to exert so much influence on the thinking of political leaders and common subjects is that they invite people to engage them, to interpret the clues strewn throughout the city and its mass media. In doing so, people unwittingly translate broad, and mostly unsubstantiated, theories about nefarious schemes into the very fabric of reality though everyday conversation and personal interaction. In an essay on the mass media in Thailand, Annette Hamilton writes that stories about current events, as portrayed on the news, provide the substance for "interpersonal conversations between intimates, who may re-interpret or deconstruct 'what is happening' through commonly held beliefs about the nature of power and the hidden narratives which are used as explanatory frameworks."[99] Along these lines, one finds in Thailand a constant stream of chatter on topics from "accounts of manipulation of cosmic forces by prominent politicians and power-brokers to ensure their success" to the Machiavellian intentions of foreigners.[100] In other words, people at all levels of society engage in the detection game, sure in their minds that behind the news lies a real truth about power and politics in Thai society. The power of conspiracy theories is therefore that they are highly social. They may begin at the top as a strategy to cover and justify the use of physical force or to discredit enemies in a struggle for power and wealth, but then they lure people into their web to discuss, debate, and disagree about the hidden forces behind the visible. Conspiracy theories do not cover up one reality with another. They confuse what reality might be and then bind people to the deception through their participation.[101] This is the function of conspiracy theory, itself the narrative form of modern Thai history.

VISUALIZING CONSPIRACY

Just as the shifts in post–World War II socioeconomic conditions required a new vocabulary with which to discuss politics and power, they also necessitated fresh ways to visualize the country's changing political and economic terrain. To help the reader picture the complex and shifting links between individuals and cliques that flourished after World War II, Riggs provided a number of diagrams. The one reproduced in Figure 5.1 shows the relationships between Sarit Thanarat's clique and that of Phin Chunhawan and Phao during the mid-1950s. As described above, both these cliques gained and maintained their positions through ties with Chinese businessmen and their money. Riggs also illustrates these connections in table form, listing the board memberships of each cabinet member. Both sets of relationships—intra-bureaucratic and bureaucrat-businessman—were nested in yet another network, namely the one created by the American and Thai governments. An image of this network is shown in Figure 5.2, which is

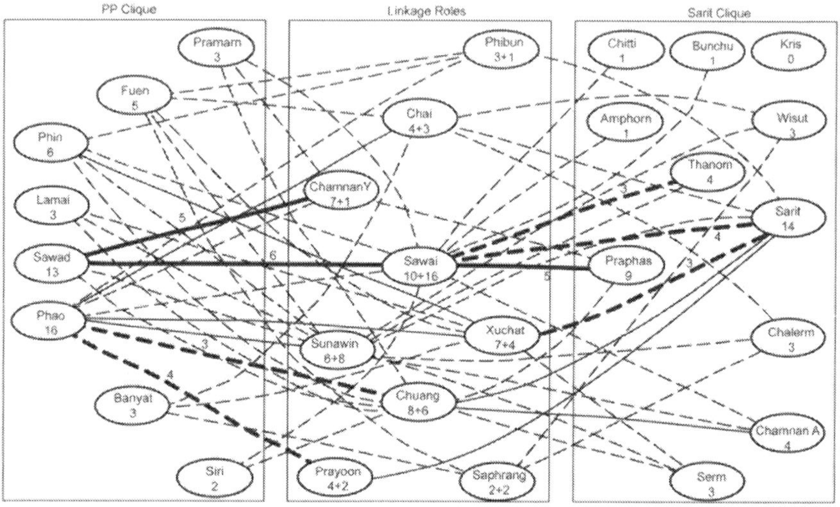

FIGURE 5.1. Diagram showing linkages between cliques in the Thai government's cabinet in the mid-1950s. From Riggs, *Bureaucratic Polity,* 1966.

from Thomas Lobe's informative study of American aid to the Thai police during the Cold War. The usefulness of diagrams like these stems from the fact that they help one imagine social phenomena that cannot generally be seen. Connections between individuals and groups are made visible by an assortment of lines linking various bubbles and boxes containing names of individuals and institutions, giving shape to networks through forms (ovals and lines) that indicate functions (flows of money and benefits described earlier), allowing ordinary citizens to perceive the myriad of forces that act behind the scenes to shape their lives. In Thailand the visual rhetoric of social scientific diagrams helped reveal a specter, one of a Cold War capitalist system that according to Fredric Jameson was "so vast that it [could not] be encompassed by the natural and historically developed categories of perception with which human beings normally orient themselves."[102] The dread, the crime waves, the feeling that control had been lost and society was disintegrating were verified visually, backed by the authority that these new visions were modern and real rather than ghostly or supernatural.

Western social scientists are not the only people with access to modernist techniques of representation. Amid mounting protests in 2010 for the elected government to step down, a Center for the Resolution of Emergency Situations (CRES) spokesman gave a press briefing on April 26 at which he

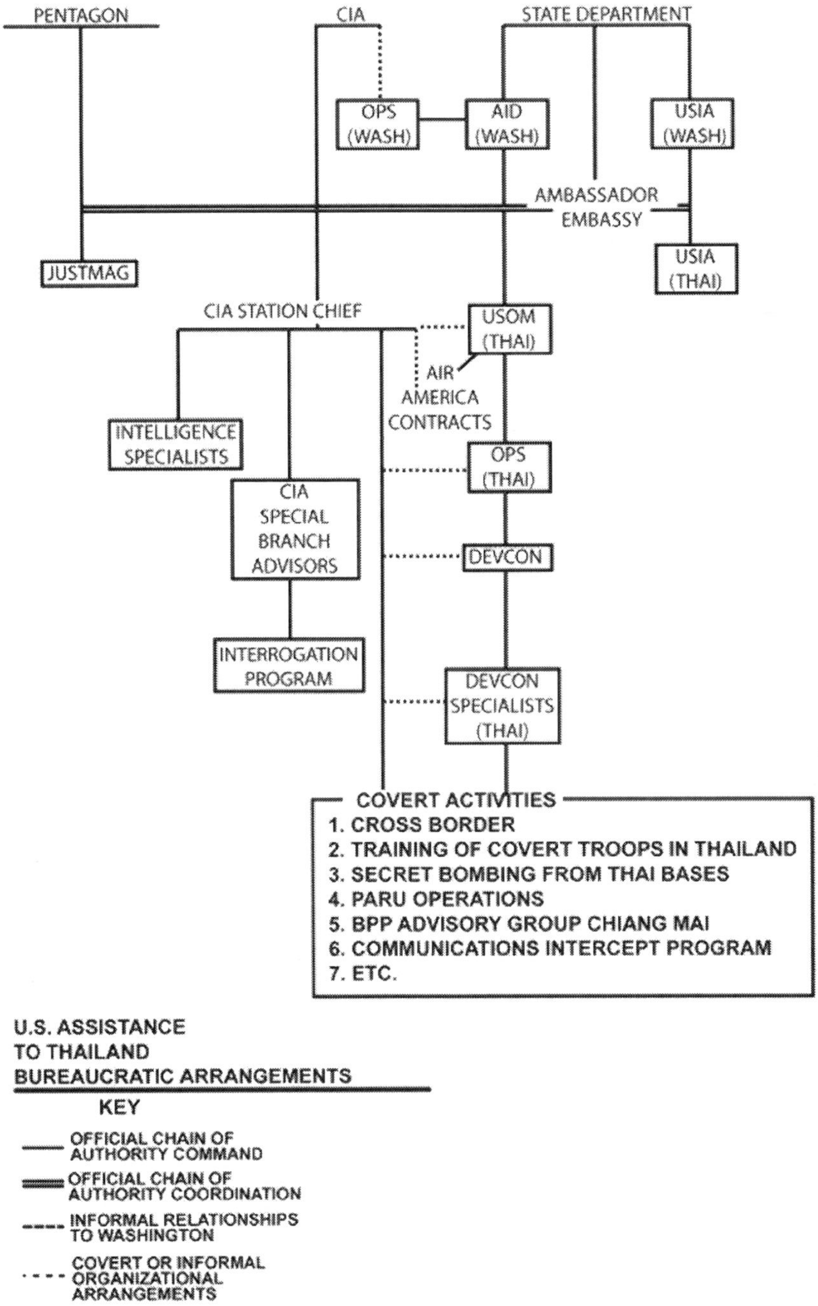

FIGURE 5.2. Diagram illustrating the connections between the American and Thai governments. From Lobe, *United States National Security Policy,* 1977.

distributed a handout with a diagram depicting a scheme to overthrow the monarchy (Figure 5.3). The diagram contains the names of a number of individuals, from an ousted prime minister and a radio DJ to a noodle restaurateur in San Francisco and various academics and publishers, in ovals connected by lines. These lines and geometric shapes are meant, as in Riggs' diagrams, to indicate the ways each individual element of a larger whole is related. Taken in its entirety, the visualization shows a picture of forces allegedly allied against the monarchy. The alleged plot's most tangible manifestation before this presentation was the phrase "Finland Plan." In a single diagram, a hidden threat to power was made real and thus accessible as a

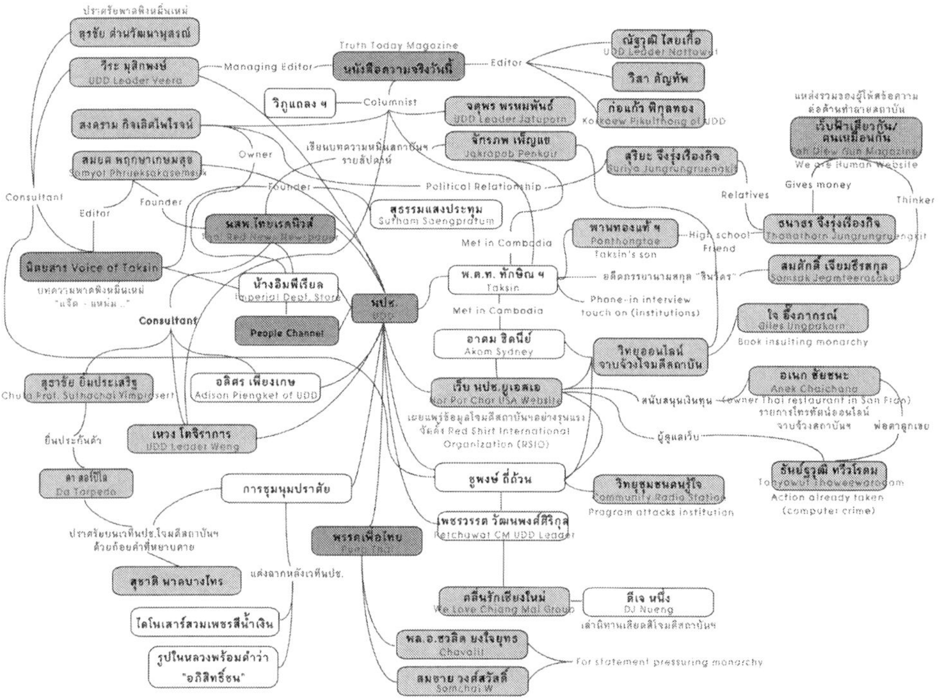

FIGURE 5.3. Diagram of a conspiracy to overthrow the monarchy, distributed by the Center for the Resolution of Emergency Situations (CRES). This image was produced after the coup of a popularly elected government in 2010 and presented during a news conference to explain the rationale behind the coup. The diagram can be found online at several different websites. This one is adapted from the version located at the Bangkok Pundit column on the Asian Correspondent website, http://asiancorrespondent.com/31566/conspiracy-against-the-monarchy/.

vast, cabalistic network with lines, circles, and text. In short, the CRES diagram gave conspiracy theory, at last, a visible form.[103]

That conspiracy theorists employ the same methods of visual persuasion found in serious academic work is not surprising. Thai governments have, over the course of the late nineteenth and twentieth centuries, become adept at adopting various foreign practices. Benedict Anderson notes,

> Once again, the observer is struck by the irony of this [American Cold War–era economic and technical] assistance—in other words, that it had its effects largely by inadvertence. At one level, it meant the introduction of American-style social science—the product of the training Thai students were getting in the United States, the growing Americanization of the structures and priorities of Thai universities, and the counterinsurgency research sponsored by American military and civil institutions in Siam.[104]

The use of modern representational techniques to prove the truth of a conspiracy theory can therefore be seen as an outgrowth of Thailand's engagement with the United States, as a form of mimicry sometimes associated with colonial subjects. Hofstadter writes,

> It is hard to resist the conclusion that this enemy [behind a conspiracy] is on many counts a projection of the self; both the ideal and the unacceptable aspects of the self are attributed to him. The enemy may be the cosmopolitan intellectual, but the paranoid will outdo him in the apparatus of scholarship, even of pedantry. Secret organizations set up to combat secret organizations give the same flattery. The Ku Klux Klan imitated Catholicism to the point of donning priestly vestments, developing an elaborate ritual and an equally elaborate hierarchy. The John Birch Society emulates Communist cells and quasi-secret operation through "front" groups, and preaches a ruthless prosecution of the ideological war along lines very similar to those it finds in the Communist enemy.[105]

In a similar manner, the development of a secret police in the early 1900s can be viewed as the Siamese state's attempt to be like the European colonial threats it feared. When strengthening the police in the 1950s, the Thai state emulated the FBI. In using a violence similar to that employed by *anthaphan* and *jao pho,* state agents copied the methods of terror favored by the kingdom's new criminal element. In adopting modernist techniques for visual representation, conspiracy theorists imitate the foreign expert, the Western social scientist, to show that the alleged plots to foment disorder were in fact rational, modern, and real.

The preceding chapters have been about how a common set of social scientific methods for producing an internationally accepted appearance of facticity was a key aspect of police modernization. That similar conventions are now the standard by which most sectors of the state present facts indicates how deeply rooted they have become. To prove the existence of a conspiracy requires the same sort of evidence—tables, lists, text, and, of course, diagrams—necessary to illustrate the truth of any other social phenomenon, from a crime wave to the potential efficacy of higher income taxes. The production of this evidence then becomes a key concern for the theory's adherents. In 1947, after a coup drove Pridi and Prime Minister Thamrongnawasat out of the country, the post-coup Phibun government issued a white paper stating that two Chinese "born in Siam in the town of Ayuthia [*sic*]" were planning a large-scale Chinese invasion of the kingdom. The white paper charged that these two Chinese planned to set up a "South China," of which Pridi would have been named president. It then went on to connect a series of events—the 1944 resignation of Phibun, the death of the king, the signing of a treaty with China, and a plot to overcome the army—into a coherent narrative about the recent past that proved the truth of the alleged plot.[106] Recall also that in the news reports cited above, the police and the government would claim each time they arrested suspected conspirators that they had found a treasure trove of documentation. Indeed, the "paranoid style," writes Hofstadter, is rational and document based:

> The higher paranoid scholarship is nothing if not coherent—in fact the paranoid mind is far more coherent than the real world. It is nothing if not scholarly in technique. McCarthy's 96-page pamphlet, *McCarthyism*, contains no less than 313 footnote references, and Mr. Welch's incredible assault on Eisenhower, *The Politician*, has one hundred pages of bibliography and notes. The entire right-wing movement of our time is a parade of experts, study groups, monographs, footnotes, and bibliographies.[107]

The conspiracy theories of Cold War Thailand are similarly proved, with reports and diagrams.

I have described the way modern ideas about facticity in the criminal justice system have become tied to formal conventions developed over the twentieth century and specific mechanical technologies of representation.

The techniques and conventions used to judge an image as realistic or accurate have become naturalized, so that most people no longer question them. Alan Sekula advises, however, that one should not exaggerate the power of "optical realism."[108] Images themselves, as realistic as they may appear, are no guarantee that the public will see them as true. Rosalind Morris' discussion of photographs of dead bodies from the Thai military's attack on the Krue Sae mosque in 2004 is relevant here. That year, a group of men that the military claimed were separatist insurgents took refuge in the mosque in Thailand's south. After a standoff, the military forcibly cleared the mosque, killing the men inside. Photographs of the attack were leaked. The military claimed that the photographs, proof of the violence they administered, had been doctored.[109] The police's subsequent autopsies of the dead men showed, they claimed, that traces of heroin had been found in their blood. The military then went to the press, using this as part of their justification for the use of deadly force; violence was necessary for the government's war on drugs and terrorism and for the maintenance of national stability. The photos were the location of competing interpretations about a particular historical event.[110] What the episode also shows is that when the enemy (here, the public) has proof (photographs) of military brutality, the state attacks the evidence. It then hits back with its own scientific and modern forms of proof (the autopsy). When agents of the Thai state offer forensic evidence to justify the use of excessive force, they connect brutality to technology and scientific modernity. The resulting alliance of violence and visual practice within an overarching narrative framework of conspiracy theory creates a split between formalistic realism and facticity, the connection that undergirds modernist modes of representation. The outcome, one that state agents seem unable to fully grasp, is that the aesthetic rules that have been so painstakingly developed and taught, including to the police, over the course of the twentieth century and that were meant to anchor life and the law to truth come to be seen as little more than an epistemological cover for corruption and tyranny. The tragedy of all this is that in many cases the juicy rumors, full of intrigue and innuendo, that pass for political discourse in Thailand likely contain more than a bit of truth. The problem is that the mechanisms for discerning what exactly is factual have been undermined after decades of obfuscation and the use of brute force. I do not mean to imply here that there are no facts, only that it is increasingly difficult to tell with any certainty what they are in today's Thailand. As a result, people continue to seek solace in the relative certainty of predictions made by diviners and fortunetellers. "We are all sufferers from history," says Hofstadter, "but the paranoid is a double sufferer, since he is afflicted not only by the real world, with the rest of us, but by his fantasies as well."[111]

The conviction that behind the visible lie hidden, malevolent individuals and forces pushes people into a game of constant detection and interpretation to locate and name these furtive agents of history. It is a condition, to cite Robert Wilson, that can best be described with the phrase "guerilla ontology." By this he means a literary technique that mixes fact and fiction such that "the reader must decide on each page 'How much of this is real and how much is put-on?' "[112] In real life, it means that people perpetually question official accounts of current events and look instead to alternative explanations that, in Thailand, often involve hidden masterminds or supernatural agents. In the process, the forces that might be said to actually drive history—material relations, technological change—fall away, replaced by unnamable, powerful, and ill-intentioned figures. In this state, everything becomes a potential clue—the color of the shirt a particular politician wears to a function or a remark made casually in a private setting—for cobbling together a coherent story about the way things *really* work. In a society where life for so many people is simply a series of small injustices, the routine humiliations of daily existence make perfect sense as the result of the machinations of nefarious, shadowy figures, resilient to modern forms of representation. Today, everyone is a detective.

Conclusion

As the first trial in the Sherry Ann Duncan case began, a letter dated June 3, 1988, stamped "Secret, Urgent" (*lap duan*), arrived at the provincial court at Samut Prakan, where the trial was taking place. The letter, from the commander of the Central Investigation Bureau, asked that the charges against the four men accused of murdering Sherry Ann be dropped. It stated that an investigation by the Crime Suppression Division initiated by the one of the police's first suspects, Winai Chaiphanit, had uncovered important evidence that showed that the four men on trial were not involved in the young woman's death. According to the evidence, the real perpetrators were still at large. The police requested that the court dismiss charges against the four men before any "injustice" was done.[1] The judge in the case consulted with the special prosecutor for Samut Prakan. The special prosecutor considered previous cases, Attorney General Office rules, and procedural codes including Ministry of Interior document number 31/9, dated October 28, 1954, which stated that the police do not have the authority to investigate cases after a trial begins.[2] The special prosecutor therefore pronounced the Crime Suppression Division's files inadmissible and recommended that the hearing continue. The information contained in the report, marked "Very Secret" (*lap mak*) in red at the top and bottom of the cover page, remained as designated, undisclosed to the broader criminal justice system.[3]

A piece of paper traveled across time, linking one historical context, a period of military rule in 1954, with another, a period of civilian government in Thailand in 1995, to help decide the fate of four men accused of a murder that occurred in 1986. Documents move from one location to another, from the past to the present, and the idea is that as they travel, so, too, do the concepts they contain. Certainly, as shown by the examples in this study of the way the police and other agents of the legal system in Thailand

(and elsewhere) use documents, these actors operate as if a document's meaning and function are stable. Yet, the history of artifacts such as fingerprints, maps, and photographs shows that the stability of meaning in documents is in many ways "constructed"; the ability of images or text on paper to operate across various times and places is an effect produced by rules and conventions that guide the ways in which people can make sense of and use them. Documents function in part because they are part of a larger, rule-bound economy of representations subject to the demands of markets, politics, and institutional needs. Images, whether photographs, maps, or diagrams, are a special part of this economy and, as the preceding chapters show, they have come to take on an increasingly prominent and influential role in the operation of the criminal justice system in Thailand. For these reasons, I have approached historical questions about policing and the law in terms of visual culture.

Other scholars and interested individuals have also studied the visual culture of Southeast Asia. When people first began working with images from the region, the focus was primarily on gathering, cataloging, and describing different types and aspects of visual arts, mostly from a limited set of images such as the religious paintings found in Buddhist temples. John Bowring's 1857 account of Siam and its people, for example, included a long, detailed description of the torture scenes he saw in monasteries in Bangkok.[4] There are also numerous studies of Buddhist iconography from throughout the region published in English and Thai from the early twentieth century onward. Accordingly, Justin McDaniel, who has also written on religious imagery, notes that early studies of visual culture by scholars of Southeast Asia tended to concentrate "primarily on the images produced by the elite and made before the twentieth century."[5]

However, more recent work on Southeast Asia, particularly in anthropology, has reflected the "visual turn" in the humanities and social sciences that took place around the 1990s, enlarging the field of scholarly inquiry beyond elite cultural production.[6] Karen Strassler studies personal photography in Yogyakarta to show how photographic images function to link nationalist discourses with those of the self.[7] Doreen Lee takes an analytical lens to the visual practices of young political protesters in 1998 in Jakarta to show how their creations, from graffiti to political posters, influenced the dramatic events at the end of Suharto's New Order.[8] James T. Siegel examines photographs of criminals from the Indonesian tabloid newspaper *Pos Kota* to shed light on what he calls the nationalization of death in the aftermath of the 1965 killings that preceded the removal of Sukarno from office.[9]

Alan Klima looks at photographs of dead bodies as a meditation tool in Thailand, and Rosalind Morris has written incisively on photographs taken of the "Black May" government crackdown on civilian protesters in Bangkok in 1992.[10] Studies like these indicate an increasing awareness and curiosity about visual culture, even if their focus has been primarily on photography.

They also show that as the range of visual artifacts has expanded to "nonart" objects, so, too, have the ways in which scholars treat images and their production. From a seemingly nonideological cataloging and describing of iconographic elements in paintings and sculpture, scholars have moved to more politically conscious critiques of images and their role in contemporary social, political, and economic life. Along these lines, one prominent approach has been to see images and image making as a form of power tied to ideological domination. Certainly, following Edward Said's influential work on colonial representations of the Middle East, connections between practices of representation and power have become clearer. As Said has so forcefully shown, the collection and dissemination of information about colonial subjects were techniques that underwrote the imperial project by shaping European ideas about the gender, race, and class of their subjects.[11] It makes sense that Bowring was interested in sensationalizing the paintings of Buddhist hells that he came across during his stay in Bangkok. For Bowring, colonial officials, and orientalists (often one and the same), these sorts of images were indicative of a premodern sensibility, superstitious and irrational, that could and should be corrected.[12]

As technologies of representation evolved and it became easier to capture images of colonial subjects, Europeans and Americans were able to quickly expand their project of documentation. Christopher Capozolla's essay on American photographer Dean Worcester's work in the Philippines during the early twentieth century shows how photographs taken on the islands reflected "Worcester's preoccupation with classifying the 'primitive' racial types that he encountered in the mountain highlands and distant islands. Despite his day-to-day interactions with urban Filipinos, Worcester took the overwhelming majority of his photographs in the most remote regions of the Philippines."[13] Christopher Pinney shows that a similar process took place in British India during the middle of the nineteenth century, when early anthropologists actively pursued an "aesthetic of primitivism" in which "local subjects were photographed without clothes and often in 'tribal' makeup and costume."[14] In a telling example, Pinney describes a case in which a British zoologist working in the Andaman Islands photographed one local woman "destitute of clothes, shaved, and greased with a mixture of olive-colored mud and fat," despite having written in his personal journal that he had seen his subject dressed neatly in white every day.[15] As with the crime scene photograph, naturalism in ethnographic portraits required human help: "Official photography was enveloped in a discourse of scienticity and indexicality, but in practice vigorous efforts were often made to construct a different reality for the camera."[16] Stereotypes of natives as savage, lazy, or indolent emerged in part from ostensibly objective portrayals like these.

At the same time, Europeans pictured themselves as heroic conquerors. Sarah Monks writes that images of colonial officers in India "depict male colonists as assured and commanding managers of their servant retinues and as figures of subtle exoticism, framed as 'other' in relation both to the indigenous Indians who tend them and to the Britons back 'home' to whom their images are addressed."[17] Along the same lines, Morris cites John Thomson, a "peripatetic photographer" who traveled in Asia during the late nineteenth and early twentieth centuries, as saying that Asians thought of him as a "dangerous geomancer" whose "camera was held to be a dark mysterious instrument."[18] A similar rhetorical track was followed earlier in India, where Europeans simply assumed that their photographic equipment would stupefy the "superstitious common people" and that "uneducated Natives" could scarcely "comprehend the meaning of ordinary photos."[19] The creation of "self" and "other" takes place visually, and the study of images in Thailand and Asia more broadly has been linked, rightly so, to colonial projects of domination.

Statements like those of Thomson and other nineteenth-century colonialists are not to be taken at face value, however, as Morris is quick to note. They were often part of a larger exercise in fantasy fulfillment on the part of colonialists. As with the Thai police, photography and other visual practices, including fingerprinting and mapping, were not necessarily feared, even if they were not completely understood. The new visual practices being introduced to Siam were actually embraced, in many cases uncritically so. Recall that despite warnings against accepting photographs of crime scenes as "first-level" evidence, the police in Thailand quickly came to do just that, using photographs as if they were transparent reflections of the past. King Mongkut, meanwhile, is famous for having developed an early fascination with photography, and he was keen on having his portrait taken. He shared these photos with European dignitaries, including Queen Victoria, creating perhaps for him a sense of equivalence or solidarity with other world leaders. Morris writes, "Mongkut seems to have recognized early on that photographic portraiture had a capacity to extend the domain of his influence."[20]

The use of photography was similarly widespread and popular in British India. Pinney gives this quote from a colonial officer: "Is there a ruling chief or a petty chief in India that has not got an outfit consisting of several cameras and lenses and all the rest of it? In fact, every tenth person you meet is a photographer, or at least carries a camera in his hand, if not with a strap over his shoulder."[21] In India, the first photography shops were patronized and run by Indians as well as Europeans, so even those outside elite circles were actively engaged in putting the new technology to use. A relatively diverse group of people throughout the colonies and semicolonies were therefore involved in modern image-making practices. Though European colonialists portrayed themselves as great leaders, inventors, and masters of technology, the situation was more complicated than they made it seem.

As with studies of visual culture in the context of colonialism, research that focuses on the development of modernity and capitalism in Asia shows images performing a similar defining role, setting out the ways in which individuals might see and situate themselves in the modern world. Cosmetics companies, for example, have long relied on images of women to sell their products. In the early twentieth century, marketing firms located in places like Ohio helped create a vision of female beauty, the "modern girl," that combined leisure and luxury. This vision of an ideal type then spread, through very material objects like advertisements in newspapers, to locales as distinct from each other as India, Japan, and Burma.[22] The process continues today, with cosmetics advertisements in Thailand featuring photographs of women with bright white skin, which are disseminated and internalized as the standard of modern beauty.[23] Local notions of gender, race, and class, as well as of the nation, were and continue to be transnational, visual phenomena, acting to define the local subject.

Of course, not all people come away from an image with an identical understanding of its meaning. People may interpret images differently, potentially undermining any disciplinary effect an image might have. Writing about the Thai mass media, a key producer of visual material, Annette Hamilton states, "Modern mass media have the potential to escape from the clutches of the state, while the readings of an audience may not conform to the intention of the broadcasters and image-managers."[24] So, though government officials and advertising professionals use and control the media, there is the constant danger of subversion, which then prompts the state to redouble its efforts to regulate the production and circulation of images. Pinney's work on India shows that by the late nineteenth century, the colonial government could no longer "control and categorize the production of images," particularly ones promoting anti-British nationalism. The sheer diversity and decentralized production of images in India meant that the colonial state never had complete control in the first place.[25] On one hand, material images are a disciplinary mechanism, and, on the other, they are tools for resistance; they can be a manifestation of a state's ideology, allied with global capitalism, or evidence of local agency in opposition to some institution of authority.

To analyze images along any of these lines, scholars generally employ an accepted theory or other general framework with which to extract, analyze, and reconfigure the meaning of an image or set of pictures in a way that makes sense to themselves and their target audiences. The vocabulary of discipline and discourse and Said's notion of orientalism are two examples of such frameworks. There are many others, including Marxist and psychoanalytical ones. Interpretive work of this nature has produced in many cases marvelous and, I believe, accurate insight into cultural phenomena across the globe. I also perform such work in this study. The danger, as Franco Moretti noted about literary criticism, is that in some cases, interpretive methods that are applied too literally add "nothing to what is already known about society. It merely allows for the usual: 'also in Mallarme one can discover the mechanism of alienation.' "[26] In other words, one may read particular images as a reflection of a state's disciplinary intentions simply because that is what is expected. As Pinney points out, images in academic studies often act simply as evidence of preexisting text-based narratives about the world, as mere illustrations. This, to paraphrase Carlo Ginzburg, is akin to reading into an image what one has already learned by other means, what one believes one knows and wants to show about a particular people or phenomenon.[27] However, pointing out the potential pitfalls of interpretation is not a cry for its end, as Susan Sontag polemically called for fifty years ago.[28]

For Sontag, the need to consider an image's form rather than interpret its meaning had to do with intellectual objections to contemporary art criticism, which she felt had become self-indulgent and overly complicated, obscuring any merits that a work of art might have. My motives are more practical and stem from the ways that agents in modern legal systems, and other realms of daily life, actually understand and use images. As the Thai police's visual practices show, images perform a range of functions. Sometimes they are indexical, sometimes they are symbolic, and sometimes they are both. And sometimes they act as aids for creating new knowledge. Simply put, images do more than represent. Reading them for meaning is just one way to approach them. For the most part, scholars studying visual culture in Southeast Asia understand and acknowledge this, though usually indirectly. In describing photos of the 1992 protests against military dictatorship in Bangkok and the 2004 killings at Krue Sae Mosque in southern Thailand, Morris writes that photographs "tend toward an iconicity that exceeds their status as photographs. That is, they seem not only to be endemically marked by the moment of their production, but to represent it in a distilled and abstracted form."[29] In other words, the photos she examines are both symbols (of, say, injustice or state authority) and indexes for a concrete, tangible thing (dead bodies). Strassler, meanwhile, writes that popular usage of the camera can create new "imaginative worlds" for the people that are photographed.[30] This conclusion is similar to Pinney's, who vividly shows the generative capacity of Indian studio photography. Earlier, Alan Sekula noted that because photos can be used instrumentally "to capture and illustrate the body/anatomy," they give rise to a "new typology, a generalized type."[31] Meanwhile, McDaniel argues that images at a temple in Bangkok have "agency," an idea that can be traced to a handful of writers, the most well known perhaps being the anthropologist of art Alfred Gell.[32] In all these cases, images are credited with specific qualities and outcomes—excess, novel imaginative worlds, new typologies, and agency—that transcend the images themselves. Acknowledging the generative aspect of images, I have tried in this book to put images to work as tools, just as their makers do. It is an earnest attempt to complement interpretive methods by attending to the material form of images.[33]

To do this, I have taken inspiration from research conducted in the field of science and technology studies. Before the visual turn of the 1990s, people interested in the practices of scientists and engineers had already been studying and writing about their visualization techniques. In an article from 1977, Eugene S. Ferguson states, "Pyramids, cathedrals, and rockets exist not because of geometry, theory of structures, or thermodynamics, but because they were first a picture—literally a vision—in the minds of those who built them."[34] These imaginings were then committed to paper: "Beginning with the Renaissance of the fifteenth century, a vast body of technical knowledge has been recorded and conveyed in the form of drawings and pictures. As soon as printed books superseded manuscript codices, large numbers of identical illustrations began to be reproduced. The circle of technologists whose minds could be engaged by a particular problem or stimulated by a particular idea was thus indefinitely enlarged."[35] Michael Lynch writes that "objects and relationships which were initially invisible become visible and palpable as a result of highly technical skills and complex instruments" and that visual representations constitute a "scientific object materially, make it sensible, analyzable, measurable, and examinable."[36] The first aspect to understand in generating new knowledge about the physical world, then, is that simply making things material and visible plays a key role in scientific discovery. The same holds true when examining the function of images in the legal system of modern Thailand.

Discovery is possible in science and in criminal investigation because once out in the world, visualizations become tools to be worked with. One way is, quite bluntly, as a crude instrument for the justification of the use of force. Thongchai Winichakul writes that the map of the nation acted as a tool used by the government in Bangkok to integrate the Lao region into the Siamese realm and that it became a "lethal instrument to concretize the projected desire [of government elites] on the earth's surface."[37] Local elites outside of Bangkok understood this threat instinctively, as indicated in their resistance to having their fiefdoms mapped, which they saw as a prelude to losing property.[38] Images are also tool-like because they allow people to move, manipulate, and work with them, and thus with ideas about the world, in order to arrive at a conclusion or generate knowledge that is not inherent in the image itself. The entire surface of an image, as a diagrammatic tool, becomes active and open to "creative misuse."[39] As I've shown, the police take pictures, draw diagrams, and make maps, tables, and lists. They then use these images by comparing them, marking them up, measuring elements within them, making various manipulations of what is depicted, and combining them with other images and texts (and now sound in videos). Sanga Kittikhajon writes in his police manual that the "usefulness of a crime scene map is that it allows you to consider things like how a perpetrator entered and left a crime scene or the particular behavior or actions of a criminal. It allows you to come up with an accurate picture of the case."[40] With reenactments, the police are able to test hypotheses in the process of creating images of the past. Maps and other visualizations are cognitive tools; detectives are able to think through various ideas about a crime by making and using visual representations. These representations could then travel through the legal system, from crime scene or police lab to courts of law and into the popular press. Once removed from the specific historical conditions of their production, documents become like a set of "reference books . . . a producer rather than just a product, comparable to the sorts of tables used by astrologers and other specialists to inform the 'man in the street' about the nature of the universe in which he finds himself."[41] The upshot is that conclusions made about the past cannot be predetermined, since visualizations shape the outcomes of criminal procedures in ways that are open-ended and sometimes difficult to predict. Visualizations are generative in the way that others have alluded to precisely because they function as tools. Focusing on visual practices and conceptualizing material images as such simply provides a way to talk about this creative capacity in a concrete manner.

For images to operate as tools, there needs to be a common understanding of what different symbols mean and how they work. This, over time, generally means that conventions are developed to guide the production, reception, and use of an image. Realism in visual representation, for example, has long been a goal for both the police and scientists. Lynch writes, "As the history of art shows, artistic realism includes an abundance of painterly techniques and stylistic conventions which do not simply fall in line along a continuum from 'non-realistic' to 'completely realistic.' Scientific realism is no less nuanced than artistic realism, and, in fact, scientists have often made use of artistic conventions and techniques for documenting observations and illustrating texts."[42] The same is true for visualizations that make their way into modern legal systems. The examples of crime scene photography in this study show that the realism of visualizations made by the police stems in part from a set of conventions that have evolved over the past century. So have standards for scale and symbolic representations on maps and diagrams. Casting a historical eye on form shows that what constitutes an image's facticity is historically specific; there is nothing necessarily formalist, in the derogatory sense, about the study of form.[43] As the posing of suspects for reenactments, the emphasis on the right color of ink to use on forms, the instructions for using proper camera angles, and the instances of misdocumentation indicate, the police are often quite conscious of the formalism of their work.

To say that things like legal facts are "constructed" and that the police often treat images formalistically is not to say that knowledge about past crimes is created out of thin air and therefore that real facts do not exist and cannot be judged. Instead, facts about crime are, as Lynch notes, the result of the interaction of tools and social environment, people and things.[44] The emphasis on representational practices and the materiality of facts points more to the social nature of knowledge than to the conclusion that nothing matters because everything is fabricated. That is not the point of my study, which describes how police investigators, judges, and laymen go about their work using visual tools and how these tools structure the way in which people can imagine the past and therefore shape legal outcomes. Thinking about and through documents in terms of their aesthetics is a way of approaching history that complements practices of interpretation; understanding that form is what underlies a material image's ability to bear meaning gives a more complete picture of how such images work in real life than either interpretation or formal analysis alone would be able to provide. It may be that this idea—that one might glean from a study of form a hint about the epistemological frameworks of a group of people or a time period—is as naive as any other method of looking at images (or texts), but the potential for learning about how the law functions, about how people know things visually, make it worth the effort.

Now that I have summed up why a historian might want to approach images in terms of aesthetics and as tools, I may draw from the preceding chapters a few conclusions about historical change in Thailand and about modern practices of knowledge production more broadly. Bruno Latour writes, "A new visual culture redefines both what it is to see, and what there is to see."[45] What I've described about the different ways the police investigated crime at the end of the nineteenth century and the beginning of the twentieth—their conceptions of what a clue is and how to capture and present it in a court of law—constitutes just such a change. The new visual culture of policing continued to develop through the middle of the twentieth century, resulting in practices like the reenactment and artifacts like the images used in the Sherry Ann trials. They continue to evolve even now, in part because the actors and things that make up the practice of criminal detection are neither static nor a closed set. Journalists, fiction writers, newspapers, and films are all part of a wider network of people, things, and ideas about crime, criminality, and detection. Police-produced maps, photographs, and diagrams of crime spread out into society through the mass media, just as the media helped influence what those visualizations looked like. The scientific revolution in policing that government officials hoped to initiate beginning in the late nineteenth century produced a very serious transformation in the way that Thais could represent the world.

This transformation, furthermore, was part of a transnational shift that took place in a number of other countries. Jennifer Mnookin's work on the use of visual materials in American and European courts shows how photographs and maps became common in legal proceedings for civil cases. As in Thailand, initial skepticism became acceptance and eventually visual evidence became just another unremarkable aspect of the law. Though photographs, and even maps and diagrams, did not exist previously as a single category of evidence, by the 1880s they had become widespread in all types of cases, spurring the development of a new "epistemological category," that of visual representations, which existed somewhere between "illustration and proof." With this category came a "culture of construction." That is, lawyers and others went out and "made" evidence. Building a case was no longer simply about locating witnesses or objects, but about creating a representation. Evidence was constructed as well as collected, causing the jury to function as "virtual witnesses."[46] In the United States and countries in Europe, a shift in how facts were represented in the law took place in the nineteenth and twentieth centuries, and this led to qualitative changes in the way the police and the public understood crime and the way modern justice systems now operate. The changes that took place in Thailand were part of an international phenomenon.

It has become almost axiomatic that it is through power that one knows and that knowing is a form of power over those people and things that become the objects of knowing. In the messy cities and sparsely settled countryside of Siam, information took form in and moved through informal networks that were often inaccessible to the mandarins of Bangkok. Systems used to generate and organize that information, that is, "knowledge" (and thus power), were in the hands of a diffuse group of players. The ability of the central government, or the state (itself a system of representations), to know and thus discipline had not yet been established across the geo-body of Siam, in part because the state and the geo-body had not yet created themselves. From an examination of the development of the police, it is clear that the central government did in fact see knowledge, or at least information, as a critical aspect of society worth controlling as part of its bid to consolidate authority over the kingdom. The government's response to the problem of multiple and diffuse networks of knowledge production and nonstandard forms of information took shape as an attempt to establish a state surveillance apparatus, one inspired by the detective agencies of England, France, and the United States. In its attempts to know and detect, however, the object of surveillance created was not a pliant, auto-submissive, modern subject. Instead, government reforms in policing and administrative practices brought into being a paper-based, mechanically reproduced, and commercially circulated world in which new methods of modern detection could be employed. The state and its detectives, along with the mass media, called forth a new space through their crime scene maps, photographs, statistics, and other texts.

This world, rather than being inhabited by rational, modern beings methodically deriving the truth from material clues, is one characterized by men and women whose imaginations are riddled with paranoia, haunted by rumor, driven by gossip, and organized by conspiracy theories. Today, conflicts of all sorts seem explained less easily by "rational" thought than by recourse to theories that a self-identified modern person might deem absurd. The folk epistemologies that the city and the archive were meant to erase or control did not disappear. Instead, the new police and media practices privileged some methods of generating knowledge over others, made some forms of information acceptable in courts of law, turned others into facts, and made still others into fictions. Recourse to whispering ghosts (*phi krasip*) that tell their caretakers (*phu liang phi*) the location of stolen goods or reveal the identities of culprits has declined in favor of scientific investigation practices such as autopsies and chemical analyses. In other instances, people have shown a tendency to rely *more* on explanations involving what might be considered supernatural beings, objects, and forces.[47] Astrological charts, along with other long-standing diagrams used for divination and prognostication, remain popular methods of generating information about the unknown that people use alongside the more recent innovations. So although this book has been about the development of modern forms of knowledge in the field of criminal detection, it should not be read as a tale of how science or some other branch of Western rationality has come to supplant local epistemologies, even if that may have been in many instances the intention of royals, their foreign advisers, and other elites. In detective training manuals, early police reformers like Eric St. John Lawson and Luang Phisitwithayakan stressed that it was people, not magic, working with their tools and smarts that solved crime. Yet the country's most famous policeman, Khun Phantharakratchadet (1898–2006), often relied on magical talismans.[48] In today's Thailand, men and women, elites and commoners, politicians and private-sector professionals continue to conceptualize their actions in terms of conspiratorial narratives that connect various worlds past, present, future, human, and nonhuman. The scientific revolution in policing that was hoped for in the 1920s created a virtual world on paper through which state power is exercised as much as it has effected change in how people conceptualize the natural world.

In 1977, Jack Goody published *Domestication of the Savage Mind*. In it, he argued, in part, that there is no physical or inherent biological difference between a modern and a traditional human being, between hot and cold cultures, between savage and domesticated minds: "We speak in terms of primitive and advanced, almost as if human minds themselves differed in their structure like machines of an earlier and later design."[49] He says instead that differences do exist between societies and cultures, but these are material and in the system of communications more than in the structure of the mind.[50] In other words, differences between societies and between groups within societies reside in part with the tools they have for communicating. Speech on paper, or another surface, allows people to edit, rearrange, and play with their ideas and thus have an impact on rationality, on how one makes sense of the world. In many ways, then, what the preceding chapters have shown parallels Goody's argument. There are differences between how Thais thought about crime and policing before 1892 and after 1932 and between how Thais and Europeans think about these things still today. These dissimilarities, however, do not reside in one's "cultural essence" so much as in the tools and practices of communication, of forms, that materialize different objects and different possibilities for reality. The images that the police and others generate to represent reality do more than that. They create the past and thus shape the possibilities for what lies ahead. People make images. These images then make the world.

Epilogue

In the years following the second trial in the murder of Sherry Ann Duncan, the government passed a series of legal reforms as part of the promulgation of a new constitution (the 1997 version) that addressed specific concerns raised by the case. Article 237, for example, required that the police bring a suspect to trial within forty-eight hours of arrest and limited their power to conduct warrantless searches. In the Sherry Ann case, the four defendants were arrested and then held for weeks as the police conducted their investigation. Article 246 stipulated that suspects have the right to receive compensation for the time during which they were detained if found innocent. This was known as the Sherry Ann article, owing to the tragic events that befell the four men while incarcerated. After the coup of 2006 that removed Thaksin Shinawatra from power, a new law of the land was issued—the 2007 Constitution of Thailand. This constitution, the country's seventeenth (including charters), was much more circumspect in its detailing of rights in criminal cases. In it, a few of the basic tenets introduced after the Sherry Ann case were retained, including the right to an "uncomplicated" and efficient trial (part 4, section 40 of the 2007 constitution) and the principle that the accused shall not, before being convicted of any crime, be treated as a "convict" (part 4, section 9). Other rights retained, albeit in general terms only, include the right to be treated properly during the entire judicial process, the right to not have to testify against oneself, and the right to the protection and assistance of the state. Compensation for essential expenditures of defendants is also provided for in cases where the accused is not found guilty. In both instances, 1997 and 2007, reforms were procedural, altering (theoretically, anyway) the practices of actors in the criminal justice system. The reenactment was left untouched, and it remains to this day a key part of the Thai legal, cultural, and social landscape.

NOTES

INTRODUCTION

1. This account is assembled from information in trial documents from *Khadi choeri aen dankhaen fong kao* [The case of Sherry Ann Duncan, first trial] and *Khadi choeri aen dankhaen fong mai* [The case of Sherry Ann Duncan, second trial] at the Library and Museum of the Attorney General's Office of Thailand (LMAG), news reports from *Thai rat* [Thai state] and *Deli nio* [Daily news], and the following secondary sources: Criminal Law Institute, *Raingan kan sewana thang wichakan rueang khadi choeri-aen . . . krabuan kan yuttitham ja khum khrong sitthi seriphap khong phu borisut dai yangrai* [Report from seminar on the case of Sherry Ann . . . How will the justice system protect the rights and freedoms of the innocent?] (Bangkok: Office of the Attorney General, 1996); Jarun Wathanasin, *Choeri-aen* [Sherry Ann] (Bangkok: Nation Multimedia Group, 2001); and Rut Manthira, *Jap phae buchayan khayao wongkan yuttitham sathuean wai* [Arresting a scapegoat, shaking up the circles of justice] (Bangkok: Namfon, 1996). The police's photographs of the reenactment of Pramoen's testimony are located in the case files for the first and second trials. I was granted permission to read through the files but was not allowed to publish the photographs mentioned here.
2. The term "epistemological history" is from Lorraine Daston, who defines it as a "history of the categories that structure our thought, pattern our arguments and proofs, and certify our standards for explanation" that attempts to "discover the preconditions for making a thing or idea possible." Lorraine Daston, "Historical Epistemology," in *Questions of Evidence: Proof, Practice, and Persuasion across the Disciplines,* ed. James Chandler, Arnold Davidson, and Harry Harootunian (Chicago: University of Chicago Press, 1994), 282.
3. Rosalind Morris, "Photography and the Power of Images in the History of Power," in *Photographies East: The Camera and Its Histories in East and Southeast Asia,* ed. Rosalind Morris (Durham, NC: Duke University Press, 2009), 140.
4. Jennifer Mnookin, "The Image of Truth: Photographic Evidence and the Power of Analogy," *Yale Journal of Law and the Humanities* 10 (1998): 2–3.
5. Lorraine Daston and Peter Galison, "The Image of Objectivity," *Representations* 40 (Autumn 1992): 84, 98.
6. Frederik Stjernfelt, *Diagrammatology: An Investigation on the Borderlines of Phenomenology, Ontology, and Semiotics* (Dordrecht, Netherlands: Springer, 2007), ix.

7. Charles Peirce, quoted in ibid., 90.
8. Ibid., 105.
9. A complete, updated, and annotated version of King Vajiravudh's detective stories can be found in Ramajit [King Vajiravudh], *Prapruethikan khong nai thong-in rathanet* [The adventures of Thong-in Rathanet] (Bangkok: Samoson Nangsue Rahatsakhadi, 2006). The stories originally appeared in Vajiravudh's journal *Thawi panya* between 1904 and 1905 and were published under the pen name Nai Kaeo and Nai Khwan. They have been reprinted several times since and are collectively known as "Nithan Thong-in" (Tales of Thong-in), after their lead character and detective, Nai Thong-in (Mr. Thong-in).
10. Alfred Gell, *Art and Agency: An Anthropological Theory* (Oxford: Oxford University Press, 1999). Also see his article, "Vogel's Net: Traps as Artworks and Artworks as Traps," *Journal of Material Culture* 1 (1996): 15–38.
11. J. C. Eade, *The Calendrical Systems of Mainland Southeast Asia* (Leiden, Netherlands: E. J. Brill, 1995), 13.

CHAPTER 1: KINGDOM OF CRIME

Passages of this chapter are extracted from Samson Lim, "Detective Fiction, the Police, and Secrecy in Early Twentieth Century Siam," *Southeast Asia Research* 20, no. 1 (2012): 83–102, copyright © SOAS 2012. Reproduced by permission of IP Publishing Ltd.

1. *Khadi khwam 7516/2529 dam—1712/2533 daeng* [Case number 7516/2529 black—1712/2533 red], October 22, 1986, in *Khadi choeri aen dankhaen fong kao* [The case of Sherry Ann Duncan, first trial], Library and Museum of the Attorney General's Office of Thailand (LMAG).
2. "Nakrian sao hai tua taeksi luek lap pha choet khana rongrian loek klap ban" [Schoolgirl disappears: Mysterious taxi takes her away after school], *Thai rat,* July 27, 1986, front page. Note that the late edition of Thai newspapers is published with the next day's date. The late edition of *Thai rat* dated July 27, 1986, actually came out on the afternoon of July 26, 1986.
3. Testimony of Winai Chaiphanit to police, given July 31, 1986, in *Khadi choeri aen dankhaen fong kao,* LMAG.
4. The Provincial Gendarmerie was established in 1897.
5. From a compilation of accounts by foreigners in Siam during the late nineteenth century in Larry Sternstein, "Krungthep at One Hundred: Scape and Grid," *Journal of the Siam Society* 67, no. 2 (July 1979): 2.
6. Ibid., 5–6.
7. Ibid., 6.

8. NA R6 Y 13/19, *Krasuang yuttitham, san tang jangwat, khadi len kan phanan thi wat* [Sixth Reign, Ministry of Justice, provincial courts, case of gambling in a *wat*], 1911.
9. Andrew Freeman, *A Journalist in Siam* (Bangkok: White Lotus, 2007), 48.
10. Carl Bock, *Temples and Elephants: The Narrative of a Journey of Exploration through Upper Siam and Lao* (Bangkok: White Orchid Press, 1985), 82.
11. Ibid., 50.
12. Frederick Arthur Neale, *Narrative of a Residence in Siam* (Bangkok: White Lotus, 1996), 26–27.
13. Sternstein, "Krungthep," 3.
14. Adolf Bastian, *A Journey in Siam,* trans. Walter E. J. Tips (Bangkok: White Lotus, 2005), 50. Many people at the time lived in houses located along the rivers or canals that crisscrossed the city.
15. Rachel Harrison, among others, has described the early twentieth century in Siam as its "Victorian period" because of the influence of Victorian-era English culture on the Siamese elite. Rachel Harrison, "The Allure of Ambiguity: The 'West' and the Making of Thai Identities," in *The Ambiguous Allure of the West: Traces of the Colonial in Thailand,* ed. Rachel Harrison (Hong Kong: Hong Kong University Press, 2010), 1–36.
16. Bastian, *A Journey,* 51–52.
17. Larry Sternstein, "Bangkok at the Turn of the Century: Mongut and Chulalongkorn Entertain the West," *Journal of Siam Society* 54, no. 1 (1966): 64.
18. Porphant Ouyyanont, "Physical and Economic Change in Bangkok, 1851–1925," *Southeast Asian Studies* 36, no. 4 (March 1999): 443, 448–449.
19. Ibid., 465.
20. Ibid., 460.
21. Sternstein, "Bangkok," 69–70.
22. Executive Committee of the Eighth Congress of the Far Eastern Association of Tropical Medicine, *Siam in 1930: General and Medical Features* (Bangkok: White Lotus, 2000), 17. Eleven baht equaled about one English pound at the time of the congress in 1930. Foreigners typically referred to the baht as "tical" in early twentieth-century documents.
23. Porphant, "Physical Change," 444.
24. Ibid., 458.
25. Ibid.
26. Ibid.
27. G. William Skinner, *Chinese Society in Thailand: An Analytical History* (Ithaca, NY: Cornell University Press, 1957), 74.
28. Porphant, "Physical Change," 445.
29. Skinner, *Chinese Society,* 61 (table 2).
30. Constance Wilson, "Bangkok in 1883: An Economic and Social Profile," *Journal of Siam Society* 77, no. 2 (1989): 54.

31. This term comes up in reports about the late nineteenth and early twentieth centuries written later, such as those about famous historical bandits in newspapers like *Phim thai* from the 1950s.
32. "Gang Robbery at Paklat," *Bangkok Times,* May 19, 1902, from David Bruce Johnston, "Rural Society and the Rice Economy in Thailand, 1880–1930" (PhD dissertation, Yale University, 1977), 178.
33. Johnston, "Rural Society," 178.
34. Ibid., 179.
35. Cecil H. Forty, "Cremation Volume for Police Lieutenant Colonel C. H. Forty" (Bangkok, 1967), 32.
36. Ibid., 6.
37. I translate *krasuang nakhonban* as "Ministry of Local Government," following the name they used on their letterhead. Other studies have translated the name as "Ministry of the Capital" because its function was to administer Bangkok, not the provinces.
38. NA R6 N 20.5/36, *Krasuang nakhonban, nangsuephim, khao tang jangwat, khao jak phrapradaeng* [Sixth Reign, Ministry of Local Government, newspapers, provincial news, news from Phrapradaeng].
39. Ibid.
40. Jao Phraya Surasakmontri, *Prawat khong jom phon jao phraya surasakmontri* [The biography of Jao Phraya Surasakmontri] (Bangkok: Khrusapha, 1951), 164.
41. Ibid., 170.
42. "Ayutthia," *Bangkok Times,* December 14, 1892, in Johnston, "Rural Society," 169. *Monthon* is the name for the geographical unit of administration established in 1892. It is sometimes translated as "circle." Within these circles were *jangwat,* the term now translated as "province."
43. NA R6 N 20.5/5, *Krasuang nakhonban, nangsuephim, khao tang jangwat, khao jak nakhon nayok* [Sixth Reign, Ministry of Local Government, newspapers, provincial news, news from Nakhon Nayok].
44. Ibid.
45. Unless otherwise noted, the examples in the rest of this paragraph are all from NA R6 N 20.5/15, *Krasuang nakhonban, nangsuephim, khao tang jangwat, khao jak sawankhalok, phitsanulok monthon* [Sixth Reign, Ministry of Local Government, newspapers, provincial news, news from Sawankhalok, Phitsanulok Circle].
46. *Jare* (pronounced ja-ray) were officers of the Provincial Police's "internal investigation division" (*jare tamruat*) set up in 1914 (disbanded in 1923) to monitor the performance of the Provincial Gendarmerie. Most of the inspectors were Danish.
47. NA R6 N 4.1/91, *Krasuang nakhonban, krom tamruat phranakhonban lae phuthon, ratchakan thua pai, raingan wa duai jon phu rai* [Sixth Reign, Minis-

try of Local Government, Metropolitan and Provincial Police, general duties, report on banditry by Police Inspector Jarmer], October 25, 1916.

48. Unless otherwise noted, the examples in this paragraph are all from NA R6 N 20.5/9, *Krasuang nakhonban, nangsuephim, khao tang jangwat, khao jak chonburi* [Sixth Reign, Ministry of Local Government, newspapers, provincial news, news from Chonburi].

49. NA R6 N 20.5/7 *Krasuang nakhonban, nangsuephim, khao tang jangwat, khao jak nakhon ratchasima* [Sixth Reign, Ministry of Local Government, newspapers, provincial news, news from Nakhon Ratchasima].

50. NA R6 N 4.5/2, *Krasuang nakhonban, krom tamruat phranakhonban lae phuthon (jare krom tamruat), nai phan tamruat aek jao ratchabut jare raingan wa nai boriwaen jangwat lampang mi jon phu rai chuk chum thawi mak khuen kho phoem nai sip phon tamruat lae kho yup ngoen bia liang thi tat ok nan on ma phua jai samrap phoem khon khuen hai phiang pho kae kan raksa thong thi to pai* [Sixth Reign, Ministry of Local Government, Metropolitan and Provincial Police (inspector of police), Inspector Jao Ratchabut reports an increase in the number of bandits in Lampang and requests for an increase in the number of officers and funds to pay for maintenance of area], 1916. Mom Jao Khamrop is the uncle of well-known writer and newspaper publisher Kukrit Pramot.

51. NA R6 N 20.5/3, *Krasuang nakhonban, nangsuephim, khao tang jangwat, khao jak krung kao* [Sixth Reign, Ministry of Local Government, newspapers, provincial news, news from Krung Kao (Ayutthaya)].

52. NA R6 N 20.5/17, *Krasuang nakhonban, nangsuephim, khao tang nangwat, khao jak lopburi* [Sixth Reign, Ministry of Local Government, newspapers, provincial news, news from Lopburi].

53. Reginald Le May, *An Asian Arcady: The Land and Peoples of Northern Siam* (Bangkok: White Lotus, 1999), 93.

54. Ibid., 91.

55. Ibid., 91–92.

56. "Ayutthia," *Bangkok Times,* December 14, 1892, in Johnston, "Rural Society," 171.

57. This suggests that the government in Bangkok during the early days of the reform period relied in part on intelligence gathered through the emerging popular press. While the Bangkok government did begin to send government officials out to administer the provinces in the 1890s, the press often seemed to have more up-to-date information about local conditions.

58. "How to Deal with Dacoits," *Bangkok Times,* January 14, 1907, in Johnston, "Rural Society," 151.

59. NA R6 N 20.5/5.

60. NA R6 N 20.5/4, *Krasuang nakhonban, nangsuephim, khao tang jangwat, khao jak ratchaburi* [Sixth Reign, Ministry of Local Government, newspapers, provincial news, news from Ratchaburi].

61. NA R6 N 4.2/21, *Krasuang nakhonban, krom tamruat phranakhonban lae phuthon, prakat lae phorobo, khwam hen rueang rabiap kan tamruat phuthon 2460–2464* [Sixth Reign, Ministry of Local Government, Metropolitan and Provincial Police, announcements and royal decrees, opinion on the system of Provincial Police, 1917–1921], 1918.
62. Letter from Police Major Sisao, Inspector for Region Four, Nongkhai, to Police Major Phraya Khathathonabodi Siratchaban Mueang, Chief Inspector, in NA R6 N 4.5 ก/4, *Krasuang nakhonban, krom tamruat phranakhonban lae phuthon (jare tamruat), truat ratchakan* [Sixth Reign, Ministry of Local Government, Department of the Metropolitan Police and the Provincial Gendarmerie (inspector of police), inspecting police work, not enough police in Nakhon Phanom, Monthon Udon], June 30, 1916.
63. NA R6 N 20.5/15.
64. Ibid.
65. Krom Phraya Damrong Rajanubhab, "Rueang sonthana kap phu rai plon" [Interview with a bandit], in cremation volume for Phra Tamruat Tri Phraya Aphichitchanyut (given name Jaroen Sawettanan) (Bangkok: Sophonphiphatthanakon, 1925), 4. The translation of *nakleng* is not a straightforward task, as the term has multiple connotations that have changed over time. The George Bradley McFarland *Thai-English Dictionary* (Stanford, 1944) defines *nakleng* variously as "a rogue; a rascal; a ruffian, a dishonest and unprincipled person; a knave, a scamp, a true sport" (Johnston, "Rural Society," 139), but others have given it, and masculinity in Thai society more broadly, a more nuanced look. See, for example, Pattana Kitiarsa, "Lives of Hunting Dogs: 'Muai Thai' and the Politics of Thai Masculinities," *South East Asia Research* 13, no.1 (March 2005): 57–90, and Craig J. Reynolds, "Rural Male Leadership, Religion and the Environment in Thailand's Mid-South, 1920s–1960s," *Journal of Southeast Asian Studies* 42, no. 1 (2011): 39–57.
66. Damrong, "Interview with a Bandit," 4.
67. Phirasak Chaidaisuk, *Chat sua wai lai* [Once a tiger, always a tiger], (Bangkok: Matichon Press, 2008), 117. Phirasak provides a good discussion on the relationship between bandits and local officials during the Fifth Reign in which he describes the complicated arrangements of power and patronage at the local level and resistance to the centralizing state in Bangkok.
68. Jao Phraya Surasakmontri, *Biography*, 176.
69. NA R6 N 20.5/9.
70. "The Treaty of Friendship and Commerce between the Kingdom of Siam and the British Empire," signed April 18, 1855. For a summary of the treaty's provisions, see James Ingram, *Economic Change in Thailand, 1850–1970* (Palo Alto, CA: Stanford University Press, 1971), 34–35.
71. Extraterritoriality ended gradually with the signing of a revised bilateral treaty with the United States in 1920. Between 1920 and 1926, revised treaties with

other countries followed, so that by the end of that decade, extraterritoriality had technically been eliminated.

72. Forty, "Cremation Volume," 30. The Bow Street Runners are the famous forerunners to the London Metropolitan Police (established in 1829). The Runners operated in the mid-eighteenth and early nineteenth centuries, helping magistrates at the Bow Street magistrates' court to serve warrants and arrest criminals.
73. Ibid., 30.
74. Ibid., 55.
75. Ibid., 56.
76. Sampheng is in the area thought of as the Chinese district of the city, but, as mentioned earlier, Constance Wilson's analysis of the 1883 Postal Census for Bangkok shows that the Chinese were spread throughout the capital. Wilson, "Bangkok in 1883."
77. Indeed, as Tamara Loos shows in *Subject Siam: Family, Law, and Colonial Modernity in Thailand* (Ithaca, NY: Cornell University Press, 2006), the Siamese government adopted strategies from European colonial powers to gain control over areas in the south.
78. Forty, "Cremation Volume," 31.
79. Rotsukhon Jaratsi, "Botbat khong kharatchakan chao tang prathet nai krom tamruat nai samai somburananasithirat" [The role of foreign civil servants in the police department under the absolute monarchy] (master's thesis, Chulalongkorn University, Bangkok, 1977), 34.
80. See *Wachirayan* 15 (1896): 1526–1550; *Wachirayan* 16 (1896): 1608–1641; *Wachirayan* 17 (1896): 1733–1752; and *Wachirayan* 18 (1896): 1824–1837.
81. A similar situation existed with respect to the police in other locations in Asia. Fredrick Wakeman shows in *Policing Shanghai, 1927–1937* (Berkeley: University of California Press, 1996), for example, that the police were seen as a means of illustrating to foreign governments that the Chinese could take care of their own security and be modern at the same time.
82. Prior to the reform period, government agencies were organized into "right" and "left" groups, each with similar powers, but with different areas of jurisdiction in the kingdom.
83. Rotsukhon, "The Role of Foreign Civil Servants," 48–49.
84. NA R7 M 11/1, *Krasuang mahathai, plian nam krom lae nam tamnaeng athibodi krom tamruat phranakhonban lae tamruat phuthon* [Seventh Reign, Ministry of Interior, Provincial, Metropolitan, and Investigative Police, changing the head of the department and head of the Metropolitan and Provincial Police], 1926.
85. "Kotmai polit 53 kho sueng ja raksa nathi nai phranakhon nok phranakhon" [Fifty-three rules for the police to uphold in and outside Phranakhon], in Sathian Lailak, ed., *Prachum kotmai prajam sok lem 9* [Collected laws, volume 9] (Bangkok: Daily Mail, 1876), 92–96.

86. Eric St. John Lawson, "Police and Provincial Gendarmerie," in *Twentieth Century Impressions of Siam: Its History, People, Commerce, Industries, and Resources,* ed. Arnold Wright and Oliver T. Breakspear (Bangkok: White Lotus, 1994), 107.
87. Ibid.
88. In 1893, French and Siamese forces engaged in a gun battle at the mouth of the Chao Phraya River. The Siamese lost the fight and were forced to give up their claims to sovereignty over areas along the eastern bank of the Mekong River.
89. Wiwana Thewachalaangkun, "Naiyobai khong rat kap kan tamruat phuthon phoso 2440–2465" [Government policy and the gendarmerie, 1897–1922] (master's thesis, Silapakon University, Bangkok, 1984), 17–19.
90. The British were the French's chief colonial rivals in mainland Southeast Asia in the early twentieth century.
91. Wiwana, "Gendarmerie," 53.
92. Population estimate from http://www.populstat.info/Asia/thailand.htm.
93. Wiwana, "Gendarmerie," 61–62.
94. Lawson, "Police," 111.
95. Wiwana, "Gendarmerie," 64–65, 69.
96. Letter from Luang Phraya Phetinthara to Jao Phraya Yommarat in NA R6 N 4.5/6, *Krasuang nakhonban* (*jare krom tamruat*), *rong rian nai tamruat* [Sixth Reign, Ministry of Local Government, metropolitan and provincial (police inspector of police), police academy], September 6, 1916.
97. Announcement in *Royal Gazette,* no. 32, October 17, 1915, 314, "Royal Announcement on the Consolidation of the Provincial Gendarmerie and the Metropolitan Constabulary." The name of the department was changed to *krom tamruat* (or simply "police department") after 1932. Yommarat was the minister of local government from 1908 to 1922.
98. NA R7 M 11/1.
99. Ministry of Interior document number 349/2480, dated February 3, 1938, in "Prawat kiao kap kan sop suan khadi aya khong phanakngan sop suan fai pokkhrong nai phumiphak" [History related to investigating criminal cases by civilian investigators in the provinces], in *Krom kan pokkhrong* [Civil administration] (Bangkok: Krommakan Pokkhrong, 1984), 4–5. This power was lost and regained several times afterward.
100. The *kong mon* consisted of Mon people, hence its name. Its primary purpose was to monitor the activities of the Burmese army in the border regions between the two countries. The Mon, whose population was relatively large in border areas with Burma, were enlisted specifically because they could travel to and from Burma and tap into existing networks of information there without attracting undue attention from the British Burmese authorities. See Thawisak Suphasa, "Kan jatkan lae botbat khong tamruat nai krungthep ratchasamai phrabat somdet phrajulajomklao jao yu hua" [The establishment

and role of the police in Bangkok during the reign of King Chulalongkorn] (master's thesis, Srinakharinwirot University, Bangkok, 1978), 26. The *kong mon* was eventually disbanded under King Chulalongkorn because, by the 1880s, the threat of war with the Burmese had become low. In addition, the costs of keeping the unit operational became too high. Mon informers were transferred to regular police posts in the Metropolitan Constabulary after 1892. The use of a particular ethnic group, such as the Cham or Karen, as informers began as early as the reign of King Narai (r. 1656–1688), but these, like the use of the Mon, were to gain intelligence about foreign governments rather than about Siamese subjects (see NA R5–6 PL, *Banchi samruat ekkasan yep lem chut samnao phraratchahatlekha, muat thi 1 trawen* [Collected royal correspondences from the Fifth and Sixth Reigns, section 1, the constabulary], 1892, 20–21).

101. NA R5 N 8.1/1, *Krasuang nakhonban, krom kong trawen, ratchakan thua pai, khwam hen thi ja jatkan krom kong trawen* [Sixth Reign, Ministry of Local Government, Metropolitan Constabulary, general duties, opinion regarding the establishment of a police department], 1892.

102. NA R5 N 8.1/47, *Krasuang nakhonban, krom kong trawen ratchakan thua pai, rueang senabodi mi khamsang thueng phraya inthara phra thephaphon luang wisetthani luang wiphatpranun wa kong raksa tai taeng khon ok sotnaem jap phu rai tha amphoe kamnan hen nangsue samkhan khue mi phranam senabodi lae tra sing laeo ko hai amphoe kamnan pen thura chuai jap phu rai duai* [Fifth Reign, Ministry of Local Government, Metropolitan Constabulary, general duties, correspondence from minister of local government to Phraya Inthara, Phra Thephaphon, Luang Wisetthani, and Luang Wiphatpranun regarding the sending out of secret investigators to catch criminals: if a local official is presented a document with an official seal, that local official should assist in the arrest of criminals], 1892.

103. NA R5 N 8.2ก/6, *Krasuang nakhonban, krom kong trawen, kharatchakan chao tang prathet, phra ong jao chanthatchuthathan kho hai mom chao mahamad mura pen kong trawen* [Fifth Reign, Ministry of Local Government, Metropolitan Constabulary, foreign nationals in government service, Phra Ong Jao Chanthatchuthathan requesting Mom Jao Mohammed Mura be allowed to serve in the constabulary], 1899.

104. Thawisak, "The Establishment of the Police in Bangkok," 267.

105. Forty, "Cremation Volume," 34.

106. NA R5 N 102, Fifth Reign, Ministry of Local Government, report on the police administration of Bangkok town, northern and southern suburbs and railway district, 1903 [in English], 19.

107. Tej Bunnag, "The Provincial Administration of Siam from 1892 to 1915: A Study of the Creation, the Growth, the Achievements, and the Implications for Modern Siam, of the Ministry of the Interior under Prince Damrong Rachanuphap" (PhD dissertation, Oxford University, 1968), 224.

108. "Raingan prachum thesaphiban roso 126" [Report for provincial administration meeting, 1907], in *Thesaphiban* [Provincial administration journal] 4, no. 22 (1908): 143.
109. The change in the terms used for the detective police, from *kong sot naem* to *krom nak suep,* may also indicate the change in ideas about what it was the unit was supposed to do. *Sot naem* means to spy or infiltrate and gather information, whereas *nak suep* refers to the more modern figure of the private detective who relies on logic and evidence.
110. NA R6 N 4.1/2, *Krasuang nakhonban, krom tamruat phranakhonban lae phuthon, ratchakan thua pai, khwam hen phraya athikonprakat lae nai losan thiprueksa nai rueang tamruat lap* [Sixth Reign, Ministry of Local Government, Metropolitan and Provincial Police, general duties, opinion of Phraya Athikonprakat and general adviser Mr. Lawson on the secret police], 1918.
111. NA R7 M 11/5 *Krasuang mahathai, krom tamruat phuthon nakhonban phuban, tang tamruat phuthon klang* [Seventh Reign, Provincial Gendarmerie, Metropolitan Police, and detective police, establishing a central investigation division], 1928.
112. Ibid.

CHAPTER 2: FACTS ABOUT CRIME

This chapter is derived, in part, from Samson Lim, "The Case of Volunteer 8: Proof, Violence, and History in Thai Society," *Critical Asian Studies* 43, no. 3 (2011): 399–420, http://www.tandfonline.com/doi/abs/10.1080/14672715.2011.597333.

1. Pridi Phanomyong, *Pathakatha rueang panha kiao kae kan long atchaya phu kratham phit kotmai* [Problems related to punishing people who break the law], lecture given on August 10, 1928, published in festschrift for Samunwinathoramontri Na Susanluang at Wat Thepsirinarat, 1931, 119.
2. The ideas of a natural-born criminal and a criminal type became popular in the late nineteenth century. These were notions popularized by criminologists of the Italian School for Positivist Criminology and its founder, Cesare Lombroso. Lombroso and his followers believed that criminals were born as such and that a person's physical features were signs of this innate criminality. On this topic, he wrote voluminously. Many of his ideas on criminality are summarized in Cesare Lombroso, *Criminal Man: According to the Classification of Cesare Lombroso* (New York: Knickerbocker Press, 1911). Also influential in advancing the idea that physical appearance could be used for policing purposes was Alphonse Bertillon, inventor of Bertillonage, a system of identification of criminals based on the measurement of physical features. The efforts of Lombroso and Bertillon were part of a larger

movement at the time to rationalize, or make scientific, the practice of criminal investigation.

3. Luang Bannasanprasit (given name Sithi Rojanawiphat), *Lak lae withikan suep suan tai suan khadi aya* [Rules and techniques for investigating criminal cases] (Bangkok: Aksonniti, 1929), 19–22. After World War II, however, there is evidence that some began to think otherwise. Sanga Kittikhajon, an officer in the police science section in the 1950s, wrote, for example, that one of the causes of crime was genetics. He cited research by Gregor Mendel on inheritance and concluded that people with relatives that are criminals are more likely to be born criminals. Sanga then proposed three solutions for this problem: sterilization, special education, and penal colonies that would separate born criminals from the rest of society. See Sanga Kittikhajon, *Withayakan tamruat kiao kap kan suep suan* [Police methods related to investigation] (Bangkok: Prasoetakson, 1953), 3.
4. Data from NA R6 N 4.1/125, *Krasuang nakhonban, krom tamruat phranakhonban lae phuthon, ratchakan thua pai, raingan wa duai kan prap jon phu rai* [Sixth Reign, Ministry of Local Government, Metropolitan and Provincial Police, general duties, report on efforts against bandits], June 1917. Of course, having a high conviction rate doesn't necessarily mean the police and the justice system are particularly efficient. It could simply be that the system is stacked against the accused.
5. NA R6 N 4.1/164, *Krasuang nakhonban, krom tamruat phranakhonban lae phuthon, ratchakan thua pai* [Sixth Reign, Ministry of Local Government, Metropolitan and Provincial Police, general duties], a report on the work of the police and the gendarmerie and on criminal statistics of Siam for 1918 by Police Lieutenant General Lawson (in English), 1919.
6. NA R6 N 4.5ก/11, *Krasuang nakhonban, krom tamruat phranakhonban lae phuthon (jare tamruat), truat ratchakan, nai phan tamruat tho troloe jare prajam monthon nakhon sawan wa dai truat kan tamruat nai jangwat kamphaengphet jangwat tak lae amphoe mae sot mi jon phu rai mak khuen thang jangwat* [Sixth Reign, Ministry of Local Government, Metropolitan and Provincial Police (inspector of police), inspecting police work, the police inspector for Nakhon Sawan reports that crime is up in Khamphaengphet, Tak, and Mae Sot], September 16, 1916.
7. NA R6 N 4.1/160, *Krasuang nakhonban, krom tamruat phranakhonban lae phuthon, ratchakan thua pai, khwam hen jat ratchakan krom tamruat phranakhonban lae phuthon* [Sixth Reign, Ministry of Local Government, Metropolitan and Provincial Police, general duties, opinions on the establishment of the Metropolitan Police and the Provincial Gendarmerie], 1919.
8. NA R6 N 4.1/224, *Krasuang nakhonban, krom tamruat phranakhonban lae phuthon, ratchakan thua pai, raingan prachum krommakan phijarana kho ratchakan kiao duai krom tamruat phuthon lae tamruat phranakhon* [Sixth

Reign, Ministry of Local Government, Metropolitan and Provincial Police, general duties, meeting of officials to consider issues related to the Provincial Gendarmerie and the Metropolitan Police], July 25, 1923.

9. NA R6 N 4.1/164.
10. NA R6 N 4.1/93, *Krasuang nakhonban, krom tamruat phranakhonban lae phuthon, ratchakan thua pai, khwam hen phraya sunthonphiphit rueang nai roi tri yom boek khwam taek tang kap amphoe bangkapi rueang phu rai plon ban phai nai amphoe bangkapi* [Sixth Reign, Ministry of Local Government, Metropolitan and Provincial Police, general duties, conflicting reports on investigation of a robbery in Bangkapi], November 24, 1916.
11. NA K 0301.1.21/2 (*lem* 1), *Krasuang kan khlang* [Ministry of Finance], Office of the Financial Adviser, Law and Justice, "Reports of Ministry of Justice for the Years R.S. 121 (1902–03), 122 (1903–04), 123 (1904–05), 124 (1905–06), 125 (1906–07), 126 (1907–08)."
12. Phraya Manawaratchasewi *Lak kan suep suan khadi aya* [The foundations for investigating criminal cases] (Bangkok: Bamrung Nukunlakit, 1929), 3–4.
13. NA R6 N 4.1/164.
14. NA K 0301.1.22/1, *Krasuang kan khlang* [Ministry of Finance], Office of the Financial Adviser, Police and Jails (in English), report of violent crime of Bangkok, suburbs and railway divisions for the fourth quarter, year 120 (1901–1902), ending March 31, 1902. The emphasis on tools, or lack thereof, would be echoed in the 1950s and 1960s, when the police would embark on another modernization campaign under the auspices of the U.S. government. This will be discussed in Chapter 5.
15. Letter from Luang Phraya Phetinthara to Jao Phraya Yommarat in NA R6 N 4.5ก/9, *Krasuang nakhonban, krom tamruat phranakhonban lae phuthon (jare tamruat), truat ratchakan, jare prajam monthon chiang mai ok truat ratchakan mi khwam hen wa khuan yup loek rong phak* [Sixth Reign, Ministry of Local Government, Metropolitan and Provincial Police (inspector of police), inspecting police work, inspector of police for Chiang Mai recommends the closure of a police station], August 25, 1916.
16. Simon A. Cole, *Suspect Identities: A History of Fingerprinting and Criminal Identification* (Cambridge, MA: Harvard University Press, 2001), 14–15.
17. NA R6 N 4.1/164.
18. David Bruce Johnston, "Rural Society and the Rice Economy in Thailand, 1880–1930" (PhD diss., Yale University, 1977), 178.
19. The term "geo-body" is from Thongchai Winichakul, *Siam Mapped: A History of the Geo-body of a Nation* (Honolulu: University of Hawai'i Press, 1994).
20. Jennifer Mnookin, "The Image of Truth: Photographic Evidence and the Power of Analogy," *Yale Journal of Law and the Humanities* 10 (1998): 8.
21. The first handheld cameras were called detective cameras because they were designed to be hidden (e.g., under hats or in lapels), and the popularity of these

machines coincided with the processing technology and mail-in services of Eastman Kodak. See Tom Gunning, "Embarrassing Evidence," in *Collecting Visible Evidence,* ed. Jane Gaines and Michael Renov (Minneapolis: University of Minnesota Press, 1999), 47.

22. John Tagg, *The Burden of Representation: Essays on Photographies and Histories* (Minneapolis: University of Minnesota Press, 1993), 60.
23. Mnookin, "The Image of Truth," 8.
24. Ibid., 11.
25. Cole, *Suspect Identities,* 20.
26. Ibid., 21–22.
27. Anek Nawigamune, *Prawat kan thai rup yuk raek khong thai* [History of early photography in Thailand] (Bangkok: Sarakhadi Phap, 2005), 15.
28. Thawisak Suphasa, "Kan jatkan lae botbat khong tamruat nai krungthep ratchasamai phrabat somdet phrajulajomklao jao yu hua" [The establishment and role of the police in Bangkok during the reign of King Chulalongkorn] (master's thesis, Srinakharinwirot University, 1978), 271.
29. Eric St. John Lawson, *Police Manual* (Bangkok: American Presbyterian Mission Press, 1906). A copy of the book can be found in NA K 0301.1.22/6, Ministry of Finance, Office of the Financial Adviser, Police and Jails, police manual (in English).
30. Phra Sisena (given name Kit Katchachiwa), *Withi suep suan jon phu rai lem 1* [Methods for investigating criminals, vol. 1] (Bangkok: Phraratchapantit, 1917), 339–340.
31. Letter from Phraya Athikonprakat to Eric Lawson dated June 27, 1918, in NA R6 N 4.1/2, *Krasuang nakhonban, krom tamruat phranakhonban lae phuthon, ratchakan thua pai, khwam hen phraya athikon lae nai losan thi prueksa nai rueang tamruat lap* [Sixth Reign, Ministry of Local Government, Metropolitan and Provincial Police, general duties, opinion of Phraya Athikon and Mr. Lawson on the secret police].
32. Letter from Eric Lawson to Jao Phraya Yommarat dated September 3, 1920, in NA R6 N 4.1/2.
33. Letter from Basil Thomson to Prince Paribatra in NA R7 M 11/7, *Krasuang mahathai, tamruat phuthon nakhonban phuban, tang tamruat phuban* [Seventh Reign, Ministry of Interior, Provincial, Metropolitan, and Investigative Police, establishing the detective police], January 11, 1929.
34. Phra Sisena, *Methods,* 42.
35. Ibid., 161–162.
36. Udom Latphli, *Withayakan tamruat bang rueang* [On various police methods], in *Krom tamurat* [Police Department], *Botkhwam prakop khwam ru kiao kap tamruat* [Collected articles on the police], a cremation volume printed in honor of Phraya Athikonprakat (given name Lui Jatikawanit) at Wat Thepsirintherawat, Bangkok, May 9, 1955, 76.

37. Sanga, *Police Methods,* 471.
38. Ibid., 471–472.
39. Ibid., 472.
40. Ibid., 120–123.
41. Luang Bannasanprasit, *Rules and Techniques,* 172.
42. The Chinese had been using fingerprints since about 200 BCE as signatures in contracts.
43. See Cole, *Suspect Identities,* for a detailed treatment of the history of the fingerprint.
44. Letter from Eric Lawson to Stewart Black dated February 10, 1906, in NA R5 Y 4.1/39, *Krasuang yuttitham, fem thi prueksa kotmai, khadi khwam* [Fifth Reign, Ministry of Justice, files of the legal adviser Stewart Black, case files].
45. Letter from Prince Rabi to Henri Laurent in NA R5 Y 4/75, *Krasuang yuttitham, fem thi prueksa kotmai* [Fifth Reign, Ministry of Justice, files of the legal adviser Stewart Black], 1909.
46. NA R6 N 4.1/164.
47. Letter from Phraya Athikonprakat to Eric Lawson in NA R6 N 4.1/2.
48. Letter from Henri Laurent to Prince Rabi in NA R5 Y 4/75, March 7, 1909.
49. NA R6 N 4.1/164.
50. Eric St. John Lawson, "Police and Provincial Gendarmerie," in *Twentieth Century Impressions of Siam: Its History, People, Commerce, Industry, and Resources,* ed. Arnold Wright and Oliver Breakspear (Bangkok: White Lotus, 1994), 109. See also NA R5 N 8.6/26, *Krasuang nakhonban, krom kong trawen (raingan tang-tang), raingan krom kong trawen prajam pi soko 122* [Fifth Reign, Ministry of Local Government, Metropolitan Constabulary (miscellaneous reports), annual report for the police constabulary for 1902], March 31, 1901, to May 20, 1902.
51. Lawson, "Police," 108.
52. Somphong Jaengrew, "Kamnoet tamruat santiban nai prawatsat kanmueang thai samai 2475" [The origins of the special branch in the political history of Thailand during the 1932 period], *Silapa watthanatham* [Art and culture], November 2008, 127.
53. Rotsukhon Jaratsi, "Botbat khong kharatchakan chao tang prathet nai krom tamruat nai samai somburananasithirat" [The role of foreign civil servants in the police department under the absolute monarchy] (master's thesis, Chulalongkorn University, Bangkok, 1977), 145.
54. Luang Phisitwithayakan, "Lai nio mue phu rai nai thi koet het" [Fingerprints at the scene of a crime], *Tamruat* [Police] 1, no. 3 (February 1931): 236. Luang Phisitwithayakan would go on to become the head of the Science Section of the *santiban* after 1932. He was purged, however, when army general Phibun Songkhram came to power through a military coup in 1938.
55. Luang Bannasanprasit, *Rules and Techniques,* 169.

56. NA R6 N 4.6/16, *Krasuang nakhonban, krom tamruat phranakhonban lae phuthon, rong rian roi tamruat phon tamruat, lak sut kan fuekhat song son rong rian phon trawen* [Sixth Reign, Ministry of Local Government, Metropolitan and Provincial Police, police academy, basic training and teachings at school for constabulary], 1916.
57. NA R6 N 4.1/56, *Krasuang nakhonban, krom tamruat phranakhonban lae phuthon, ratchakan thua phai, raingan jak kong phaet sukhaphiban* [Sixth Reign, Ministry of Local Government, Metropolitan and Provincial Police, general duties, report from the Office of the Medical Officer of the Department of Local Sanitation], 1915.
58. Phirasak Chaidaisuk, *Chat suea wai lai* [Once a tiger, always a tiger] (Bangkok: Matichon Press, 2008), 174.
59. Ibid., 77.
60. Ibid., 145.
61. Letter from Eric Lawson to Stewart Black in NA R5 Y 4/89, *Krasuang yuttitham, fem thi prueksa kotmai* [Fifth Reign, Ministry of Justice, files of legal adviser Stewart Black], January 11, 1909. "Foil" and "counterfoil" refer to the practice of entering complaints in duplicate with one copy or portion of the report retained as a record of a complaint having been made.
62. Lawson, "Police," 107.
63. Letter from Eric Lawson to Stewart Black in NA R5 Y 4/89.
64. See, for example, Phra Sisena, *Methods,* 339–340, and Lawson, *Police Manual,* 166.
65. NA R6 N 4.1/197, *Krasuang nakhonban, krom tamruat phranakhonban lae phuthon, ratchakan thua pai* [Sixth Reign, Ministry of Local Government, Metropolitan and Provincial Police, general duties, documents related to sending a delegation to Moulmein and Penang to talk to the British about capturing bandits operating near the border], March 13, 1922.
66. *Lak inthaphat,* in *Nitipratya thai: Prakat phraratchaprarot lak inthaphat phrathammasat lae "On the Laws of Mu'ung Thai or Siam"* [Thai legal theory: Royal announcements, the Lak Inthapat, and "On the Laws of Mueang Thai or Siam"] (Bangkok: Samnakngan Kong Thun Sanapsanun Kan Wichai, 2005), sections 30–31. The Law of the Three Seals is the name for the collected laws of Siam that date back to the Ayutthaya period (ca. 1350–1789). The version that most refer to today is one that was compiled and revised during the early Bangkok period (ca. 1782–present).
67. Section 44 of the *Laksana phayan* says that *tralakan* should write out a witness's testimony and have the witness either accept or reject the written account. Section 32 of the *Lak inthaphat* also refers to the writing of testimony.
68. Lawson, "Police," 109.
69. Nai Janthana [Malai Chuphinit], *Suea fai sip thit* [Tiger Fai of the ten directions] (Bangkok: Samnakphim Krathom, 1998), 33.

70. Michel Foucault, *State, Territory, Population: Lectures at the Collège de France, 1977–1978* (New York: Picador, 2009), 337.
71. Letter from Luang Phraya Phetinthara to Jao Phraya Yommarat in NA R6 N 4.5ก/17, *Krasuang nakhonban, krom tamruat phranakhonban lae phuthon (jare tamruat), truat ratchakan, jare tamruat phuthon nakhon chiang mai raignan wa dai ok truat kan rong phak mue tamruat phuthon tambon mueang naeng hen kan pho somkhuan thuk yang tae banchi khadi aya bang rong phak ko dai tham bang rong phak ko mai dai tham mi kham sang hai tham tham thuk rong phak* [Sixth Reign, Ministry of Local Government, Metropolitan and Provincial Police (inspector of police), inspecting police work, inspector of Chiang Mai city reports that the work of police stations is satisfactory but that not all stations have a record book and orders that all stations use one], March 26, 1917.
72. Letter from Luang Phraya Phetinthara to Jao Phraya Yommarat in NA R6 N 4.5ก/9.
73. NA R6 N 4.5ก/10, *Krasuang nakhonban, krom tamruat phranakhonban lae phuthon (jare tamruat), truat ratchakan, nai phan tamruat tho satainoe jare tamraut phak tai nai monthon surat thani lae jangwat songkhla jangwat phuket monthon pattani hen wa kitjakan tang tang bokphrong mak* [Sixth Reign, Ministry of Local Government, Metropolitan and Provincial Police (inspector of police), inspecting police work, the inspector of the south reports many deficiencies in police work], November 3, 1916.
74. NA R6 N 4.5ก/11.
75. Letter from chief inspector of police to Jao Phraya Yommarat regarding the misconduct of the district administration in *amphoe* Pong in Nan province in NA R6 N 4.5ก/13, *Krasuang nakhonban, krom tamruat phranakhonban lae phuthon (jare tamruat), truat ratchakan* [Sixth Reign, Ministry of Local Government, Department of the Metropolitan Police and the Provincial Gendarmerie (inspector of police), inspecting police work], 1916.
76. *Chiwit lae ngan khong ari liwira* [The life and work of Ari Liwira] (Bangkok: Siam Phanitchayakan, 1963), n.p.
77. Wiwana Thewachalaangkun, "Naiyobai khong rat kap kan tamruat phuthon phoso 2440–2465" [Government policy and the gendarmerie, 1897–1922] (master's thesis, Silapakon University, Bangkok, 1984), 172.
78. Rotsukhon, "The Role of Foreign Civil Servants," 57–58.
79. Ibid., 108.
80. Ibid., 99–100.
81. NA R6 N 4.1/224, July 25, 1923.
82. Rotsukhon, "The Role of Foreign Civil Servants," 152.
83. Wiwana, "Gendarmerie," 112.
84. NA R6 N 4.1/261, *Krasuang nakhonban, krom tamruat phranakhonban lae phuthon, ratchakan thua pai, tamnan jat tang kong tamruat phuthon prajam*

kan [Sixth Reign, Ministry of Local Government, Metropolitan and Provincial Police, general duties, on the establishment of the Provincial Gendarmerie], ca. 1923.

85. Wiwana, "Gendarmerie," 134.
86. Ibid., 136. Hence the need to subject the police to fingerprint surveillance.
87. Cecil H. Forty, "Cremation Volume for Police Lieutenant Colonel C. H. Forty" (Bangkok, 1967), 58.
88. Wiwana, "Gendarmerie," 87.
89. Rotsukhon, "The Role of Foreign Civil Servants," 181.
90. NA R7 M 11/3, *Krasuang mahathai, krom tamruat phuthon nakhonban phuban, rong rian tamruat* [Seventh Reign, Ministry of Interior, Metropolitan, Provincial, and Investigative Police, police academy], July 22, 1927, and NA R6 N 4.1/253, *Krasuang nakhonban, krom tamruat phranakhonban lae phuthon, ratchakan thua pai, prakat kong trawen* [Sixth Reign, Ministry of Local Government, Metropolitan and Provincial Police, general duties, announcement on the Metropolitan Constabulary], ca. 1923.
91. Letter from Luang Phraya Phetinthara to Jao Phraya Yommarat in NA R6 N 4.5/6, *Krasuang nakhonban (jare krom tamruat), rong rian nai tamruat* [Sixth Reign, Ministry of Local Government, inspector of police, police academy], September 6, 1916.
92. Letter from Mom Jao Khamrop to Luang Phraya Phetinthara, March 8, 1917, in ibid.
93. Memo by Luang Phraya Phetinthara, March 5, 1917, in ibid.
94. NA R6 N 4.6/5 *Krasuang nakhonban, rong rian roi tamruat phon tamruat, hua kho samrap pathakatha rong rian phon trawen* [Sixth Reign, Ministry of Local Government, police school, subjects for lectures], March 1, 1914.
95. NA R6 N 4.6/6 *Krasuang nakhonban, rong rian roi tamruat phon tamruat, kho bangkhap rong rian fuekhat nai muat pi 130* [Sixth Reign, Ministry of Local Government, police school, regulations for officer training for 1911], 1911.
96. Letter from Mom Jao Khamrop, chief of police, to Luang Buretphathungkit, head of the police training academy in Bangkok, in NA R6 N 4.6/16, May 25, 1916.
97. Luang Phisitwithayakan, *Tamruat kap lak kan suep suan* [The police and the rules of investigation] (Bangkok: Police Department, 1935), 114.
98. Luang Bannasanprasit, *Rules and Techniques*, 142.
99. Lawson, *Police Manual*. He goes on about the left hand as well.
100. NA R5 Y 10/20, *Krasuang yuttitham, san dika, tang damnaeng kammakan 1 kammakan sawaengha lai mue 2 kammakan wat duang sang* [Fifth Reign, Ministry of Justice, Supreme Court, designating two officials: 1. Official to look for fingerprints and 2. official for the Duang Sang temple], 1910.
101. Luang Phisitwithayakan, *The Police and the Rules*, 126.
102. Phra Sisena, *Methods*, 172.

103. Luang Bannasanprasit, *Rules and Techniques,* 161–162.
104. Luang Phisitwithayakan, *The Police and the Rules,* 77–78.
105. Ibid., 82.
106. Sanga, *Police Methods,* 473.
107. The phrase "grammar of murder" comes from Karla Oeler, *A Grammar of Murder: Violent Scenes and Film Form* (Chicago: University of Chicago Press, 2009), which tells a history of murder scenes and the development of tropes used to visualize murder in film.
108. Lawson, *Police Manual,* 54.
109. Lorraine Daston, "Historical Epistemology," in *Questions of Evidence: Proof, Practice, and Persuasion across the Disciplines,* ed. James Chandler, Arnold Davidson, and Harry Harootunian (Chicago: University of Chicago Press, 1994), 283.

CHAPTER 3: CRIMINAL MAPPINGS

1. From *Khadi khwam 7516/2529 dam—1712/2533 daeng* [Case number 7516/2529 black—1712/2533 red], October 22, 1986, in *Khadi choeri aen dankhaen fong kao* [The case of Sherry Ann Duncan, first trial], Library and Museum of the Attorney General's Office of Thailand (LMAG).
2. NA R6 N 4.1/164, *Krasuang nakhonban, krom tamruat phranakhonban lae phuthon, ratchakan thua pai* [Sixth Reign, Ministry of Local Government, Metropolitan and Provincial Police, general duties], a report on the work of the police and the gendarmerie and on criminal statistics of Siam for B.E. 2463 by police lieutenant general Lawson (in English), 1919.
3. NA K 0301.1.22/1, Ministry of Finance, Office of the Financial Adviser, Police and Jails, report of violent crime of Bangkok, suburbs and railway divisions for the fourth quarter, year 120 (1901–1902), ending March 31, 1902 (in English).
4. Wiwana Thewachalaangkun, "Naiyobai khong rat kap kan tamruat phuthon phoso 2440–2465" [Government policy and the gendarmerie, 1897–1922] (master's thesis, Silapakon University, Bangkok, 1984), 61–62.
5. This was also the case in Europe. Douglass Starr, in *The Killer of Little Shepherds: A True Crime Story and the Birth of Forensic Science* (New York: Alfred Knopf, 2010), writes that the police in many parts of France during the late nineteenth century did not investigate crimes at the location where they happened but relied instead on "denunciations, rumor, and innuendo, even when physical evidence pointed to the contrary. They would round up suspects on the merest suspicion and hold them in jail until, police hoped, one of them cracked" (33). He also notes that criminal investigation practices in England lagged "years behind" those of the Continent (39), and that Dr. Jean Alexandre

Eugene Lacassagne, a pioneer in forensic medicine in France, published several articles on how to conduct crime scene investigations, something that had yet to become common practice (17).

6. Eric St. John Lawson, *Police Manual* (Bangkok: American Presbyterian Mission Press, 1906).
7. Phra Sisena uses the phrase *than thi* for location of a crime. Phra Sisena (Kit Katchachiwa), *Withi suep suan jon phu rai lem 1* [Methods for investigating criminals, vol. 1] (Bangkok: Phraratchapantit, 1917), 42.
8. Luang Phisitwithayakan uses the phrase *sathan thi koet het* (place where an event happens). Luang Phisitwithayakan, *Tamruat kap lak kan suep suan* [The police and the rules of investigation] (Bangkok: Police Department, 1935), 42. Luang Phisitwithayakan studied police science at the University of Lausanne, Switzerland, forensics and police techniques at Lyons in France, ballistics at the School of Criminology in Brussels, Belgium, and underwent basic police training (*wichakan tamruat*) in England and Ireland. He was also an instructor of criminal investigation at the Siamese police academy (*rong rian nakrian nai roi tamruat*).
9. Sanga Kittikhajon, *Withayakan tamruat kiao kap kan suep suan* [Police methods related to investigation] (Bangkok: Prasoetakson, 1953), 21.
10. Udom Latphli, *Withayakan tamruat bang rueang* [On various police methods], in *Krom tamurat* [Police Department], *Botkhwam prakop khwam ru kiao kap tamruat* [Collected articles on the police], a cremation volume printed in honor of Phraya Athikonprakat (given name Lui Jatikawanit) at Wat Thepsirintherawat, Bangkok, May 9, 1955, 73.
11. Sanga, *Police Methods*, 25.
12. Phra Sisena, *Methods*, 45.
13. Luang Phisitwithayakan, *The Police and the Rules*, 68.
14. Luang Bannasanprasit (Sithi Rojanawiphat), *Lak lae withikan suep suan tai suan khadi aya* [Rules and techniques for investigating criminal cases] (Bangkok: Aksonniti, 1929), 1.
15. The seven factors are people, objects, proofs (testimony, documents, and other things), the crime scene, peculiarities or odd behavior, proclivity to criminal activity or a history of crime, and circumstantial factors. Ibid., 28–29.
16. Ibid., 183.
17. Phraya Manawaratchasewi, *Lak kan suep suan khadi aya* [The foundations of investigating criminal cases] (Bangkok: Bamrung Nukunlakit, 1929), 131.
18. Luang Phisitwithayakan, *The Police and the Rules*, 77–78.
19. Luang Phisitwithayakan, *Prachachon atja chuai ratchakan tamruat dai yangrai (thang withayu krajai siang)* [How citizens can help the police (a radio address)], in *Nangsue ngan napanakit khong nang phijanwonlakit* [Commemorative volume for Miss Phijanwonlakit] (Bangkok, 1934), 35–36.
20. Sanga, *Police Methods*, 21–25.

21. Police manuals provided specific instructions on how to store, transport, and present material objects like these as well, indicating that their presentation has an aesthetic component, though to a lesser degree compared to maps.
22. Lawson, *Police Manual,* 100.
23. Ibid.
24. Phra Sisena, *Methods,* 42.
25. Luang Phisitwithayakan, *The Police and the Rules,* 82.
26. Luang Bannasanprasit, *Rules and Techniques,* 160–162.
27. Thongchai Winichakul, *Siam Mapped: A History of the Geo-body of a Nation* (Honolulu: University of Hawai'i Press, 1994).
28. Luang Bannasanprasit, *Rules and Techniques,* 160–162.
29. Sanga, *Police Methods,* 249.
30. Ibid., 462–463, 465–466.
31. A version of this story can be found in Ramajit [King Vajiravudh], *Prapruethikan khong nai thong-in rathanet* [The adventures of Thong-in Rathanet], ed. Rattanachai Lueangwongngam (Bangkok: Samoson Nangsue Rahatsakhadi, 2006), 151–174. The story was originally published in the journal *Thawi panya* 3, no. 15 (June 1905).
32. Incidentally, I could find no similar crime scene map in any of the early editions of Poe's story.
33. Luang Withayathikonsak, "Khwam phajon phai khong soe roboet beden paowen" (The adventures of Sir Robert Baden-Powell), in *Senasueksa lae phae withayasat* [Military studies and the spread of science] 5, no. 5 (1921): 503.
34. Sir Robert Baden-Powell, *My Adventures as a Spy* (London: Arthur Pearson, 1915). Baden-Powell was an officer in the British Army and the founder of the Scout Movement.
35. Letter from Prince Paribatra to King Prajadhipok in NA R7 MT 11/5, *Krasuang mahathai, tamraut phuthon nakhonban phuban, tang tamruat phuthon klang* [Seventh Reign, Ministry of Interior, the Provincial, Metropolitan, and Investigative Police, setting up a central investigation division], May 16, 1928.
36. Luang Bannasanprasit, *Rules and Techniques*, 161.
37. Starr, *Killer of Little Shepherds,* 104.
38. Ibid., 105.
39. Phraya Samosonsaphakan, "Suep saphakan," *Wachirayan* 35 (July 1897): 3500. Phraya Samosonsaphakan was evidently a student of or an aide to Henry Alabaster, a translator for the British consulate general in Siam during the late nineteenth century.
40. On early twentieth-century detective fiction in Siam, see Samson Lim, "Detective Fiction, the Police, and Secrecy in Early Twentieth Century Siam," *Southeast Asia Research* 20, no. 1 (2012): 83–102.
41. Phra Phinit Chonkhadi, *Nithan tamruat* [The story of the police] (Bangkok: Thai Watthana Phanit, 1963), 39.

42. Op-ed, *Krungthep deli me,* December 22–31, 1912, in NA R6 N 20.6/4, *Krasuang nakhonban, nangsuephim, botkhwam nai nangsuephim* [Sixth Reign, Ministry of Local Government, newspapers, articles in newspapers].
43. Michael Lynch, "Science in the Age of Mechanical Reproduction: Moral and Epistemic Relations between Diagrams and Photographs," *Biology and Philosophy* 6 (1991): 211–212.
44. Michael Lynch, "Discipline and the Material Form of Images: An Analysis of Scientific Visibility," *Social Studies of Science* 15, no. 1 (February 1985): 42.
45. Phra Sisena, *Methods,* 44–45.
46. Luang Bannasanprasit, *Rules and Techniques,* 159–174.
47. Luang Phisitwithayakan, *The Police and the Rules,* 72–73.
48. Ibid., 62.
49. Phraya Manawaratchasewi, *The Foundations,* 129.
50. Sanga, *Police Methods,* 10.
51. Ibid., 21.
52. Phra Sisena, *Methods,* 45.
53. Luang Phisitwithayakan, *Suep khadi luek lap* [Investigating mysterious crimes], in cremation volume for military and police officers who died in service during the Boworadet Rebellion of 1933, cremation ceremony at Sanam Luang, February 18, 1933.
54. Thongchai, *Siam Mapped,* 115, 121–122, 127.
55. Scientific objects have a similar biography, as Lorraine Daston shows in *Biographies of Scientific Objects* (Chicago: University of Chicago Press, 2000).
56. Luang Bannasanprasit, *Rules and Techniques,* 183.
57. Phra Sisena, *Methods,* 3.
58. Ibid., 25.
59. Ibid., 26–28.
60. Sanga, *Police Methods,* 15.
61. On castration, see "Sterilization Looms as Penalty," *Bangkok Post,* June 19, 1959.
62. Human Rights Watch, "Not Enough Graves: The War on Drugs, HIV/AIDS, and Violations of Human Rights," June 2004, http://www.hrw.org/reports/2004/thailand0704/4.htm.
63. Sanga, *Police Methods,* 100, 106–107.
64. Ibid., 8–9.
65. Personal interview with former head of Central Investigation Department, March 14, 2011.
66. Phraya Manawaratchasewi, *The Foundations,* 21.
67. A group of men supposedly led by Pridi Phanomyong attempted a coup on February 26, 1949. The prime minister at the time, Major General Phibun Songkhram, had called a state of emergency just before the attempted coup, and this gave the military and the police far-ranging powers for arrest and detention.

68. Testimony of Captain Yongyudh Damrongchai given on November 8, 1957, in *Khadi kha phu uen dai doi jethana (4 ratthamontri)* [The case of the murder of four former ministers], LMAG.
69. Judgment of the Criminal Court, September 30, 1962, in ibid.
70. Testimony of Captain Yongyudh Damrongchai, in ibid.
71. The analogy here is deliberate rather than merely rhetorical. David Engel has shown through ethnographic research how urbanization, industrialization, and internal migration have eroded traditional community-based mechanisms for conflict resolution and the promotion of social harmony. This has, he argues, led people to increasingly see supra-local phenomena like karma, fate, and spirits as causal agents in human affairs. In other words, the public nature of criminal detection may in fact perform a function parallel to that of traditional, locally based mechanisms for social justice, but at a national level. I will return to Engel's points later in this chapter. See David Engel, "Landscapes of the Law: Injury, Remedy, and Social Change in Thailand," *Law and Society Review* 43, no. 1 (2009): 61–94, and also his "Globalization and the Decline of Legal Consciousness: Torts, Ghosts, and Karma in Thailand," *Law and Social Inquiry* 30, no. 3 (2005): 469–514.
72. Kullasap Gesmankit, "Preface," in King Lithai, *Traibhumikatha: The Story of the Three Planes of Existence*, trans. Thai National Team (Bangkok: ASEAN Committee on Culture and Information, 1987), 13.
73. Klaus Wenk, *Thai Literature: An Introduction* (Bangkok: White Lotus, 1995), 2.
74. Nidhi Eoseewong, "The World of Lady Nophamat," in *Pen and Sail: Literature and History in Early Bangkok,* trans. Chris Baker, Benedict Anderson, Craig J. Reynolds, Hong Lysa, Pasuk Phongpaichit, Patrick Jory, and Ruth McVey (Chiang Mai, Thailand: Silkworm Books, 2005), 227–254.
75. Ibid., 244.
76. Ibid., 251.
77. Tony Day and Craig J. Reynolds, "Cosmologies, Truth Regimes, and the State in Southeast Asia," *Modern Asian Studies* 34, no. 1 (February 2000): 8.
78. Nidhi, "Lady Nophamat," 247.
79. Ibid., 246.
80. Ibid., 245.
81. Pattamakorn Bullstaporn, "Khwam ru nai tamra phrommachat" [The knowledge of the Phrommachat] (master's thesis, Chiang Mai University, 1996), 1–2. The oldest complete version, from 1901, was published several times, with some print runs going as high as 6,000 copies. Approximately 18,000 copies were published between 1901 and 1911. All together, the *tamra phrommachat* has been printed more than one hundred times, totaling more than 200,000 copies.
82. Ibid., 18.
83. Ibid., 106–108.

84. Engel, "Globalization," 472.
85. Mikhail Bakhtin, "Forms of Time and of the Chronotope in the Novel," in *The Dialogic Imagination: Four Essays by M. M. Bakhtin,* trans. Michael Holquist and Caryl Emerson (Austin: University of Texas Press, 1981), 84.

CHAPTER 4: MURDER, REENACTED

Passages of the section "Origins of an Idiom" are extracted from Samson Lim, "Murder! in Thailand's Vernacular Press," *Journal of Asian Studies* 73, no. 2 (May 2014): 359–376. Copyright © 2001 The Association for Asian Studies, Inc. Reprinted with the permission of Cambridge University Press.

1. Carlo Ginzburg, "Clues: Roots of an Evidential Paradigm," in *Clues, Myths, and the Historical Method,* trans. John Tedeschi and Anne C. Tedeschi (Baltimore: Johns Hopkins University Press, 1992), 100.
2. Carlo Ginzburg, "From Aby Warburgh to E. H. Gombrich: A Problem of Method," in ibid., 29.
3. Cited in Carlo Ginzburg, "Checking the Evidence: The Judge and the Historian," in *Questions of Evidence: Proof, Practice, and Persuasion across the Disciplines,* ed. James Chandler, Arnold Davidson, and Harry Harootunian (Chicago: University of Chicago Press, 1994), 294.
4. Cited in Robin W. Winks, "What Is Evidence? The Relativist View," in *The Historian as Detective: Essays on Evidence,* ed. Robin W. Winks (New York: Harper and Row, 1969), 11–12.
5. Ibid.
6. From the website of the Chiangsan Police Department, http://chiangsan.chiangrai.police.go.th/detective%20lesson4.html. This website is no longer available.
7. Pattaravit Obsuwan, "Kan tham phaen prathutsakam prakop kham rap sarap-hap nai robop kotmai thai" [Crime science reconstruction by the accused to support confession of the accused in the Thai legal system] (master's thesis, Thammasat University, 2007), 103. Erika Fry, who generously provided me the text of the interview on October 15, 2008, conducted the *Bangkok Post* interview. For the article, see Erika Fry, "Arresting Theatre," *Bangkok Post,* August 10, 2008.
8. Luang Bannasanprasit (Sithi Rojanawiphat), *Lak lae withikan suep suan tai suan khadi aya* [Rules and techniques for investigating criminal cases] (Bangkok: Aksonniti, 1929), 160.
9. Luang Phisitwithayakan, *Suep khadi luek lap* [Investigating mysterious cases], in cremation volume for military and police officers who died in service during the Boworadet Rebellion of 1933. Cremation ceremony at Sanam Luang on February 18, 1933.

10. Luang Phisitwithayakan, *Suep khadi luek lap* [Investigating mysterious cases], in cremation volume for military and police officers who died in service during the Boworadet Rebellion of 1933. Cremation ceremony at Sanam Luang on February 18, 1933, 18.
11. Phao Sriyanond, "Khwam rusuek khong khaphajao" [My feelings], in Sanga Kittikhajon, *Withayakan tamruat kiao kap kan suep suan* [Police methods related to investigation] (Bangkok: Prasoetakson, 1953), ก.
12. Douglass Starr refers to examples that took place in the late 1800s in France in *The Killer of Little Shepherds: A True Crime Story and the Birth of Forensic Science* (New York: Alfred Knopf, 2010). Basil Thomson was a well-known officer at Scotland Yard during the early twentieth century who was charged toward the end of his career with committing an act of public indecency with a woman at Hyde Park. He denied the allegations, saying that he was conducting research for a book. As noted in Chapter 2, he was also an adviser to the Siamese police force in the early twentieth century.
13. August Vollmer, "Revision of the Atcherley Modus Operandi System," *Journal of the American Institute of Criminal Law and Criminology* 10, no. 2 (August 1919): 229.
14. Gene E. Carte and Elaine H. Carte, *Police Reform in the United States: The Era of August Vollmer, 1905–1922* (Berkeley: University of California Press, 1975), 2.
15. August Vollmer, "The Bureau of Criminal Records," *Journal of the American Institute of Criminal Law and Criminology* 11, no. 2 (August 1920): 171.
16. Carte and Carte, *Police Reform,* 23.
17. Vollmer, "Revision," 233.
18. Carlo Ginzburg, "Clues," 106–108.
19. Si Ui's embalmed body is on display at the Medical Museum at Sirirat Hospital in Bangkok.
20. "Phaen prathutsakam ngong khao khatakon pha ok dek" [Criminal methods section confused in case of murderer who split child's torso], *Phim thai rai wan,* February 1, 1958, front page.
21. *Kotmai phijarana khadi aya* [Criminal procedural code] (1935), section 134.
22. Ibid., section 232, and Supreme Court Decision 35/2532.
23. Pattaravit, "Crime Scene Reconstruction," 85, 110. He cites Supreme Court Decision 1346/2530, 890.
24. Police rules cited in Pattaravit, "Crime Scene Reconstruction," 107–108. Emphasis added.
25. Ibid., 107.
26. Ibid. The phrase in Thai is *sadaeng tha thang nai kan kratham khwam phit tam chan ton tang tang doi laiat.*
27. Ibid., 108. See also p. 85, where he cites Wong Wiraphong, *Kan ruapruam lae kan nam suep phayan lakthan nai khadi ukchakan* [Compiling and investigating evidence in serious cases] (Bangkok: Dusit Samphan, 1963), 172.

28. Personal interview with former head of the Central Investigation Bureau at his house on March 14, 2011.
29. Aphisak Thongnaphakhun and Jutharat Ua-amnoey, *Kan prachathan kap kan khum khrong sithi khong phu tong ha nai kan nam chi thi koet het prakop kham rap saraphap* [Vigilantism and the protection of the rights of suspects in the practice of pointing out a location of a crime to support a confession]. Draft paper provided by authors, 2010, 7–8. The phrase they use is "reenactments": "thue pen lak batibat khong phanakngan kan sop suan thi chua wa mi khwam samkhan lae mi suan chuai nai kan khon ha khwam jing nai khan ton kan sop suan" [it (the reenactment) is a basic practice of the investigative police that is held to be important and aids in the search for truth in crime investigations].
30. Ginzburg, "Representing the Enemy," 29.
31. Phraya Manawaratchasewi, *Kan tai suan lae kan phijarana rueang kha nai pin aekaraphanit thi jangwat janburi* [The investigation and deliberation of the case of the murder of Mr. Pin Aekaraphanit in Janthaburi province] (Bangkok, 1930), photo pages not numbered.
32. Account from Hayi Khiat [pseud.], *Ai bunpheng phu rai samkhan hip lek* [Bunpheng, the villain of the iron trunk] (Bangkok: Bangkok Press, 1919). The subtitle of this *lamtat* (a type of performance, typically by two people who tell a story as a dialogue or repartee) reads "Pen rueang luek lap sap son" [A mysterious, complex story]. There is now a statue of Bunpheng at the temple in Bangkok where he was executed.
33. Anek Nawigamune, *Dao rai nai adit* [Criminals in the past] (Bangkok: Saeng Daet, 1995), 103.
34. From Piyakanit Hongthong, *Nangsue chue sayam sanuk khao* [A book called fun news of Siam] (Bangkok: Kanya Publishing, 1988), 39.
35. Ibid., 83.
36. "Rueang khong nangsuephim mueang thai pen bunthuek khwam khong phu sonjai nangsuephim khon nueng" [The story of newspapers in Thailand: A record by an interested person], in *Chiwit lae ngan khong ari liwira* [Life and work of Ari Liwira] (Bangkok: Siam Phanitchayakan), 1963, n.p.
37. Andrew Freeman, *A Journalist in Siam* (Bangkok: White Lotus, 2007), 58, 60.
38. "The Story of Newspapers," n.p.
39. Freeman, *A Journalist,* 107.
40. Ibid., 87.
41. Christopher P. Wilson, *Cop Knowledge: Police Power and Cultural Narrative in Twentieth-Century America* (Chicago: University of Chicago Press, 2000), 73.
42. Freeman, *A Journalist,* 199.
43. Data from the National Library of Thailand support the idea that the vernacular press experienced a period of growth in the early twentieth century. A total of 7 non-daily serials were started during the reigns of Rama III (r. 1824–1851)

and Rama IV (Mongkut, r. 1851–1868), 47 under Rama V (Chulalongkorn, r. 1868–1910), 127 under Rama VI (Vajiravudh, r. 1910–1925), and 160 under Rama VII (r. 1925–1935). One hundred forty-eight were started prior to 1932, the year of the revolution. While these often lasted only a year or two, it is clear that there was a print-media boom in the early twentieth century.

44. Freeman, *A Journalist,* 102.
45. Recall from Chapter 2 that the police did not have their own photography unit until 1932.
46. "The Story of Newspapers," n.p.
47. See Thawon Suwan, *Fa thalai nam muek* [Navigating a sea of ink] (Bangkok: Matichon Press, 2007).
48. Thawon, *Sea of Ink,* 37.
49. Ibid., 169.
50. Rodney Tasker, "Questions of Justice," *Far Eastern Economic Review,* August 27, 1998, 28.
51. David Engel, "Globalization and the Decline of Legal Consciousness: Torts, Ghosts, and Karma in Thailand," *Law and Social Inquiry* 30, no. 3 (2005): 508.
52. Personal interview with former head of Central Investigation Department, March 14, 2011.
53. Anecdotal evidence shows that while the publicity did not improve the image of the police with the public in general, the strategy may have been effective in making physical force a legitimate option. In a memo dated December 11, 1966, a researcher working for the United States Operations Mission in Thailand wrote that a group of villagers in northeastern Thailand spoke about their problems related to cattle rustling. The villagers were asked, "Why don't you ask for police assistance?" They replied that the police were not effective, that sometimes the police would catch a thief but the thief would be acquitted and then rob again. One villager opined, "If they [the villagers] were the police they would kill every robber they captured." One asked, "Why didn't the police improve the law about robbery?" This man wanted the police to have more authority to suppress crimes: "Every robber should be killed or shot by the police when he was arrested." Memo from Mai Chuepaeng, Research Division, to Dr. Toshio Yatsushiro, USOM/Thailand, "Cattle Rustling and the Police," December 30, 1966.
54. The recent troubles in Britain with Rupert Murdoch's *News of the World,* where it was alleged that agents of the paper paid bribes to the police for information, suggest that the close relationship between the police and the press is a global phenomenon.
55. From Narong Phoemphun, *Poet phum chiwit kamphon wacharaphon jao pho thai rat* [In praise of the life of Kamphon Wacharaphon: Godfather of *Thai rat*] (Bangkok: Black and Grey, 1989), 91.
56. Aphisak and Ua-amnoey, "Vigilantism," 8.

57. Text of interview provided by Erika Fry. Personal correspondence, October 15, 2008.
58. Police officers or civilian volunteers, meanwhile, play victims. There is even a Thai film, *The Victim* (2006), about an aspiring actress hired by police to act out the role of female victims in reenactments. In the film, the ghost of one victim possesses the actress and helps the police solve a murder case.
59. In a belated trial that took place ten years after the crime for a group of police officers accused of murdering four former government ministers in 1949, police investigators conducted the reenactment of witness testimony at 1:00 a.m., the time of the murder. The intention was to re-create as closely as possible the conditions during the night of the crime. The investigators also used the cars that were originally involved in transporting the ministers when they were shot dead at point-blank range. *Khadi kha phu uen dai doi jethana (4 rattha-montri)* [The case of the murder of four former ministers], Library and Museum of the Attorney General's Office of Thailand (LMAG).
60. Franco Moretti, "Clues," in *Signs Taken for Wonders: Essays in the Sociology of Literary Forms,* trans. Susan Fischer, David Forgacs, and David Miller (London: Verso, 1983), 149.
61. Aphisak and Ua-amnoey, "Vigilantism," 111.
62. Phra Sisena (given name Kit Katchachiwa), *Withi suep suan jon phu rai lem 1* [Methods for investigating criminals, vol. 1] (Bangkok: Phraratchapantit, 1917), 186.
63. Luang Phisitwithayakan, *Investigating Mysterious Cases,* 17.
64. Sanga Kittikhajon, *Withayakan tamruat kiao kap kan suep suan* [Police methods related to investigation] (Bangkok: Prasoetakson, 1953), 18.
65. Chalothon [pseud.], "Plon 617" [Plundering 617], *Phim thai rai pak,* 2nd half, April 1957, 20–22, 44–46.
66. Chris Baker and Pasuk Phongpaichit, trans., *The Tale of Khun Chang Khun Phaen: A Siamese Epic of Love, War, and Tragedy* (Seattle: University of Washington Press, 2012), 939.
67. Translated text from interview with retired criminal court judge conducted on November 25, 2010. Text provided by Viengrat Nethipho via e-mail on November 29, 2010.
68. Ibid.

CHAPTER 5: HISTORY OF CONSPIRACY

Passages of the sections "Brave New World" and "The Dark Hand of Influence" are extracted from Samson Lim, "Murder! in Thailand's Vernacular Press," *Journal of Asian Studies* 73, no. 2 (May 2014): 359–376. Copyright © 2001 The Association for Asian Studies, Inc. Reprinted with the permission of Cambridge University Press.

1. Thak Chaloemtiarana, *Thailand: The Politics of Despotic Paternalism* (Ithaca, NY: Cornell Southeast Asia Program, Cornell University, 2007), 24.
2. Alexander MacDonald, *Bangkok Editor* (New York: Macmillan, 1949), 46.
3. Ibid., 81.
4. Tulsathit Taptim, "It's a Good Time to Be a Conspiracy Theorist," *Nation,* April 27, 2011.
5. Voranai Vanijaka, "The Hand That Rocks the Cradle," *Bangkok Post,* August 15, 2010, http://bangkokpost.com/opinion/opinion/191120/the-hand-that-rocks-the-cradle.
6. Gordon Fairclough, "Thailand: Hidden Hands," *Far Eastern Economic Review,* June 19, 1994, http://search.proquest.com/docview/208214530?accountid=12492.
7. Search conducted on January 4, 2015. Search limits included full text, newspapers, historical newspapers, and magazines. The results are from English-language sources on the database, so they do not reflect content in the vernacular press. They do, however, give an indication of the continued use of the terms in thinking about current events in Thailand.
8. J. Alexander Caldwell, *American Economic Aid to Thailand* (Toronto: Lexington Books, 1974), 29.
9. "Government Defends Grant of Funds to Police Department," *Bangkok Post,* November 3, 1950.
10. Theodore J. Curtis, "A Brief History of USOM Support to the Thai National Police Department," a report prepared by the United States Operations Mission to Thailand, Agency for International Development, Bangkok, Thailand, July 1973, 5.
11. Ibid., 1.
12. John W. Finney, "US Pays Thailand 50-Million a Year for Vietnam Aid," *New York Times,* June 8, 1970.
13. "Thai Police Force Bigger than Army," *New York Times,* July 23, 1951, 2. According to the numbers in the article, the police did not actually have more members than the armed forces combined, but the point remains that the police rivaled all branches of the armed forces combined in terms of size by the early 1950s.
14. Curtis, "Brief History," 4.
15. Ibid., 8.
16. Ibid., 12.
17. Ibid., 15.
18. Jutharat Ua-amnoey, e-mail to author, May 3, 2010.
19. Daniel Fineman, *A Special Relationship: The United States and Military Government in Thailand, 1947–1958* (Honolulu: University of Hawai'i Press, 1997), 123. Phao is notorious primarily because he oversaw the use of police officers as a political and personal weapon to silence critics of his work. He also used his

position in the force to enrich himself. Both these points will be touched on again later in the chapter.

20. Mizutani Yasuhiro, "A Modern Thai State Stumbling: The Expansion of the Police in Thailand from the 1930s to 1940s" [in Japanese], *Southeast Asian Studies* 43, no. 2 (September 2009): 206.
21. Phao Sriyanond, "Khwam rusuek khong khaphajao" [My feelings], in Sanga Kittikhajon, *Withayakan tamruat kiao kap kan suep suan* [Police methods related to investigation] (Bangkok: Prasoetakson, 1953), ก–ข.
22. Ibid., ค.
23. Sanga Kittikhajon, *Withayakan tamruat kiao kap kan suep suan* [Police methods related to investigation] (Bangkok: Prasoetakson, 1953), 37.
24. "First Detection Class Opened," *Bangkok Post,* February 15, 1954.
25. Chumsai Chaiwat, "Botbat thang kanmueang khong phon tamruat aek phao siyanon, phoso 2490–2500" [The role of Phao Sriyanond in politics, 1947–1957] (master's thesis, Chulalongkorn University, 1995), 33–35.
26. Somkit Santhunsing, "Ho withayakan tamruat" [The police science lab], in *Krom tamruat* [Police Department], *Botkhwam prakop khwam ru kiao kap tamruat* [Collected essays on topics related to the police], cremation volume printed in honor of Phraya Athikonprakat (given name Lui Jatikawanit) at Wat Thepsirintherawat, Bangkok, May 9, 1955, 284–286.
27. Ibid., 295. The exact year for which these figures hold is not clear in Somkit's article.
28. Ibid., 282–283.
29. Curtis, "Brief History," 24.
30. "Thailand Getting First Mobile Crime Laboratory This Month," *Bangkok Post,* October 13, 1959.
31. Curtis, "Brief History," 26.
32. Ibid., 26.
33. Samrit Sukhumwat, "Foreword 2," in Sanga, *Police Methods,* ญ.
34. NA [2]SR 0201.22.4/2, Committee to Consider the Economic Situation after the War, folder 1.
35. NA [2]SR 0201.22.4/14, Committee to Consider the Economic Situation after the War.
36. NA [2]SR 0201.22.4/2, Committee to Consider the Economic Situation after the War, folder 2.
37. NA [2]SR 0201.22.4/2, Committee to Consider the Economic Situation after the War, folder 1. For more on corruption in the rice industry after the war, see Thak, *Despotic Paternalism,* 21–22.
38. Chris Baker and Pasuk Phongpaichit, *Thailand: Economy and Politics,* 2nd ed. (Selangor, Malaysia: Oxford University Press, 2002), 197.
39. Chalong Soontravanich, "Small Arms, Romance, and Crime and Violence in Post World War II Thai Society," *Southeast Asian Studies* 43, no. 1 (2005): 31.

40. Baker and Pasuk, *Thailand,* 283.
41. Chalong, "Small Arms," 31.
42. Quoted in Baker and Pasuk, *Thailand,* 283.
43. Thak, *Despotic Paternalism,* 60–61.
44. Ibid., 60.
45. MacDonald, *Bangkok Editor,* 57.
46. Ibid., 58.
47. Kasian Tejaphira provides a table that lists political murders of the late 1940s and 1950s in *Commodifying Marxism: The Formation of Modern Thai Radical Culture, 1927–1958* (Kyoto: Kyoto University Press, 2001), 85.
48. Benedict Anderson calls the murders carried out by agents of the state "personal" murders because they are part of an "intra-upper-class" competition for power carried out behind closed doors. He sees this pattern of political violence lasting from 1932 to 1958, when Sarit comes to power. After that point, the targets of murder expand "outward and downward" into society. Benedict Anderson, "Murder and Progress in Modern Siam," in *Exploration and Irony in Studies of Siam over Forty Years* (Ithaca, NY: Cornell Southeast Asia Program, Cornell University, 2014), 103–104. See also his "Withdrawal Symptoms" in the same volume, in which he states that Phao and Sarit carried out their murders "administratively, behind closed doors" (75). The point is that the murders carried out in the open during the 1976 massacre of students at Thammasat was a qualitatively different sort of violence, perpetrated as a very public punishment of subversive elements of the liberal Left (75).
49. Testimony of Police Lieutenant Boonsom Atphadung given on December 3, 1957, in *Khadi kha phu uen dai doi jethana (4 ratthamontri)* [The case of the murder of four former ministers], Library and Museum of the Attorney General's Office (LMAG).
50. Testimony of Police Seargent Kiatisak Phuangthiang given on November 20, 1957, in ibid.
51. Benjamin Baston, *The Tragedy of Wanit* (Singapore: Journal of Southeast Asian Studies Special Publications Series No. 1, 1990), 19.
52. On Haji Sulong's life and disappearance see James Ockey, "Individual Imaginings: The Religio-nationalist Pilgrimages of Haji Sulong Abdulkadir al-Fatani," *Journal of Southeast Asian Studies* 42, no. 1 (2011): 89–119, esp. 117n109.
53. "Sixth Man Sought in Aree Murder," *Bangkok Post,* March 23, 1953.
54. Thak, *Despotic Paternalism,* 60.
55. Fineman, *Special Relationship,* 133.
56. Ibid., 134–135.
57. Ibid., 136–137.
58. Fred Riggs, *Thailand: The Modernization of a Bureaucratic Polity* (Honolulu: University of Hawai'i Press, 1966).

59. Tillman Durdin, "Thailand's Regime Shows Its Defects," *New York Times,* April 6, 1952.
60. Ibid.
61. Riggs, *Bureaucratic Polity,* 271–272.
62. Fineman, *Special Relationship,* 151.
63. Ibid., 162.
64. "Cola War Opening Here in March," *Bangkok Post,* February 19, 1953.
65. Thak, *Despotic Paternalism,* 224.
66. Riggs, *Bureaucratic Polity,* 253–254.
67. Craig Reynolds et al. provide a good way to conceptualize the loosely unified character of the Thai state in "Time's Arrow and the Burden of the Past: A Primer on the Thai Un-state," *Sensate* (2012), http://sensatejournal.com/2012/05/craig-reynolds-et-al-times-arrow/.
68. Fineman, *Special Relationship,* 158.
69. This version of events is adapted from accounts in several sources, including newspaper reports and memoirs, which differ, sometimes significantly, in their details. In some accounts there is only one gunman. In others, Ari was upstairs sleeping in his bedroom when the gunman (or gunmen) arrived at his bungalow. In cases of discrepancy, I have followed the narrative presented in Thawon Suwan, *Fa thalai nam muek* [Navigating a sea of ink] (Bangkok: Matichon Press, 2007), 199–224, which he claims are based on police interviews of witnesses.
70. Ibid., 220.
71. Narong Phoemphun, *Poet pum chiwit kamphon wacharaphon jao pho thai rat* [In praise of the life of Kamphon Wacharaphon: Godfather of *Thai rat*] (Bangkok: Black and Grey, 1989), 87. The term "soul shaking" (*khayao khwan*) was a common expression used in the press when writing about violence in the 1950s and 1960s.
72. "Kanchanburi Men Nabbed in Phetburi," *Bangkok Post,* March 10, 1953.
73. "Kanburi Police Say Their Trip Official," *Bangkok Post,* March 13, 1953.
74. Phinit was recalled from retirement to handle the investigation of the death of King Ananda in 1946.
75. "Sixth Man Sought in Aree Murder," *Bangkok Post,* March 23, 1953.
76. Attajak Sattayanurak, who gives the best and only account of what he calls "third-party politics," dates the emergence of phrases like "third hands" to the Sarit period, or 1957 onward. See his *Mue thi sam nai prawatsat kan mueang thai* [Third hands in Thailand's political history] (Bangkok: Khop Fai, 2006).
77. Viengrat Nethipo indicates that this term is first used in the paper *Thai rat* in February 1976 to describe a crime boss in Petchaburi province, south of Bangkok. Unpublished research notes provided by author in personal correspondence, 7.
78. Ibid. See also Attajak, *Third Hands.*

79. *Sia* is a term used for a wealthy entrepreneur who is typically of Chinese ancestry.
80. From *Siang ang thong,* August to December 1960 and March 18, 1960.
81. Examples include March 8, "Influence from Illegal Logging Boss [*ithiphon mai thuean*] behind [*bueang lang*] the Multiple Murder of Volunteer 8's Family"; March 14, "*Thai rat* Threatened Not to Report on Shooting Death of Volunteer's Friend, Influential Boss's [*jom ithiphon*] Gunman Laying Low"; March 14, "Influential Boss's Underlings in Volunteer's Friend's Shooting Death at Odds"; March 22, "Influential Boss's Gunman in Assassination of Volunteer's Friend Arrested"; March 24, "Influential Boss's Lackeys [*klum ithiphon*] Intimidate Special Investigation Unit in Shooting Death of Volunteer's Friend"; and March 25, "Police Suggest Moving Men of Influence in Case of Volunteer's Friend's Shooting Death."
82. Thak, *Despotic Paternalism,* 23.
83. MacDonald, *Bangkok Editor,* 143–144.
84. Robert Textor's multivolume study on supernatural objects in Thailand is perhaps the most complete catalog of the Thai spirit world in English. See Robert B. Textor, *Roster of the Gods: An Ethnography of the Supernatural in a Thai Village* (New Haven, CT: Human Relations Area Files, 1973).
85. Mark Fenster, *Conspiracy Theories: Secrecy and Power in American Culture* (Minneapolis: University of Minnesota Press, 2008), 1, 7.
86. "Thailand Holds 11 as Red Plotters," *New York Times,* August 27, 1953.
87. "Key Subversive Suspect Captured in Thailand," *Los Angeles Times,* July 6, 1954.
88. "Premier Suspects Plot in Thailand," *New York Times,* August 23, 1957.
89. "Reds in Thailand Kill Police Aides," *New York Times,* November 27, 1965.
90. George McArthur, "Uneasy Thai Regime Sees Devious Conspiracy," *Los Angeles Times,* October 24, 1976.
91. Attajak gives a comprehensive list of stories in the vernacular press that employ terms like "dark hand" in his *Third Hands.*
92. Richard Hofstadter, "The Paranoid Style in American Politics," *Harper's,* November 1964, 81, 85–86.
93. Thongchai Winichakul, *Siam Mapped: A History of the Geo-body of a Nation* (Honolulu: University of Hawai'i Press, 1997).
94. Somkiat Wanthana, "The Politics of Modern Thai Historiography" (PhD dissertation, Monash University, 1986), 329. Thak writes that this man was Democrat Party MP Liang Chaiyakan, who was arrested afterward.
95. Somsak Jiamthirasakul, "*Prisana karani sawanakhot*" [Mysterious case of regicide], *Fah diao kan* [Same sky] 6, no. 2 (April–June 2008): 123–124.
96. Thak, *Despotic Paternalism,* 24.
97. "Rumors," *Bangkok Post,* June 28, 1958.
98. Fineman, *Special Relationship,* 220.
99. Annette Hamilton, "Rumours, Foul Calumnies, and the Safety of the State: Mass Media and National Identity in Thailand," in *National Identity and Its*

Defenders: Thailand Today, ed. Craig Reynolds (Chiang Mai: Silkworm, 2002), 292.

100. Ibid., 293. See also Wassana Nanuam, *Lap luang phrang phak phitsadan* [Secrets, trickery, and camouflage: The improbable phenomena] (Bangkok: Post Books, 2008), which describes many of the "supernatural" tactics engaged in by politicians and others in recent political turmoil.
101. Michael T. Taussig, *Defacement: Public Secrecy and the Labor of the Negative* (Stanford, CA: Stanford University Press, 1999), 72.
102. Fredric Jameson, *The Geopolitical Aesthetic: Cinema and Space in the World System* (Bloomington: Indiana University Press, 1992), 2.
103. The Finland Plan is the name of an alleged compact made between Thaksin Shinawatra and the crown prince in Helsinki as to how to share power after the current monarch dies.
104. Benedict Anderson, "Introduction to *In the Mirror,*" in *Exploration and Irony in Studies of Siam over Forty Years* (Ithaca, NY: Cornell Southeast Asia Program, Cornell University, 2014), 90.
105. Hofstadter, "The Paranoid Style," 85.
106. MacDonald, *Bangkok Editor,* 178. Both Pridi and Thamrongnawasat were of Chinese ancestry and were born in Ayutthaya.
107. Hofstadter, "The Paranoid Style," 86.
108. Alan Sekula, "The Body and the Archive," in *Critical Histories of Photography,* ed. Richard Bolton (Cambridge, MA: MIT Press, 1992), 351.
109. Rosalind Morris, "Photography and the Power of Images in the History of Power," in *Photographies East: The Camera and Its Histories in East and Southeast Asia*, ed. Rosalind Morris (Durham, NC: Duke University Press, 2009), 140.
110. Ibid., 149.
111. Hofstadter, "The Paranoid Style," 86.
112. Robert Anton Wilson, *Illuminati Papers* (Berkeley, CA: Ronin Publishing, 1997), 2.

CONCLUSION

1. Letter from Prathin Santipraphop, commander of the Central Investigation Bureau, to the state prosecutor of Samut Prakan province, June 3, 1988, in trial documents for *Khadi choeri aen dankhaen fong kao* [The case of Sherry Ann Duncan, first trial], Library and Museum of the Attorney General's Office of Thailand.
2. Letter from special district attorney to Provincial Court of Samut Prakan, June 15, 1988, in ibid.
3. Cover letter dated October 17, 1995, Crime Suppression Division, in ibid.

4. K. I. Matics, "Hell Scenes in Thai Murals," *Journal of the Siam Society* 67, no. 2 (1979): 35–39.
5. Justin McDaniel, "The Agency between Images: The Relationships among Ghosts, Corpses, Monks, and Deities at a Buddhist Monastery in Thailand," *Material Religion* 7, no. 2 (2011): 246.
6. The notion of "visual culture" is one that scholars in art history and cultural studies began debating in the 1990s, when the term first began to circulate. See, for example, the "Visual Culture Questionnaire," *October* 77 (Summer 1996): 25–70.
7. Karen Strassler, *Refracted Visions: Popular Photography and Indonesian Modernity* (Durham, NC: Duke University Press, 2010).
8. Doreen Lee, "Anyone Can Do It: Aesthetic Empowerment, Urban Citizenship, and the Naturalization of Indonesian Graffiti and Street Art," *City and Society* 25, no. 3 (2013): 304–327.
9. James T. Siegel, *A New Criminal Type in Jakarta: Counter-revolution Today* (Durham, NC: Duke University Press, 1998).
10. See Alan Klima, *Funeral Casino: Meditation, Massacre, and Exchange with the Dead in Thailand* (Princeton, NJ: Princeton University Press, 2002), and Rosalind Morris, "Photography and the Power of Images in the History of Power," in *Photographies East: The Camera and Its Histories in East and Southeast Asia*, ed. Rosalind Morris (Durham, NC: Duke University Press, 2009), 121–160.
11. Edward Said, *Orientalism* (New York: Vintage Books, 1979).
12. The conventions for representational practices that existed in the colonies stood out as an area in which this correction would take place. Christopher Pinney's excellent work on photography in India, for example, shows that British colonialists in nineteenth-century India saw modern representational conventions as "a means of dismantling the Hindu world-view." Technical conventions, such as single-point perspective, "emerged as the key that would unravel an Indian resistance to the powers of observation." British advocates of art schooling wanted Indians to draw objects "correctly" and thus to move them away from their "dreamworld." Christopher Pinney, *Photos of the Gods: Printed Image and Political Struggle in India* (London: Reaktion Books, 2004), 18–19. This parallels the attempts of government officials to effect police reform through visual practices in Thailand.
13. Christopher Capozolla, "Photography and Power in the Colonial Philippines II," Visualizing Cultures website, http://ocw.mit.edu/ans7870/21f/21f.027/photography_and_power_02/dw02_essay01.htm.
14. Christopher Pinney, *Camera Indica: The Social Life of Indian Photographs* (Chicago: University of Chicago Press, 1997), 46.
15. Ibid.
16. Ibid.
17. Sarah Monks, "Introduction: Visual Culture in British India," *Visual Culture in Britain* 12, no. 3 (2011): 272.

18. Rosalind Morris, "Introduction," in Morris, *Photographies East,* 1. Thomson photographed King Mongkut during his stay in Siam.
19. Pinney, *Camera Indica*, 24.
20. Morris, "Photography and Power," 124.
21. Pinney, *Camera Indica*, 72.
22. Tani Barlow, "The Modern Girl around the World: Cosmetics Advertising and the Politics of Race and Style," in *The Modern Girl around the World: Consumption, Modernity, and Globalization*, ed. Alys Eve Weinbaum, Lynn M. Thomas, Priti Ramamurthy, Uta G. Poiger, Madeleine Yue Dong, and Tani E. Barlow (Durham, NC: Duke University Press, 2008), 25–54. On Burma, see Chie Ikeya, *Refiguring Women, Colonialism, and Modernity in Burma* (Honolulu: University of Hawai'i Press, 2010).
23. Walter Persaud, "Gender, Race, and Global Modernity: A Perspective from Thailand," *Globalizations* 2, no. 2 (September 2005): 210–227.
24. Annette Hamilton, "Rumours, Foul Calumnies, and the Safety of the State: Mass Media and National Identity in Thailand," in *National Identity and Its Defenders: Thailand Today*, ed. Craig Reynolds (Chiang Mai: Silkworm, 2002), 280.
25. Pinney, *Photos of the Gods*, 12, 116.
26. Franco Moretti, "Clues," in *Signs Taken for Wonders: Essays in the Sociology of Literary Forms*, trans. Susan Fischer, David Forgacs, and David Miller (London: Verso, 1983), 132.
27. Carlo Ginzburg, "From Aby Warburgh to E. H. Gombrich: A Problem of Method," in *Clues, Myths, and the Historical Method,* trans. John Tedeschi and Anne C. Tedeschi (Baltimore: Johns Hopkins University Press, 1992), 17–59, cited in Pinney, *Photos of the Gods*, 117.
28. Susan Sontag, "Against Interpretation," in *Against Interpretation and Other Essays* (New York: Picador, 2001).
29. Morris, "Photography and Power," 131.
30. Strassler, *Refracted Visions*, 219.
31. Alan Sekula, "The Body and the Archive," in *Critical Histories of Photography*, ed. Richard Bolton (Cambridge, MA: MIT Press, 1992), 345.
32. McDaniel, "The Agency between Images." Gell argues that art objects mediate social agency, motivate individuals to make "abductions" or inferences, and are catalysts for action. Alfred Gell, *Art and Agency: An Anthropological Theory* (Oxford: Oxford University Press, 1998), 7.
33. Some of Moretti's work, including *Graphs, Maps, and Trees: Abstract Models for Literary History* (London: Verso, 2007); "The Slaughterhouse of Literature," *Modern Language Quarterly* 61, no. 1 (March 2000): 207–227; and *Atlas of the European Novel, 1800–1900* (London: Verso, 1999) do this well, combining formal analysis with interpretive methods for the study of literature.

34. Eugene S. Ferguson, "The Mind's Eye: Nonverbal Thought in Technology," *Science* 197, no. 4306 (August 26, 1977): 827.
35. Ibid., 828.
36. Michael Lynch, "Discipline and the Material Form of Images: An Analysis of Scientific Visibility," *Social Studies of Science* 15, no. 1 (February 1985): 37, 43.
37. Thongchai Winichakul, *Siam Mapped: A History of the Geo-body of a Nation* (Honolulu: University of Hawai'i Press, 1994), 129–130.
38. Ibid., 118.
39. John Bender and Michael Marrinan, *The Culture of Diagram* (Palo Alto, CA: Stanford University Press, 2010), 23.
40. Sanga Kittikhajon, *Withayakan tamruat kiao kap kan suep suan* [Police methods related to investigation] (Bangkok: Prasoetakson, 1953), 464.
41. Jack Goody, *Domestication of the Savage Mind* (Cambridge: Cambridge University Press, 1977), 156.
42. Michael Lynch, "Science in the Age of Mechanical Reproduction: Moral and Epistemic Relations between Diagrams and Photographs," *Biology and Philosophy* 6 (1991): 207.
43. Lynch defines aesthetics in scientific representation much as I do for legal representations. They are "conventions and standards for crafting illustrations and assessing their visual qualities." Ibid., 210.
44. Lynch, "Discipline," 60.
45. Bruno Latour, "Drawing Things Together," in *Representation in Scientific Practice* (Cambridge, MA: MIT Press, 1990), 30.
46. Jennifer Mnookin, "The Image of Truth: Photographic Evidence and the Power of Analogy," *Yale Journal of Law and the Humanities* 10 (1998): 64–65.
47. On the whispering ghost and its decline (as well as the relative decline of other supernatural objects), see Robert B. Textor, *Roster of the Gods: An Ethnography of the Supernatural in a Thai Village* (New Haven, CT: Human Relations Area Files, 1973). On the increase in the belief in spirits and other supernatural causes in accidents and misfortunes see David M. Engel, "Landscapes of the Law: Injury, Remedy, and Social Change in Thailand," *Law and Society Review* 43, no. 1 (2009): 61–94.
48. See Craig Reynolds, "Rural Male Leadership, Religion and the Environment in Thailand's Mid-South, 1920s–1960s," *Journal of Southeast Asian Studies* 42, no. 1 (2011): 39–57, for a detailed discussion on the life of Khun Phanthararatchadet and his use of supernatural objects in police work.
49. Goody, *Domestication*, 1.
50. Ibid., 16.

BIBLIOGRAPHY

ARCHIVAL SOURCES

National Archives of Thailand

The National Archives of Thailand (NA) generally organizes documents from before 1932 according to reign. Within each reign, documents are typically grouped according to ministry or other institution. Documents are given an index code following the first letter of the name of the ministry or agency. Accordingly, NA R5 N means National Archives, Documents from the Fifth Reign, Ministry of Local Government (*nakhonban*), and NA R6 Y means National Archives, Documents from the Sixth Reign, Ministry of Justice (*yuttitham*). The number that follows this indicates a subtopic within the collection.

Ministry of Finance (*Krasuang kan khlang*)

NA K 0301.1.21—Office of the Financial Adviser, Law and Justice
NA K 0301.1.22—Office of the Financial Adviser, Police and Jails

Ministry of Interior (*Krasuang mahathai*)

NA R7 M 11—Provincial, Metropolitan, and Investigative Police

Ministry of Justice (*Krasuang yuttitham*)

NA R5 Y 4—Files of the Legal Adviser Stewart Black
NA R5 Y 4.1—Files of the Legal Adviser Stewart Black, Case Files
NA R5 Y 10—Supreme Court
NA R6 Y 13—Provincial Courts

Ministry of Local Government (*Krasuang nakhonban*)

NA R5 N 8.1—Metropolitan Constabulary, General Duties
NA R5 N 8.2ก—Metropolitan Constabulary, Foreign Nationals in Government Service
NA R5 N 8.6—Metropolitan Constabulary (Miscellaneous Reports)
NA R5 N 102—Report on the Police Administration of Bangkok Town, Northern and Southern Suburbs and Railway District, 1903 [in English]
NA R6 N 4.1—Metropolitan and Provincial Police, General Duties

NA R6 N 4.2—Metropolitan and Provincial Police, Announcements and Royal Decrees
NA R6 N 4.5—Metropolitan and Provincial Police (Inspector of Police)
NA R6 N 4.5ก—Metropolitan and Provincial Police (Inspector of Police), Inspecting Police Work
NA R6 N 4.6—Metropolitan and Provincial Police, Police Academy
NA R6 N 20.5—Newspapers, Provincial News
NA R6 N 20.6—Newspapers, Articles in Newspapers

Office of the Secretary of the Prime Minister

NA [2]SR 0201.22.4—Committee to Consider the Economic Situation after the War

Royal Secretariat (*Phraratchalekhanukan*)

NA R5–6 PL Section 1—The Constabulary

Library and Museum of the Attorney General's Office of Thailand

Documents at the Library and Museum of the Attorney General's Office of Thailand are kept in boxes grouped according to case name.
Khadi choeri aen dankhaen fong kao [The case of Sherry Ann Duncan, first trial]
Khadi choeri aen dankhaen fong mai [The case of Sherry Ann Duncan, second trial]
Khadi kha phu uen dai doi jethana (4 ratthamontri) [The case of the murder of four former ministers]

Newspapers and Magazines

Bangkok Daily Mail, 1928–1930
Bangkok Post, 1946–1959, 1973, 2000–present
Deli me, 1954
Deli nio, 1986
Krungthep deli me, 1928–1929
Los Angeles Times, 1954, 1976
Nation, 2011
New York Times, 1951–1953, 1957, 1965, 1970, 1974
Phim thai bueang lang khao, 1956–1957
Phim thai lang khao sapada, 1953
Phim thai rai duean, 1954
Phim thai rai pak, 1957
Phim thai rai wan, 1958
Sayam nikon, 1949

Senasueksa lae phae withayasat, 1921
Siang ang thong, 1960
Tamruat, 1921
Thai rat, 1961–1970, 1973, 1980–1990, 2000–present
Thesaphiban, 1908–1931
Wachirayan, 1896

SECONDARY SOURCES

Anderson, Benedict. "Introduction to *In the Mirror*." In *Exploration and Irony in Studies of Siam over Forty Years,* 77–99. Ithaca, NY: Cornell Southeast Asia Program, Cornell University, 2014.

———. "Murder and Progress in Modern Siam." In *Exploration and Irony in Studies of Siam over Forty Years,* 101–115. Ithaca, NY: Cornell Southeast Asia Program, Cornell University, 2014.

———. "Withdrawal Symptoms." In *Exploration and Irony in Studies of Siam over Forty Years,* 47–76. Ithaca, NY: Cornell Southeast Asia Program, Cornell University, 2014.

Anek Nawigamune. *Dao rai nai adit* [Criminals in the past]. Bangkok: Saeng Daet, 1995.

———. *Prawat kan thai rup yuk raek khong thai* [History of early photography in Thailand]. Bangkok: Sarakhadi Phap, 2005.

Aphisak Thongnaphakhun and Jutharat Ua-amnoey. *Kan prachathan kap kan khum khrong sithi khong phu tong ha nai kan nam chi thi koet het prakop kham rap saraphap* [Vigilantism and the protection of the rights of suspects in the practice of pointing out a location of a crime to support a confession]. Draft paper, 2010.

Attajak Sattayanurak. *Mue thi sam nai prawatsat kan mueang thai* [Third hands in Thailand's political history]. Bangkok: Khop Fai, 2006.

Baden-Powell, Sir Robert. *My Adventures as a Spy.* London: Arthur Pearson, 1915.

Baker, Chris, and Pasuk Phongpaichit, trans. *The Tale of Khun Chang Khun Phaen: A Siamese Epic of Love, War, and Tragedy.* Seattle: University of Washington Press, 2012.

———. *Thailand: Economy and Politics.* 2nd ed. Selangor, Malaysia: Oxford University Press, 2002.

Bakhtin, Mikhail. "Forms of Time and of the Chronotope in the Novel." In *The Dialogic Imagination: Four Essays by M. M. Bakhtin,* translated by Michael Holquist and Caryl Emerson, 84–258. Austin: University of Texas Press, 1981.

Barlow, Tani. "The Modern Girl around the World: Cosmetics Advertising and the Politics of Race and Style." In *The Modern Girl around the World: Consumption, Modernity, and Globalization,* edited by Alys Eve Weinbaum, Lynn M.

Thomas, Priti Ramamurthy, Uta G. Poiger, Madeleine Yue Dong, and Tani E. Barlow, 25–54. Durham, NC: Duke University Press, 2008.

Bastian, Adolf. *A Journey in Siam.* Translated by Walter E. J. Tips. Bangkok: White Lotus, 2005.

Baston, Benjamin. *The Tragedy of Wanit.* Singapore: Journal of Southeast Asian Studies Special Publications Series No. 1, 1990.

Bender, John, and Michael Marrinan. *The Culture of Diagram.* Palo Alto, CA: Stanford University Press, 2010.

Bock, Carl. *Temples and Elephants: The Narrative of a Journey of Exploration through Upper Siam and Lao.* Bangkok: White Orchid Press, 1985.

Caldwell, J. Alexander. *American Economic Aid to Thailand.* Toronto: Lexington Books, 1974.

Capozolla, Christopher. "Photography and Power in the Colonial Philippines II." Visualizing Cultures. http://ocw.mit.edu/ans7870/21f/21f.027/photography_and_power_02/dw02_essay01.htm.

Carte, Gene E., and Elaine H. Carte. *Police Reform in the United States: The Era of August Vollmer, 1905–1922.* Berkeley: University of California Press, 1975.

Chalong Soontravanich. "Small Arms, Romance, and Crime and Violence in Post World War II Thai Society." *Southeast Asian Studies* 43, no. 1 (2005): 26–46.

Chiwit lae ngan khong ari liwira [The life and work of Ari Liwira]. Bangkok: Siam Phanitchayakan, 1963.

Chumsai Chaiwat. "Botbat thang kanmueang khong phon tamruat aek phao siyanon, phoso 2490–2500" [The role of Phao Sriyanond in politics, 1947–1957]. Master's thesis, Chulalongkorn University, 1995.

Cole, Simon A. *Suspect Identities: A History of Fingerprinting and Criminal Identification.* Cambridge, MA: Harvard University Press, 2001.

Criminal Law Institute. *Raingan kan sewana thang wichakan rueang khadi choeriaen. . . . krabuan kan yuttitham ja khum khrong sitthi seriphap khong phu borisut dai yangrai* [Report from seminar on the case of Sherry Ann. . . . How will the justice system protect the rights and freedoms of the innocent?]. Bangkok: Office of the Attorney General, 1996.

Curtis, Theodore J. "A Brief History of USOM Support to the Thai National Police Department." A report prepared by the United States Operations Mission, Agency for International Development, Thailand, July 1973.

Daston, Lorraine. *Biographies of Scientific Objects.* Chicago: University of Chicago Press, 2000.

———."Historical Epistemology." In *Questions of Evidence: Proof, Practice, and Persuasion across the Disciplines,* edited by James Chandler, Arnold Davidson, and Harry Harootunian, 282–289. Chicago: University of Chicago Press, 1994.

Daston, Lorraine, and Peter Galison. "The Image of Objectivity." *Representations* 40 (Autumn 1992): 81–128.

Day, Tony, and Craig J. Reynolds. "Cosmologies, Truth Regimes, and the State in Southeast Asia." *Modern Asian Studies* 34, no. 1 (February 2000): 1–55.

Eade, J. C. *The Calendrical Systems of Mainland Southeast Asia.* Leiden, Netherlands: E. J. Brill, 1995.

Engel, David M. "Globalization and the Decline of Legal Consciousness: Torts, Ghosts, and Karma in Thailand." *Law and Social Inquiry* 30, no. 3 (2005): 469–514.

———. "Landscapes of the Law: Injury, Remedy, and Social Change in Thailand." *Law and Society Review* 43, no. 1 (2009): 61–94.

Executive Committee of the Eighth Congress of the Far Eastern Association of Tropical Medicine. *Siam in 1930: General and Medical Features.* Bangkok: White Lotus, 2000.

Fairclough, Gordon. "Thailand: Hidden Hands." *Far Eastern Economic Review,* June 19, 1994.

Fenster, Mark. *Conspiracy Theories: Secrecy and Power in American Culture.* Minneapolis: University of Minnesota Press, 2008.

Ferguson, Eugene S. "The Mind's Eye: Nonverbal Thought in Technology." *Science* 197, no. 4306 (August 26, 1977): 827–836.

Fineman, Daniel. *A Special Relationship: The United States and Military Government in Thailand, 1947–1958.* Honolulu: University of Hawai'i Press, 1997.

Forty, Cecil H. "Cremation Volume for Police Lieutenant Colonel C. H. Forty." Bangkok, 1967.

Foucault, Michel. "Of Other Spaces, Heterotopias." *Architecture, Mouvement, Continuité* 5 (1984): 46–49. http://foucault.info/documents/heteroTopia/foucault.heteroTopia.en.html.

———. *State, Territory, Population: Lectures at the Collège de France, 1977–1978.* New York: Picador, 2009.

Freeman, Andrew. *A Journalist in Siam.* Bangkok: White Lotus, 2007.

Fry, Erika. "Arresting Theatre." *Bangkok Post,* August 10, 2008.

Gell, Alfred. *Art and Agency: An Anthropological Theory.* Oxford: Oxford University Press, 1998.

———. "Vogel's Net: Traps as Artworks and Artworks as Traps." *Journal of Material Culture* 1 (1996): 15–38.

Ginzburg, Carlo. "Checking the Evidence: The Judge and the Historian." In *Questions of Evidence: Proof, Practice, and Persuasion across the Disciplines,* edited by James Chandler, Arnold Davidson, and Harry Harootunian, 290–303. Chicago: University of Chicago Press, 1994.

———. "Clues: Roots of an Evidential Paradigm." In *Clues, Myths, and the Historical Method,* translated by John Tedeschi and Anne C. Tedeschi, 96–125. Baltimore: Johns Hopkins University Press, 1992.

———. "From Aby Warburgh to E. H. Gombrich: A Problem of Method." In *Clues, Myths, and the Historical Method,* translated by John Tedeschi and Anne C. Tedeschi, 17–59. Baltimore: Johns Hopkins University Press, 1992.

———. "Representing the Enemy: Historical Evidence and Its Ambiguities." In *Evidence,* edited by Andrew Bell, John Swenson-Wright, and Karin Tybjerg, 29–47. Cambridge: Cambridge University Press, 2008.

Goody, Jack. *Domestication of the Savage Mind.* Cambridge: Cambridge University Press, 1977.

Gunning, Tom. "Embarrassing Evidence." In *Collecting Visible Evidence,* edited by Jane Gaines and Michael Renov, 46–64. Minneapolis: University of Minnesota Press, 1999.

Hamilton, Annette. "Rumours, Foul Calumnies, and the Safety of the State: Mass Media and National Identity in Thailand." In *National Identity and Its Defenders: Thailand Today,* edited by Craig Reynolds, 277–307. Chiang Mai: Silkworm, 2002.

Harrison, Rachel. "The Allure of Ambiguity: The 'West' and the Making of Thai Identities." In *The Ambiguous Allure of the West: Traces of the Colonial in Thailand,* edited by Rachel Harrison, 1–36. Hong Kong: Hong Kong University Press, 2010.

Hayi Khiat [pseud.]. *Ai bunphengphu rai samkhan hip lek* [Bunpheng, the villain of the iron trunk]. Bangkok: Bangkok Press, 1919.

Hofstadter, Richard. "The Paranoid Style in American Politics." *Harper's,* November 1964.

Human Rights Watch. "Not Enough Graves: The War on Drugs, HIV/AIDS, and Violations of Human Rights." June 2004. http://www.hrw.org/reports/2004/thailand0704/4.htm.

Ikeya, Chie. *Refiguring Women, Colonialism, and Modernity in Burma.* Honolulu: University of Hawai'i Press, 2010.

Ingram, James. *Economic Change in Thailand, 1850–1970.* Palo Alto, CA: Stanford University Press, 1971.

Jameson, Fredric. *The Geopolitical Aesthetic: Cinema and Space in the World System.* Bloomington: Indiana University Press, 1992.

Jao Phraya Surasakmontri. *Prawat khong jom phon jao phraya surasakmontri* [The biography of Jao Phraya Surasakmontri]. Bangkok: Khrusapha, 1951.

Jarun Wathanasin. *Choeri-aen* [Sherry Ann]. Bangkok: Nation Multimedia Group, 2001.

Johnston, David Bruce. "Rural Society and the Rice Economy in Thailand, 1880–1930." PhD diss., Yale University, 1977.

Kasian Tejaphira. *Commodifying Marxism: The Formation of Modern Thai Radical Culture, 1927–1958.* Kyoto: Kyoto University Press, 2001.

Khamphiphaksa khadi pratutsarai to phrabat somdet phraparamentaramaha ananthamahidon ratchakan thi 8 [Court verdict in the case of criminal violence committed against King Ananda Mahidol], case numbers 1878/2491-black and 1266/2494-red, with a foreword by Police Lieutenant General Phra Phinit Chonkhadi. Bangkok: Krung Sayam Kanphim, 1974.

Khatha Dam [pseud.]. *Kha nak nangsue phim* [The murder of a newspaperman]. Thonburi, Thailand: Thanakanphim, 1971.

Klima, Alan. *Funeral Casino: Meditation, Massacre, and Exchange with the Dead in Thailand.* Princeton, NJ: Princeton University Press, 2002.

Kotmai phijarana khadi aya [Criminal procedural code of the Kingdom of Siam]. Promulgated March 7, 1934, by the House of Representatives, effective October 1, 1935.

"Kotmai polit 53 kho sueng ja raksa nathi nai phranakhon lae nok phranakhon" [Fifty-three rules for the police to uphold in and outside of Phranakhon]. In *Prachum kotmai prajam sok lem 9* [Collected laws, volume 9], ed. Sathian Lailak, 92–96 (Bangkok: Daily Mail, 1875).

Kotmai tra sam duang [The law of the three seals]. Bangkok: Khrusapha, 1963.

Krom Phraya Damrong Rajanubhab. "Rueang sonthana kap phu rai plon" [Interview with a bandit]. In cremation volume for Phra Tamruat Tri Phraya Aphichitchanyut (given name Jaroen Sawettanan), 1–42 (Bangkok: Sophonphiphatthanakon, 1925).

Kullasap Gesmankit. "Preface." In King Lithai, *Traibhumikatha: The Story of the Three Planes of Existence*, translated by Thai National Team, 11–15. Bangkok: ASEAN Committee on Culture and Information, 1987.

Lak inthaphat [Indra's instructions]. In *Nitipratya thai: Prakat phraratchaprarot lak inthaphat phrathammasat lae "On the Laws of Mu'ung Thai or Siam"* [Thai legal theory: Royal announcements, the Lak Inthapat, and "On the Laws of Mueang Thai or Siam"], 13–58. Bangkok: Samnakngan Kong Thun Sanapsanun Kan Wichai, 2005.

Latour, Bruno, "Drawing Things Together." In *Representation in Scientific Practice,* 19–68. Cambridge, MA: MIT Press, 1990.

Lawson, Eric St. John. *Police Manual.* Bangkok: American Presbyterian Mission Press, 1906.

———. "Police and Provincial Gendarmerie." In *Twentieth Century Impressions of Siam: Its History, People, Commerce, Industries, and Resources,* edited by Arnold Wright and Oliver T. Breakspear, 107–111. Bangkok: White Lotus, 1994.

Lee, Doreen. "Anyone Can Do It: Aesthetic Empowerment, Urban Citizenship, and the Naturalization of Indonesian Graffiti and Street Art." *City and Society* 25, no. 3 (2013): 304–327.

Le May, Reginald. *An Asian Arcady: The Land and Peoples of Northern Siam.* Bangkok: White Lotus, 1999.

Lim, Samson. "The Case of Volunteer 8: Proof, Violence, and History in Thai Society." *Critical Asian Studies* 43, no. 3 (2011): 399–420.

———. "Detective Fiction, the Police, and Secrecy in Early Twentieth Century Siam." *Southeast Asia Research* 20, no. 1 (2012): 83–102.

———. "Murder! in Thailand's Vernacular Press." *Journal of Asian Studies* 73, no. 2 (May 2014): 359–376.

King Lithai. *Traibhumikatha: The Story of the Three Planes of Existence.* Translated by Thai National Team. Bangkok: ASEAN Committee on Culture and Information, 1987.

Lobe, Thomas. *United States National Security Policy and Aid to the Thailand Police.* Denver: University of Denver, Graduate School of International Studies, 1977.

Lombroso, Cesare. *Criminal Man: According to the Classification of Cesare Lombroso.* New York: Knickerbocker Press, 1911.

Loos, Tamara. *Subject Siam: Family, Law, and Colonial Modernity in Thailand.* Ithaca, NY: Cornell University Press, 2006.

Luang Bannasanprasit (Sithi Rojanawiphat). *Lak lae withikan suep suan tai suan khadi aya* [Rules and techniques for investigating criminal cases]. Bangkok: Aksonniti, 1929.

Luang Phisitwithayakan. *Tamruat kap lak kan suep suan* [The police and the rules of investigation]. Bangkok: Police Department, 1935.

———. "Lai nio mue phu rai nai thi koet het" [Fingerprints at the scene of a crime]. *Tamruat* [Police] 1, no. 3 (February 1931): 233–245.

———. *Prachachon atja chuai ratchakan tamruat dai yangrai (thang withayu krajai siang)* [How citizens can help the police (a radio address)]. In *Nangsue ngan napanakit khong nang phijanwonlakit* [Commemorative volume for Miss Phijanwonlakit]. Bangkok, 1934.

———. *Suep khadi luek lap* [Investigating mysterious cases]. In cremation volume for military and police officers who died in service during the Boworadet Rebellion of 1933. Cremation ceremony at Sanam Luang on February 18, 1933.

Luang Withayathikonsak. "Khwam phajon phai khong soe roboet beden paowen" [The adventures of Sir Robert Baden-Powell]. *Senasueksa lae phae withayasat* [Military studies and the spread of science] 5, nos. 1–6 (1921): 38–43, 129–142, 309–316, 362–374, 499–505, 575–582.

Lynch, Michael. "Discipline and the Material Form of Images: An Analysis of Scientific Visibility." *Social Studies of Science* 15, no. 1 (February 1985): 37–66.

———. "Science in the Age of Mechanical Reproduction: Moral and Epistemic Relations between Diagrams and Photographs." *Biology and Philosophy* 6 (1991): 205–226.

MacDonald, Alexander. *Bangkok Editor.* New York: Macmillan, 1949.

Matics, K. I. "Hell Scenes in Thai Murals." *Journal of the Siam Society* 67, no. 2 (1979): 35–39.

McDaniel, Justin. "The Agency between Images: The Relationships among Ghosts, Corpses, Monks, and Deities at a Buddhist Monastery in Thailand." *Material Religion* 7, no. 2 (2011): 242–267.

Mizutani Yasuhiro. "A Modern Thai State Stumbling: The Expansion of the Police in Thailand from the 1930s to 1940s." [In Japanese.] *Southeast Asian Studies* 43, no. 2 (September 2009): 191–209.

Mnookin, Jennifer. "The Image of Truth: Photographic Evidence and the Power of Analogy." *Yale Journal of Law and the Humanities* 10 (1998): 1–74.

Monks, Sarah. "Introduction: Visual Culture and British India." *Visual Culture in Britain* 12, no. 3 (2011): 269–275.

Moretti, Franco. *Atlas of the European Novel, 1800–1900*. London: Verso, 1999.

———. "Clues." In *Signs Taken for Wonders: Essays in the Sociology of Literary Forms,* translated by Susan Fischer, David Forgacs, and David Miller, 130–156. London: Verso, 1983.

———. *Graphs, Maps, and Trees: Abstract Models for Literary History.* London: Verso, 2007.

———. "The Slaughterhouse of Literature." *Modern Language Quarterly* 61, no. 1 (March 2000): 207–227.

Morris, Rosalind. "Introduction." In *Photographies East: The Camera and Its Histories in East and Southeast Asia,* edited by Rosalind Morris, 1–28. Durham, NC: Duke University Press, 2009.

———. "Photography and the Power of Images in the History of Power." In *Photographies East: The Camera and Its Histories in East and Southeast Asia,* edited by Rosalind Morris, 121–160. Durham, NC: Duke University Press, 2009.

Nai Janthana [Malai Chuphinit]. *Suea fai sip thit* [Tiger Fai of the ten directions]. Bangkok: Samnakphim Krathom, 1998.

Nai Kaeo and Nai Khwan [King Vajiravudh]. *Nithan Thong-in* [The stories of Thong-in]. Bangkok, 1930.

Narong Phoemphun. *Poet pum chiwit kamphon wacharaphon jao pho thai rat* [In praise of the life of Kamphon Wacharaphon: Godfather of *Thai rat*]. Bangkok: Black and Grey, 1989.

Neale, Frederick Arthur. *Narrative of a Residence in Siam.* Bangkok: White Lotus, 1996.

Nidhi Eoseewong. "The World of Lady Nophamat." In *Pen and Sail: Literature and History in Early Bangkok,* translated by Chris Baker, Benedict Anderson, Craig J. Reynolds, Hong Lysa, Pasuk Phongpaichit, Patrick Jory, and Ruth McVey, 227–254. Chiang Mai: Silkworm Books, 2005.

Ockey, James. "Individual Imaginings: The Religio-nationalist Pilgrimages of Haji Sulong Abdulkadir al-Fatani." *Journal of Southeast Asian Studies* 42, no. 1 (2011): 89–119.

Oeler, Karla. *A Grammar of Murder: Violent Scenes and Film Form*. Chicago: University of Chicago Press, 2009.

Pattamakorn Bullstaporn. "Khwam ru nai tamra phrommachat" [The knowledge of the Phrommachat]. Master's thesis, Chiang Mai University, 1996.

Pattana Kitiarsa. "Lives of Hunting Dogs: 'Muai Thai' and the Politics of Thai Masculinities." *South East Asia Research* 13, no. 1 (March 2005): 57–90.

Pattaravit Obsuwan. "Kan tham phaen prathutsakam prakop kham rap saraphap nai robop kotmai thai" [Crime science reconstruction by the accused to support confession of the accused in the Thai legal system]. Master's thesis, Thammasat University, 2007.

Persaud, Walter. "Gender, Race, and Global Modernity: A Perspective from Thailand." *Globalizations* 2, no. 2 (September 2005): 210–227.

Phao Sriyanond. "Khwam rusuek khong khaphajao" [My feelings]. In Sanga Kittikhajon, *Withayakan tamruat kiao kap kan suep suan* [Police methods related to investigation], ก–ฉ. Bangkok: Prasoetakson, 1953.

Phirasak Chaidaisuk. *Chat suea wai lai* [Once a tiger, always a tiger]. Bangkok: Matichon Press, 2008.

Phra Phinit Chonkhadi. *Nithan tamruat* [The story of the police]. Bangkok: Thai Watthana Phanit, 1963.

Phra Sisena (Kit Katchachiwa). *Withi suep suan jon phu rai lem 1* [Methods for investigating criminals, vol. 1]. Bangkok: Phraratchapantit, 1917.

Phraya Manawaratchasewi. *Kan tai suan lae kan phijarana rueang kha nai pin aekaraphanit thi jangwat janburi* [The investigation and deliberation of the case of the murder of Mr. Pin Aekaraphanit in Janthaburi province]. Bangkok, 1930.

———. *Lak kan suep suan khadi aya* [The foundations for investigating criminal cases]. Bangkok: Bamrung Nukunlakit, 1929.

Pinney, Christopher. *Camera Indica: The Social Life of Indian Photographs*. Chicago: University of Chicago Press, 1997.

———. *Photos of the Gods: Printed Image and Political Struggle in India*. London: Reaktion Books, 2004.

Piyakanit Hongthong. *Nangsue chue sayam sanuk khao* [A book called fun news of Siam]. Bangkok: Kanya Publishing, 1988.

Porphant Ouyyanont. "Physical and Economic Change in Bangkok, 1851–1925." *Southeast Asian Studies* 36, no. 4 (March 1999): 437–474.

"Prawat kiao kap kan sop suan khadi aya khong phanakngan sop suan fai pokkhrong nai phumiphak" [History related to investigating criminal cases by civilian investigators in the provinces], 3–8. In *Krom kan pokkhrong* [Civil administration]. Bangkok: Krommakan Pokkhrong, 1984.

Pridi Phanomyong. *Pathakatha rueang panha kiao kae kan long atchaya phu kratham phit kotmai* [Problems related to punishing people who break the law]. Lecture given on August 10, 1928, published in festschrift for Samunwinathoramontri Na Susanluang at Wat Thepsirinarat, 1931.

"Raingan prachum thesaphiban roso 126" [Report for provincial administration meeting, 1907]. *Thesaphiban* [Provincial administration journal] 4, no. 22 (1908): 111–154.

Ramajit [King Vajiravudh]. *Prapruethikan khong nai thong-in rathanet* [The adventures of Thong-in Rathanet]. Edited by Rattanachai Lueangwongngam. Bangkok: Samoson Nangsue Rahatsakhadi, 2006.

Reynolds, Craig J. "Rural Male Leadership, Religion and the Environment in Thailand's Mid-South, 1920s–1960s." *Journal of Southeast Asian Studies* 42, no. 1 (2011): 39–57.

Reynolds, Craig J., Yoshinori Nishizaki, Jim Glassman, Nicholas Farrelly, Pongphisoot Busbarat, Samson Lim, Tyrell Haberkorn, and Pavin Chachavalpongpun. "Time's Arrow and the Burden of the Past: A Primer on the Thai Un-state." *Sensate* (2012). http://sensatejournal.com/2012/05/craig-reynolds-et-al-times-arrow/.

Riggs, Fred. *Thailand: The Modernization of a Bureaucratic Polity.* Honolulu: University of Hawai'i Press, 1966.

Rotsukhon Jaratsi. "Botbat khong kharatchakan chao tang prathet nai krom tamruat nai samai somburananasithirat" [The role of foreign civil servants in the police department under the absolute monarchy]. Master's thesis, Chulalongkorn University, 1977.

"Royal Announcement on the Consolidation of the Provincial Gendarmerie and the Metropolitan Constabulary." *Royal Gazette,* no. 32, October 17, 1915.

"Rueang khong nangsuephim mueang thai pen bunthuek khwam khong phu sonjai nangsuephim khon nueng" [The story of newspapers in Thailand: A record by an interested person]. In *Chiwit lae ngan khong ari liwira* [Life and work of Ari Liwira], n.p. Bangkok: Siam Phanitchayakan, 1963.

Rut Manthira. *Jap phae buchayan khayao wongkan yuttitham sathuean wai* [Arresting a scapegoat, shaking up the circles of justice]. Bangkok: Namfon, 1996.

Said, Edward. *Orientalism.* New York: Vintage Books, 1979.

Samrit Sukhumwat. "Foreword 2." In Sanga Kittikhajon, *Withayakan tamruat kiao kap kan suep suan* [Police methods related to investigation], ข–ฎ. Bangkok: Prasoetakson, 1953.

Sanga Kittikhajon. *Withayakan tamruat kiao kap kan suep suan* [Police methods related to investigation]. Bangkok: Prasoetakson, 1953.

Sekula, Alan. "The Body and the Archive." In *The Contest of Meaning: Critical Histories of Photography,* edited by Richard Bolton, 343–389. Cambridge, MA: MIT Press, 1992.

Siegel, James T. *A New Criminal Type in Jakarta: Counter-revolution Today.* Durham, NC: Duke University Press, 1998.

Skinner, G. William. *Chinese Society in Thailand: An Analytical History.* Ithaca, NY: Cornell University Press, 1957.

Somkiat Wanthana. "The Politics of Modern Thai Historiography." PhD diss., Monash University, 1986.

Somkit Santhunsing. "Ho withayakan tamruat" [The police science lab]. In *Krom tamruat* [Police Department], *Botkhwam prakop khwam ru kiao kap tamruat* [Collected essays on topics related to the police], 281–290. Cremation volume printed in honor of Phraya Athikonprakat (Lui Jatikawanit) at Wat Thepsirintherawat. Bangkok, May 9, 1955.

Somphong Jaengrew. "Kamnoet tamruat santiban nai prawatsat kanmueang thai samai 2475" [The origins of the special branch of the police in the political history of Thailand during the 1932 period]. *Silapa wathanatham* [Art and culture], November 2008, 120–131.

Somsak Jiamthirasakul. "Prisana karani sawanakhot" [Mysterious case of regicide]. *Fah diao kan* [Same sky] 6, no. 2 (April–June 2008): 116–135.

Sontag, Susan. "Against Interpretation." In *Against Interpretation and Other Essays.* New York: Picador, 2001.

Starr, Douglass. *The Killer of Little Shepherds: A True Crime Story and the Birth of Forensic Science.* New York: Alfred Knopf, 2010.

Sternstein, Larry. "Bangkok at the Turn of the Century: Mongut and Chulalongkorn Entertain the West." *Journal of Siam Society* 54, no. 1 (1966): 55–71.

———. "Krungthep at One Hundred: Scape and Grid." *Journal of the Siam Society* 67, no. 2 (July 1979): 1–20.

Stjernfelt, Frederik. *Diagrammatology: An Investigation on the Borderlines of Phenomenology, Ontology, and Semiotics.* Dordrecht, Netherlands: Springer, 2007.

Strassler, Karen. *Refracted Visions: Popular Photography and Indonesian Modernity.* Durham, NC: Duke University Press, 2010.

Tagg, John. *The Burden of Representation: Essays on Photographies and Histories.* Minneapolis: University of Minnesota Press, 1993.

Tasker, Rodney. "Questions of Justice." *Far Eastern Economic Review,* August 27, 1998, 28.

Taussig, Michael T. *Defacement: Public Secrecy and the Labor of the Negative.* Stanford, CA: Stanford University Press, 1999.

Tej Bunnag. "The Provincial Administration of Siam from 1892 to 1915: A Study of the Creation, the Growth, the Achievements, and the Implications for Modern Siam, of the Ministry of the Interior under Prince Damrong Rachanuphap." PhD diss., Oxford University, 1968.

Textor, Robert B. *Roster of the Gods: An Ethnography of the Supernatural in a Thai Village.* New Haven, CT: Human Relations Area Files, 1973.

Thak Chaloemtiarana. *Thailand: The Politics of Despotic Paternalism.* Ithaca, NY: Cornell Southeast Asia Program, 2007.

Thawisak Suphasa. "Kan jatkan lae botbat khong tamruat nai krungthep ratchasamai phrabat somdet phrajulajomklao jao yu hua" [The establishment and role of the police in Bangkok during the reign of King Chulalongkorn]. Master's thesis, Srinakharinwirot University, 1978.

Thawon Suwan. *Fa thalai nam muek* [Navigating a sea of ink]. Bangkok: Matichon Press, 2007.

Thongchai Winichakul. *Siam Mapped: A History of the Geo-body of a Nation.* Honolulu: University of Hawai'i Press, 1997.

Udom Latphli. *Withayakan tamruat bang rueang* [On various police methods]. In *Krom tamurat* [Police Department], *Botkhwam prakop khwam ru kiao kap tamruat* [Collected articles on the police], 73–78. Cremation volume printed in honor of Phraya Athikonprakat (Lui Jatikawanit) at Wat Thepsirintherawat. Bangkok, May 9, 1955.

United States Operations Mission (USOM). "Cattle Rustling and the Police." December 30, 1966. Thailand Information Center, Chulalongkorn University Library, Bangkok.

"Visual Culture Questionnaire." *October* 77 (Summer 1996): 25–70.

Vollmer, August. "The Bureau of Criminal Records." *Journal of the American Institute of Criminal Law and Criminology* 11, no. 2 (August 1920): 171–180.

———. "Revision of the Atcherley Modus Operandi System." *Journal of the American Institute of Criminal Law and Criminology* 10, no. 2 (August 1919): 229–274.

Wakeman, Fredrick. *Policing Shanghai, 1927–1937.* Berkeley: University of California Press, 1996.

Wassana Nanuam. *Lap luang phrang phak phitsadan* [Secrets, trickery, and camouflage: The improbable phenomena]. Bangkok: Post Books, 2008.

Wenk, Klaus. *Thai Literature: An Introduction.* Bangkok: White Lotus, 1995.

Wilson, Christopher P. *Cop Knowledge: Police Power and Cultural Narrative in Twentieth-Century America.* Chicago: University of Chicago Press, 2000.

Wilson, Constance. "Bangkok in 1883: An Economic and Social Profile." *Journal of Siam Society* 77, no. 2 (1989): 49–58.

Wilson, Robert Anton. *Illuminati Papers.* 3rd ed. Berkeley, CA: Ronin Publishing, 1997.

Winks, Robin W. "What Is Evidence? The Relativist View." In *The Historian as Detective: Essays on Evidence,* edited by Robin W. Winks, 3–23. New York: Harper and Row, 1969.

Wiwana Thewachalaangkun. "Naiyobai khong rat kap kan tamruat phuthon phoso 2440–2465" [Government policy and the gendarmerie, 1897–1922]. Master's thesis, Silapakon University, 1984.

Wong Wiraphong. *Kan ruapruam lae kan nam suep phayan lakthan nai khadi ukchakan* [Compiling and investigating evidence in serious cases]. Bangkok: Dusit Samphan, 1963.

INDEX

Note: Page numbers in **bold** refer to figures.

ABOUT THE AUTHOR

Samson Lim is assistant professor of history at the Singapore University of Technology and Design. He completed his PhD in history at Cornell University. His research interests include documentation practices, visual and material culture, and social history in Thailand. He has published articles on policing, detective fiction, and crime news in *The Journal of Asian Studies, Critical Asian Studies,* and *Southeast Asia Research.* He is currently working on a new research project that examines the history of financial capitalism in early twentieth-century Thailand. Prior to becoming a historian, Lim worked in the field of city planning and development in Singapore and Bangkok and has lived in the Southeast Asia region for almost a decade.

OTHER VOLUMES IN THE SERIES

PRINT AND POWER:
Confucianism, Communism, and Buddhism in the Making of Modern Vietnam
Shawn Frederick McHale

INVESTING IN MIRACLES:
El Shaddai and the Transformation of Popular Catholicism in the Philippines
Katherine L. Wiegele

TOMS AND DEES:
Transgender Identity and Female Same-Sex Relationships in Thailand
Megan J. Sinnott

IN THE NAME OF CIVIL SOCIETY:
From Free Election Movements to People Power in the Philippines
Eva-Lotta E. Hedman

THE TÂY SƠN UPRISING:
Society and Rebellion in Eighteenth-Century Vietnam
George Dutton

SPREADING THE DHAMMA:
Writing, Orality, and Textual Transmission in Buddhist Northern Thailand
Daniel M. Veidlinger

ART AS POLITICS:
Re-crafting Identities, Tourism, and Power in Tana Toraja, Indonesia
Kathleen M. Adams

CAMBODGE:
The Cultivation of a Nation, 1860–1945
Penny Edwards

HOW TO BEHAVE:
Buddhism and Modernity in Colonial Cambodia, 1860–1931
Anne Ruth Hansen

CULT, CULTURE, AND AUTHORITY:
Princess Liễu Hạnh in Vietnamese History
Olga Dror

Khmer Women on the Move:
Exploring Work and Life in Urban Cambodia
Annuska Derks

The Anxieties of Mobility:
Migration and Tourism in the Indonesian Borderlands
Johan A. Lindquist

The Binding Tie:
Chinese Intergenerational Relations in Modern Singapore
Kristina Göransson

In Buddha's Company:
Thai Soldiers in the Vietnam War
Richard A. Ruth

Lục Xì:
Prostitution and Venereal Disease in Colonial Hanoi
Vũ Trọng Phụng
Translated by Shaun Kingsley Malarney

Refiguring Women, Colonialism, and Modernity in Burma
Chie Ikeya

Natural Potency and Political Power:
Forests and State Authority in Contemporary Laos
Sarinda Singh

The Perfect Business?
Anti-trafficking and the Sex Trade along the Mekong
Sverre Molland

Seeing Beauty, Sensing Race in Transnational Indonesia
L. Ayu Saraswati

Potent Landscapes:
Place and Mobility in Eastern Indonesia
Catherine Allerton

FOREST OF STRUGGLE:
Moralities of Remembrance in Upland Cambodia
Eve Monique Zucker

SOUNDING OUT HERITAGE:
Cultural Politics and the Social Practice of Quan Họ Folk Song in Northern Vietnam
Lauren Meeker

CAGED IN ON THE OUTSIDE:
Moral Subjectivity, Selfhood, and Islam in Minangkabau, Indonesia
Gregory M. Simon

GHOSTS OF THE NEW CITY:
Spirits, Urbanity, and the Ruins of Progress in Chiang Mai
Andrew Alan Johnson

ESSENTIAL TRADE:
Vietnamese Women in a Changing Marketplace
Ann Marie Leshkowich

SAVING BUDDHISM:
The Impermanence of Religion in Colonial Burma
Alicia Turner

EMBODIED NATION:
Sport, Masculinity, and the Making of Modern Laos
Simon Creak

THE LOST TERRITORIES:
Thailand's History of National Humiliation
Shane Strate

FORGING ISLAMIC POWER AND PLACE:
The Legacy of Shaykh Dā'ūd bin 'Abd Allāh al-Faṭānī in Mecca and Southeast Asia
Francis R. Bradley

THE UPROOTED:
Race, Children, and Imperialism in French Indochina, 1890–1980
Christina Elizabeth Firpo